Like Fire in the Bones

Like Fire in the Bones

Listening for the Prophetic Word in Jeremiah

WALTER BRUEGGEMANN

Edited by Patrick D. Miller

FORTRESS PRESS
Minneapolis

To the Memory

of

Warren R. Mehl

Library of Congress Cataloging-in-Publication Data

Brueggemann, Walter.
  Like fire in the bones : listening for the prophetic word in Jeremiah /
Walter Brueggemann ; edited by Patrick D. Miller.
    p. cm.
  Includes bibliographical references and index.
  ISBN-13: 978-0-8006-3561-9 (alk. paper)
  ISBN-10: 0-8006-3561-2 (alk. paper)
    1. Bible. O.T. Jeremiah—Criticism, interpretation, etc. I. Miller, Patrick D.
II. Title.
  BS1525.52.B78 2006
  224'.206—dc22

2006010165

10   09   08   07   06   1   2   3   4   5   6   7   8   9   10

Contents

Editor's Foreword

There are few books of the Old Testament about which Walter Brueggemann has not written in some depth. The breadth of his work matches the prolific output of scholarly, relevant, and helpful interpretation of scripture in book, essay, sermon, and prayer. It would be difficult, therefore, to identify any one area or book as a primary sphere or subject of his interpretive activity. Nevertheless, I am bold to suggest that if there is any book that he has probed more deeply and tellingly than all the others, devoting his energies to both commentary and essay, writing for both the academy and the church, it is the book of Jeremiah. His commentary on this prophetic book, *A Commentary on Jeremiah: Exile and Homecoming*, may well be the best of all his commentaries. At least, as someone who has also written a commentary on the book of Jeremiah, I can testify that no single work has provided more insight into the text or said what needed to be said in clear and helpful ways than Brueggemann's commentary, despite a spate of fine Jeremiah commentaries over the last twenty-five years.

What is there about this book that commands Brueggemann's attention and brings out so much astute and meaningful interpretation? If one infers from his many writings about this prophet and the book attributed to him, several possibilities arise. One is the degree to which the book gives a searing portrayal of a prophet under the constraints of both his calling and his circumstances. Surely there is no more extended depiction of prophetic existence and its precariousness than the prophet Jeremiah. At one point, after giving a summary statement of what it means to be a prophet, Brueggemann says succinctly: "Jeremiah is the most extreme case." Throughout the essays that follow here, one encounters the prophet in all his agony, doubt, and despair, and also in his relentless commitment to the calling he sought to avoid but could not. The reader will discern Brueggemann getting into Jeremiah's skin and helping us do the same. As the book makes clear, the word of the Lord that comes through this prophet is intricately linked to his own experience. Brueggemann's empathetic interpretation is such that often one cannot sharply separate the voice of the prophet and the voice of his interpreter. Jeremiah has always been a barrier against the purveyors of cheap grace, something Brueggemann abhors as much as did Bonhoeffer. He is as aware as Jeremiah that there are many who cry "Peace!" when all around there is war and suffering and death.

Brueggemann's continuing fascination with this prophet rests also in the fact that Jeremiah prophesied in a critical time in the history of Israel. As he puts it in one of his essays, Jeremiah "lived at a time of *incredible* headlines." While there is much debate over when Jeremiah's career started, there is no question that his prophetic work ranged from a time of grandeur and power in the Judean state through its downfall and into the time of exile. Jeremiah's times were as momentous and formative for Israel's story as any period in its history. So this prophet's message is to be heard against the background of large political, social, and economic upheavals. However one decides about the redaction of the book and the assignment of any particular oracle to Jeremiah, his words of judgment and hope as they are presented in the book are clearly reflective of the circumstances in which he lived and prophesied. He moves from powerful oracles condemning a complacent elite—declaring the Lord's intention to bring them down—to words of encouragement to those who have experienced God's judgment that they learn to live in their place and time of exile and to live in hope that God will restore their fortunes.

No prophet has conveyed more sharply the pathos of the prophetic calling to speak strong words to unwilling listeners and endure the consequences. His oracles and prayers, however, are also a vivid testimony to the pathos of the Lord who called him into his difficult ministry. Along with the powerful words of judgment against kings and other leaders who betrayed the covenantal demands of faithfulness are the tears of God over the people's failure to live as God's people, committed to ways of justice and righteousness, the care of the weak and the fear of the Lord. From his monumental *Theology of the Old Testament* to the present collection of essays, written over a long period of time, Brueggemann never lets us forget the true subject, the center and meaning of all of scripture, who never let Jeremiah off the hook even in his most desperate moments. The prophets were messengers—in their lives, their words, their actions. So is Brueggemann as he invites us to hear afresh the ancient word so agonistically announced by this prophet from Anathoth, not in order to understand the prophet better but to hear and respond to the one who spoke through him.

The reader never loses the author in these essays. Brueggemann is unabashed about overlaying his careful reading of texts with powerful claims about their significance for our lives. He is unable to speak about them simply as ancient words. Indeed, while he seeks to uncover the resonance of the texts with their times and circumstances, that is finally only in order to convey the powerful and often abrasive impact of these texts on our times and circumstances. He never quits preaching and is always meddling. That was Jeremiah's way. So what choice does the interpreter have? I think Brueggemann is right. The only thing that matters about the prophetic word is its relevance. Those who keep on reading will, therefore, be disturbed, moved, encouraged, and challenged. I am not sure Brueggemann has any other purpose in writing about this disturbing and challenging man of God.

As you read these essays, watch for certain features that are vehicles of Brueggemann's interpretive perception. One is his use of metaphors, surely evoked by the poetic and imaginative character of much of this prophet's speech. So one will encounter the book of Jeremiah as a "meditation upon the abyss," a "haunting book" for a haunted people, a guide for "Christians who know how to blush." Trained by James Muilenburg to pay attention to the rhetoric of the text before him, he has carried over that learning into his own modes of communication. The claim of any interpretive move is in its capacity to persuade. There is not some outside criterion of truth. Much of the effectiveness of Brueggemann's interpretation is in the rhetorical power of his communication.

Attend to Brueggemann's interweaving of texts, placing different Jeremiah passages alongside each other as well as in conversation with other books and texts of scripture. Brueggemann does not worry about getting to the New Testament. Nor does he hesitate a moment in seeing direct connections to the Gospels and Paul. While he will always argue for the complexity and varied voices of scripture, he works constantly to identify important streams of coherence and continuity that make the Bible a book and not simply a collection of ancient writings.

Be prepared to learn a great deal about the contemporary interpretation of the book of Jeremiah. There is no better guide to what is going on in Jeremianic studies than the opening essays of this volume. Even in this enterprise, however, Brueggemann does not lay out a dull scholarly review. His look at the work of others is always in order to say what matters about the book. Engaging others is not to summarize scholarship or to score points. It is in order to see the vision and hear the word.

Finally, there is an order to the arrangement of these essays, so that in reading through them in sequence one moves from a close look at how Jeremiah is being read and interpreted into a more detailed reading of texts and Jeremiah's place in the larger scheme of things, prophetic and otherwise, and finally into an explicit and intense grappling with the word of the prophet for the contemporary community of faith. There is no requirement, however, to read these discrete essays in any order. Wherever you start, you will confront the prophet in all the fullness of his word from the Lord and have to wrestle with the inescapable challenge of that word to your own time and place.

—Patrick D. Miller

Preface

The study of the book of Jeremiah has occupied me for the long time of my teaching years. My beginning in Jeremiah studies was with my teacher at Eden Seminary, Lionel Whiston Jr., who propelled me to graduate study. In graduate study at Union Seminary (New York), my first seminar was on Jeremiah with James Muilenburg, who led us into the rhetorical force and cunning of Jeremiah from which I have never extricated myself. (Muilenburg himself was at work on a Jeremiah commentary that has not yet been made available to us.)

During the course of my teaching years, Jeremiah studies have taken two dramatic turns. The first of these was in 1986 when all at once we received three careful and extensive critical commentaries on the book (Carroll, Holladay, McKeane), after a long dearth of critical commentaries in English. There is no doubt that these commentaries together gave new impetus to Jeremiah studies, most especially because the historically conservative work of Holladay and the passionate critique of ideology by Carroll together posed clear, new, and urgent questions for interpretation.

A second dramatic turn, mostly since 1986, has been a general move away from historical-critical methods to a variety of approaches that might all together be taken as "postmodern." Leo Perdue has skillfully taken recent scholarly work in Jeremiah as a case study for the ferment in method that is more broadly true in Old Testament studies.[1] The move away from historical criticism has led to (a) a turn from the person of Jeremiah to the book of Jeremiah, and consequently (b) a new appreciation of the materials in the latter part of the book that are an offer of hope for the future of Jerusalem. These newer studies, signaled in *Troubling Jeremiah*, have helped us to see that these materials are not simply reportage on the Jerusalem crisis of the sixth century, but are in fact reflections of a disputatious pastoral process of reinterpretation whereby faith can be practiced in a new social environment without old and legitimated institutional supports.[2] While this move toward new method is multifaced, it is likely that the most poignant of the new perspectives is to be found in the current work of my colleague, Kathleen O'Connor, who is in the process of rereading Jeremiah according to current theories of post-traumatic stress disorder. Much of this newer perspective is beyond my ken, but these articles will indicate the ways in which I have been underway myself toward these newer awarenesses.

The longer I have worked on the Jeremiah traditions, the more I have been struck by the incredible contemporaneity of those materials. Of course the text stands at a distance from us, and that distance must be taken seriously. But once that distance is acknowledged, much of the text sounds as though it had been written about our time and place. Specifically I have found it interpretively suggestive to see an analogue between the destruction of Jerusalem in the sixth century around which the book of Jeremiah pivots, and the crisis of 9/11 in U.S. society. I fully recognize that the disaster of 9/11 as a factual matter was a very modest one in which the actual number of lives lost was relatively small, but symbolically the significance of the event is enormous because it represents the undoing of U.S. exceptionalism, the notion that the United States by the providence of God is not subject to the laws of history as is every other nation state.[3] That same sense of exceptionalism operated in ancient Jerusalem, under the aegis of king and temple, to claim that Jerusalem was immune to the vagaries of history. That destruction of Jerusalem made the continuation of that illusion in ancient Israel impossible. *Mutatis mutandis*, the crisis of 9/11 also constitutes a recognition that U.S. exceptionalism is broken; that is why the disaster is so acute for those who practice the ideology of the United States as a privileged superpower, and why the break is so unnerving for a younger generation that has never had the occasion to question that unspoken but widely assumed claim. In both ancient Jerusalem and in contemporary U.S. society, life and faith after the loss of exceptionalism constitute a deep challenge that at the same time evokes denial and generates despair and cynical violence.

Given such an analogue that, of course, is not exact, it is easy to see why Jeremiah studies inevitably push beyond historical interpretation to contemporary engagement. Good interpretation surely moves back and forth between *critical historical awareness* and the *pursuit of meaning in contemporary context*. In these articles I evidence my continuing attempt to move back and forth between then and now, as I think canonical texts always require. I am grateful for the varieties of opportunities and invitations that made possible and necessary these several articles at the time of their writing. I hope, even as old and repetitious as they are, they will merit a contemporary rereading.

—WALTER BRUEGGEMANN

Acknowledgments

The retrieval and gathering together of these older journal articles has been a demanding task, mostly performed by others on my behalf. As usual I am grateful to Tia Foley for bringing the manuscript to fruition and all the work of reshaping these materials for publication. Ruth Marley retyped most of the materials in the face of a demanding deadline, for which I am most appreciative. I am grateful to Chris Hooker for preparing the indices, and to Neil Elliott and his colleagues at Fortress Press for pursuing yet another effort on my part. My longtime connection to the press continues to be a happy and generative one for me. Above all, I am thankful to Patrick Miller for his suggestion of this triad of volumes, and for his careful work in shaping them and seeing them all through to publication. The getting together of these articles reminds me, yet again, of how fortunate I am to have such an environment of good colleagues over a long period of work time.

I am pleased to be able to dedicate this volume to the memory of Warren Mehl, recently deceased, my longtime friend, colleague, and neighbor. When I was young, Warren was a model of ministry for me as he was handsome, witty, gentle, passionate, and thoughtful . . . not all of his virtues were transmitted to me. During my too-long term as Academic Dean at Eden Seminary, Warren was my most faithful and supportive colleague. I am thankful for his clear-headed, deep-hearted faith and his reliable embrace of faith and ministry. I give thanks for his life, even as I ponder his legacy among us.

Credits

1. "The Book of Jeremiah: Portrait of the Prophet," *Interpretation* 37 (1983): 130–45. Used by permission.

2. "Meditation upon the Abyss: The Book of Jeremiah," *Word & World* 22:4 (2002): 340–50. Used by permission.

3. "Jeremiah: Intense Criticism/Thin Interpretation," *Interpretation* 42 (1988): 268–80. Used by permission.

4. "Jeremiah: *Creatio in Extremis*," pages 152–70 in *God Who Creates: Essays in Honor of W. Sibley Towner*, ed. William P. Brown and S. Dean McBride, Jr. (Grand Rapids: Eerdmans, 2000). Used by permission.

5. "Next Steps in Jeremiah Studies," pages 367–86 in *Troubling Jeremiah*, JSOT-Sup 260, ed. A. R. Pete Diamond, Kathleen M. O'Connor, and Louis Stulman (Sheffield: Sheffield Academic, 2001). Reprinted by permission of The Continuum International Publishing Group.

6. "The Prophetic Word of God and History," *Interpretation* 48:3 (1994): 239–52. Used by permission.

7. "An Ending That Does Not End: The Book of Jeremiah," pages 117-28 in *Postmodern Interpretations of the Bible: A Reader*, ed. A. K. M. Adam (St. Louis: Chalice, 2001). Used by permission.

8. "A Second Reading of Jeremiah after the Dismantling," *Ex Auditu* 1 (1985): 156–68. Used by permission.

9. "A Shattered Transcendence: Exile and Restoration," pages 169–82 in *Biblical Theology: Problems and Perspectives, Essays in Honor of J. Christiaan Beker*, ed. Steven J. Kraftchick, Charles D. Myers Jr., and Ben C. Ollenburger (Nashville: Abingdon, 1995), 169–82. Used by permission.

10. "Haunting Book—Haunted People," *Word & World* 11 (1991): 62–68. These comments were originally delivered at the National Council of Churches in New York on September 27, 1990, on the occasion of the dedication of the New Revised Standard Version of the Bible. Used by permission.

11. "Prophetic Ministry: A Sustainable Alternative Community," *Horizons in Biblical Theology* 11 (1989): 1–33. Used by permission.

12. "A World Available for Peace: Images of Hope from Jeremiah and Isaiah," *Sojourners* 17:1 (1988): 22–26. Used by permission.

13. "'Is There No Balm in Gilead': The Hope and Despair of Jeremiah," *Sojourners* 14:9 (1985): 26–29. Used by permission.

14. "Making History: Jeremiah's Guide for Christians Who Know How to Blush," *The Other Side* 22:4 (October 1986): 21–25. Used by permission.

15. "Why Prophets Won't Leave Well Enough Alone," *U.S. Catholic*, 58:1 (1993): 6–14. Used by permission.

I.

The Word
Spoken through the Prophet

CHAPTER ONE

Jeremiah

Portrait of the Prophet

Our theme does not invite us to a new quest for the historical Jeremiah. The critical problems concerning the relation of the *person* of Jeremiah to the *book* of Jeremiah are notoriously difficult. There seems to be no great progress on that question in current scholarship. It is fair to say that current scholarship tends toward a minimalist view concerning the historical Jeremiah. That is, scholars are assigning more and more work to the redactional process, which leaves less and less material assigned to the authorship of Jeremiah and yields (according to the hypothesis) less and less reliable historical information about the prophet.

On the relation of the person to the redactional process, we may identify two tendencies. On the one hand, there is a scholarly tradition that pays attention to the person of Jeremiah and generally regards the early part of the book as coming from him and credits as historically reliable much of the material in the Baruch section of the book. *Prophecy and Religion*, by John Skinner,[1] is a powerful statement of this view, which is also the working assumption of John Bright's commentary on Jeremiah.[2] It is the inclination of William Holladay,[3] who has published a series of important articles on Jeremiah, and it is indirectly the basis of Robert R. Wilson's sociological analysis, *Prophecy and Society in Ancient Israel.*[4] This view tends to take (in broad outline) the presentation of Jeremiah offered to us.[5]

The alternative view (which currently is on the increase) pays much more attention to the redactional process and assumes that the person of Jeremiah given to us is largely a reconstruction of the Deuteronomic theologians. That inclination is very much in evidence in the analysis of Ernest W. Nicholson[6] and is carried to an extreme position in the work of Robert Carroll.[7] It is reflected in the title of A. H. J. Gunneweg's study "Confession or Interpretation,"[8] concerning the "confessions" of Jeremiah. Gunneweg concludes that what is given to us is an *interpretation* and not a direct confession of Jeremiah. The confessions are primarily "proclamations and not lyrics." And more broadly, Siegfried Herrmann draws a like conclusion: "In this large perspective, the book of Jeremiah is incomparably more than the record of the man from Anathoth. Under the impact of numerous and different materials, the book is the settlement of the past, the call to repentance, a document of hope for Israel and the future direction of YHWH for all peoples."[9]

Now these issues are most complex and cannot be resolved here, but they are not irrelevant to our subject of a portrait. It is clear that we do not have in any simple way a descriptive, biographical report. Indeed this portrait, like every portrait, is passed through the perceptions of the artist. The person of Jeremiah offered us in some sense (as is every such piece of literature) a construction of literary imagination.[10] But it is also probable that the person, memory, and impact of Jeremiah were so powerful and enduring that that personal reality presided over and shaped the imaginative reconstruction. It is thus plausible to state this premise for our study: We have an imaginative literary construction governed by a powerful person of memory. That reconstruction is not historically precise, but it is not literarily fanciful, undisciplined, or cut loose from its referent. It is not preoccupied with psychological or sociological matters that might interest us. But it is theologically intentional. And the theological intent is to articulate[11] this person of Jeremiah as a model or paradigm[12] for what a prophet is, for what a believing person is, for what Israel might be. The move *from personal history to theological model* loses something in historical accuracy (in any case not recoverable by us), but that move gains much in generative power that can summon Israel to faith in a profound crisis. Thus the redactors are not clerks who play fast and loose and who are indifferent to their subject matter. Rather, as creative theologians, they are artists making faith possible in the midst of Israel's deepest crisis. We deal with an identifiable man, one who is now articulated for the sake of God's continuing way with Israel.

Jeremiah is articulated for us as *overwhelmingly God's man*. This is the first thing one notices about him, already articulated in the superscription of 1:1-3. He is a man to whom a persistent, inescapable, and overriding word has been delivered. His life consists in coming to terms with that word, finding ways to articulate it to his contemporaries, and living with the hazardous consequences of that reality.

A person so utterly claimed by and preoccupied with the sovereign word of God is an oddity because we are modern and Jeremiah is ancient. But to be so called and identified is an inscrutable oddity in any time, including the time of Jeremiah. This set him at odds with his contemporaries. His call and his reference to YHWH gave him an angle on historical reality that left him at various times anguished, dismayed, depressed, and hopeful. His discernment of his historical moment under the rule of YHWH caused him to *dismiss in judgment* much that was valued and to *discern in hope* possibilities where his contemporaries recognized none.

Obviously this vocation as God's special agent and messenger is clearest at the outset, in the *call narrative of 1:4-10*, and the visions that follow (1:11-16). The call narrative is highly stylized. Perhaps it is shaped as a subsequent statement of authorization rather than a report of an experience.[13] However such a critical issue may be resolved, it is clear that YHWH holds initiative for Jeremiah's life.

He has been *known/consecrated/appointed* by YHWH (1:5). He has been "made holy" for God's purpose. The narrative account states the point vigorously, but no argument is made or evidence given. It is all prehistorical and prerational. It is "from the womb," which takes it beyond the reach of analysis. There is no "precalled" Jeremiah.

He has been *sent/commanded/set* for the sake of a mission (vv. 7, 10), a mission to be wrought by words (v. 9). Those words are from YHWH ("mine"). They are words of *discontinuity*, words that end what was seen to be absolute, words that *begin* what was seen to be impossible. This man is summoned to shatter and form worlds by his speech.

He is a man to whom peculiar promises have been made, promises of safety and defense (vv. 17-19). Indeed the supreme promise is made to this man; "I will be with you" (vv. 8, 19). The God who authorizes is the one who stands in solidarity, but what a strange accompanying presence it is. Jeremiah often experiences life alone, desolate, and abandoned. One draws the conclusion that often God is present and with Jeremiah only at the "eleventh hour."

It is worth noting that we have no judgment to make about the historicity of this initial narrative. It is part of the portrait. The book of Jeremiah here seeks to give a sketch of unchallengable authority, to provide a basis from which an alternative word can be spoken in the world, a word not grounded in or derived from the official, legitimating agenda of the day. This one who is utterly claimed by YHWH is subject to no other authority. His life consists in speaking from this free place of authority precisely to those who do not acknowledge it.

It could be that disproportionate attention has been paid to the so-called lamentations of Jeremiah.[14] Critical opinion about the character, intention, and function of these poems is divided. What they evidence is that the vocation of the prophet is a *conflicted way to live*. Jeremiah is completely identified with his call. That much is not in doubt.

His call yields more restlessness. It renders him homeless in the royal world where he is assigned. Jeremiah embodies and acts out the fact that YHWH's live word is not easily borne or received. The bearer of that word—whether of judgment or of hope—may anticipate rejection in the world.

The restlessness cuts still deeper. Given the conflict in the world, given the sure promise of his call, one might expect that the prophet could withdraw from *combat* (in the world) for *communion* (with his God). But the neat consignment of combat to earth and communion to heaven does not hold here. Jeremiah experiences in his own spirituality the same rawness from God that he dares to articulate to his contemporaries. One might have expected that this faithful speaker for God would receive solace for heeding God's call. So Jeremiah makes himself desperately *vulnerable* to the God who has called and sent him (15:17-18; 17:17-18), but Jeremiah's vulnerability is not met by solace. It is met by *toughness and ruthlessness* (12:5-6; 15:19-21). Jeremiah learns that YHWH has an overriding and tenacious commitment to his own purposes. The needfulness of Jeremiah will not detain YHWH's relentlessness any more than will the needfulness of Judah. To be overwhelmingly God's person here means to have vulnerability met by ruthlessness.

It is surely the case, as Abraham Heschel has seen, that Jeremiah experiences and enters into the pathos of God.[15] He knows about God's suffering love because of the covenant distorted. But that does not mean Jeremiah slides over to God's side of the question. The combative distance between YHWH and Israel is and remains a combative distance also for Jeremiah. For Jeremiah, as for Judah, this God is one who is close at hand, yet remains distant (23:23). Jeremiah's complaints may be a yearning for the closure of the distance,[16] but the cleavage wrought by YHWH's unaccommodating sovereignty must not be underestimated. This point is important, on the one hand, for understanding the kind of communion Jeremiah finds possible with his God. On the other hand, it helps us see that Jeremiah as a prophet is subjected to and involved in the very covenantal crises of his people.

Jeremiah is a man called and sent as a *speaker of words with poetic passion and stunning imagination.* Such a point might seem curious in an assessment of the man and the prophetic office; however, it is freshly appreciated among scholars that the poetic mode of prophetic speech is not accidental or incidental.[17] It is indispensable for what the prophet is about. The sovereign word of YHWH is not an absolute, everywhere and always the same. It is a particular, concrete word spoken to particular persons in particular contexts, to impact persons, to impinge upon perception and awareness, to intrude upon public policy, and if possible to evoke faithful and transformed behavior. The prophetic word is not a proposition or the announcement of set truths. It is often the playful exploration and processing of insight that is not known until it is brought to precisely the right shape of expression. It is not that such a poet has some content and then finds some words, but the finding of the right words is the way in which the faithful content is determined. The poetic language of Jeremiah is not just a skillful or an occasional cloak for an external word. It is part of the strategy for letting the live word make a difference in historical reality. Words matter—because they limit and permit the reality in which society lives. Prophets therefore attend to words in quite specific and concrete ways.[18]

We have said that Jeremiah's call is to *shatter* old worlds (bring them to an end) and to *form* and evoke new worlds (cause them to be). The shattering and forming of worlds is not done as a potter molds clay or as a factory makes products. It is done as a poet redescribes the world, reconfigures public perception, and causes people to reexperience their experience.[19] To do that requires that speech must not be conventional, reasonable, predictable; it must shock sensitivity, call attention to what is not noticed, break the routine, cause people to redescribe things that have long since seemed settled, bear surpluses of power before routine assessments.

It is clear that such a linguistic enterprise that redescribes the world is in fact subversive activity and indeed may be the primal act of subversion. Such speech functions to discredit and illegitimate the old, conventional modes of perception. When things are seen in new ways, we become aware that the old, conventional slogans (for example, Jer. 7:4) are in fact ideological cover-ups that no longer claim allegiance. Such imaginative speech evokes new sensitivities, invites people to hope, that is, to respond to social possibilities that the old administrative language has declared unthinkable, unreasonable, and impossible.[20]

There are several ways of attending to the subversive poetry of Jeremiah, which "tears down and builds" (1:10),[21] shatters and forms. First, after the manner of Jack R. Lundbom[22] and William Holladay,[23] one can pay attention to the large structural patterns of the poetry. One important gain made by their work is to observe that 1:4-10 and 20:14-18 form a major inclusio that binds the material together in a shrewd and intentional way. There are two major problems with that approach: (a) such analysis never quite accounts for everything, and one may be tempted to force things unduly; (b) one cannot determine what is the work of a redactor rather than the poet. But even with these reservations, such an analysis is sufficient to indicate that the poetic work before us is knowingly crafted. Our insistence is that such an enterprise as this carefully crafted poetry is not simply aesthetically noteworthy; it has a dangerous social function, namely to end the presumed world and evoke a new one.

Second, one may pay attention to the recurrent and varied uses of poignant metaphors and images around which the poetry clusters. It is clear that the use of words, images, and themes is carefully designed to play upon the imagination of the community. Some of the clearest examples of such a function are offered by James Muilenberg,[24] and we mention three:

a. The poetry is graphic concerning *war imagery.* These imaginative scenarios concern the terror of invading armies (4:13-17, 29; 5:15-17; 6:1-8, 22-25) and invite anguish and alarm in response to the destruction of war (4:19-21, 30-31; 5:26).

b. Jeremiah articulates the view that all of Judah's life is a lie: There are "constant tensions between the language of *mendacity* and the language of *veracity,* between what is spurious and what is authentic, between truth and falsehood."[25] Thomas W. Overholt has shown that the motif of "falsehood" is a primal one for Jeremiah, given his conviction that the entire royal establishment is a house of lies sure to fall.

c. Jeremiah delights in the language of *wound and healing* to recharacterize Israel's political situation. Remarkably, in a single poem he is able to speak about an "incurable wound" (30:12), yet "a wound to be healed" (30:17). I do not believe the incongruity is to be explained away by reference to a redactor. Rather I suggest it reflects the constructive, evocative power of this poet.

One may identify what seems to be a key theme that recurs at important places in the total literature, "to pluck up and tear down, to plant and build."[26] This theme does not function in the same way as the poetic metaphors noted above. It is not so freely developed to serve fresh impressionistic purposes. But it is always carefully placed. It appears often in the prose and so functions in a flatter and more linear form (for example, 1:10; 18:7-10; 24:4-7; 42:9-12). It may be taken as a repeated main theme of the prophetic perception by which the various metaphors may be organized.[27]

Finally one may pay attention in close detail to one particular poem to observe the poetic skill of Jeremiah at work. We may consider for example the passionate words of 4:19-20, which show the amazing art of the poet. The two verses match the internal disarray (v. 19) with external disorder (v. 20), to show the two closely interrelated. In v. 19, we have the double use of "anguish" (or "bowels"), the double use of "heart," and then the "I" is matched in Hebrew with *nephesh*, rendered again "I." The six uses show the total, massive involvement of the person. The transition to public events is made with "trumpet," followed by a series of five strong, violent public words stating the consequence of the trumpet: "war"; "disaster" (twice); the double use of *shadad*, rendered "laid waste," "destroyed."

Further we may note two parallel sounds. The word "I writhe" (*'ohivlah*) in v. 19 seems to be linked to "my tent" (*'ohalay*) in v. 20; and the word "alarm" (*teru'ath*) in v. 19 seems to be linked to "my curtain" (*yeri'othay*) in verse 20. The tightness of the language shows a profound binding of *internal upset* and *external disarray*. The intensity of the happening and the helplessness experienced in the face of it seem evident in the pace of the language. The words seem to rush and tumble in a visceral spree. The purpose of such poetic power is to let the listener experience (at least in imagination) this alternative to a world that still seems peaceful and well ordered. Indeed the prophet means to claim that the poetic scenario is closer to reality than conventional discernment can allow, a discernment that in fact denies reality.

My purpose here is not to study poetic style or to celebrate aesthetic qualities. The point rather is that Jeremiah the prophet is portrayed as a consummate artist, who uses his artistic gifts to overthrow the deathly technique and unexamined ideology of his society. That which finally "plucks up and tears down, plants and builds" is not political strategy or military power. It is the ways of faithful and authoritative imagination which cannot be administered by the regime. The sovereign formula, "Thus says the LORD," is used as verification for playful, free poetic speech by which God's way is worked against the rulers of this age.

Jeremiah's life and ministry are *profoundly engaged with public events*. There is a great deal of silliness written about Jeremiah, probably because of the so-called confessions. He is frequently portrayed as a man preoccupied with internal spiritual life, and he is often said to be the foremost articulator of "individual religion." Either of these judgments requires a highly selective if not skewed reading of the evidence. To the contrary, it is clear that Jeremiah is destined (predestined? cf. Jer. 1:5) to be a public man, preoccupied with public events, responsive to them, and convinced that those public events are the ways in which YHWH is having his say with his creation and with Israel.

Jeremiah lives at the time of one of the turning points in the public life of the known world of the Near East.[28] His long years of ministry cover the span of the rising and falling of empires. He witnessed the fall of Assyria and the destruction of hated Ninevah. He observed the desperate attempts of Egypt and Assyria to hold on to cruel power and saw them fail at Carchemesh. He watched the relentless and haughty rise of Babylon as *the* new power before whom all tremble. He brought to speech the terror of an "enemy from the north," conventionally regarded as the Scythians, perhaps reassigned to Babylon. He knew profoundly that everything is loose and being shaken and that the agent of such rising and falling is none other than YHWH.

Jeremiah knew with intensity and at risk that this world-shattering in the Near East is reflected and at risk in the public life of Judah. The redactor has suggested the public arena of God's word to Jeremiah (1:1-3), in relation to Josiah, Jehoiachim, and Zedekiah. On other grounds we know also about his involvement with Jehoiahaz and Jehoiachin. The purpose of such a summary as is given in 1:1-3 is more than chronology or historical placement. It is also more than spotting the place where God's word is disclosed. It is a way of drawing God's word closely and decisively into interaction with a quite concrete, known world. Thus to say that God's word came to Jeremiah in the year of Jehoiachim is not simply to say it comes in the years 609–598 B.C.E. Much more, it means that the word borne by Jeremiah comes precisely into the "life-world" of that king, into a world of conspiracy and self-serving that inevitably is a way to destruction. In that world Jeremiah must say what he must say.

It is difficult for us in our privatized world to appreciate the depth or scope of Judah's public experience of reality. It is not that Jeremiah was a believing man who simply read the newspapers and responded out of faith to the events around him. Rather he knew the traffic of public power to be the vehicle and means whereby YHWH is present to Israel. It is this historical reality that is the mode of revelation and is not to be known in a primary way elsewhere.[29] His conviction of the revelatory character of public events meets us abrasively in our habit of finding God in less public places, less precarious places, and in thinking of revelation as something excessively "spiritual" and intimate.

Three observations are in order concerning Jeremiah's public discernment of his prophetic role:

1. It is clear that the disclosure word given by Jeremiah is *aimed at and impinges upon public leadership.* The oracular address of Jeremiah is not as direct or pointed as is that of Amos or Micah concerning the leaders. But it is clear that he is taken seriously by Judah's leaders, especially the kings, by those who have authority to set policy and define the world. We may cite two examples of the way in which the word of Jeremiah is received. First, in chapter 36, the narrative shows the entire establishment gathered around: The scene is the dramatic encounter between the *prophetic word,* which appears vulnerable and is powerful, and the *royal leadership,* which appears powerful and is ineffective and incompetent. The narrative shows how the word of this prophet calls into question that entire world of royal self-deception.[30]

A very different evidence that Jeremiah's disclosure word is aimed at public persons and issues is found in the encounter with Zedekiah (37:16-21). Whereas the word is foisted upon Jehoiachim and resisted in chapter 36, it is fervently sought by Zedekiah in chapter 37 and is only reluctantly given. In this case the king seeks a good word and is given an evil word. But in both cases the word given is a free word that illegitimates royal claims to reality and presents an alternative reality that is unwelcome to the rulers of this age. Jeremiah is confident that YHWH works his own will among the nations, without regard to machinations of a political kind and without reference to Israel's special, traditional claims.

2. Jeremiah understands *public history as an arena of God's free activity*. He posits an important tension between the *realities* of public life ruled by God and the *appearances* of public life shaped by institutional claims. That tension is most easily recognized in the famous temple sermon (chap. 7). The temple is claimed to be a vehicle for God's presence in the world, but it is shown to be a fraudulent form of escape for the special interests that practice social oppression and then use the protected status of the temple:[31] a vehicle of God's presence in the world is shown to be a barrier—one that must be destroyed. The same exposé of public religion that blocks God's public history is articulated in 8:8-13, in which the leadership of Judah is indicted for its erosion of the norms of Torah and the iniquity of the courts.[32]

Jeremiah's polemical treatment of Judah's public life—and especially of religious life—needs to be understood in relation to his conviction of YHWH's rule of history. Not only are these institutions no adequate vehicle for YHWH; they are also no adequate resistance against YHWH. Jeremiah's God does not conform, and therefore the historical process is filled with surprise and inversions that are neither expected nor permitted by these institutional forms.

3. The most striking thing about Jeremiah's public ministry is that *he takes sides on a decisive public question* in unambiguous terms. Indeed it is *the* question before Judah's public life. The question is: What are we to make of the Babylonian threat? There were surely many alternative political readings of that reality, and there is ample evidence of conflicting views. On the one hand, there was the pro-Egyptian party, as there always was in Judah. This opinion urged that alliance with and reliance upon Egypt would give security. On the other hand, Jeremiah's contemporaries were not so far removed from Isaiah that they could not remember his council to quiet faith and sure confidence in YHWH (Isa. 7:9; 30:15).[33] Indeed it is likely that Hananiah, an alternative prophet (not to say false), stood in the line of Isaiah (Jeremiah 27–28). His argument has considerable merit, for it asserts that YHWH governs and Judah can trust him.[34]

Against both such views, Jeremiah takes the harder reading. He concludes that Babylon is the wave of the future and surely will triumph. Judah's best course is to ally itself early with this very one who appears to be a threat. Jeremiah radically rereads Judah's situation, against all the ready and popular readings, and identifies the perceived threat as the real hope.

It is important to observe that Jeremiah takes this stand on other than political grounds. The newspapers did not indicate such a judgment. Rather *Jeremiah's decisive political judgment is made on clear theological grounds.* He is able to work in the historical process in free, radical, and surprising ways. Jeremiah as a model does not suggest being an expert in a secular discipline like political science, but he knows especially about the scandalous ways of YHWH. So he announces not only that Babylon will triumph but, astonishingly, that YHWH wills the triumph of Babylon. "Pax Babylonia is the plan of YHWH."[35] The statement rings like a refrain in the prose literature:

...	I will	give	all Judah (20:4)
	I will	deliver	the people in this city (21:7)
	I would	tear	you off and
		give	you into the hand of those who seek your life into the hand of those of whom you are afraid (22:24-25)
Now	I have	given	all these lands (27:6, cf. vv. 12-13, 16-22)
Behold	I am	giving	this city (34:2)
You—	shall be	delivered	(37:17)
This city	shall be	given	into the hand of (Nebuchadrezzar/ the army of) the king of Babylon (38:3, cf. v. 23).

Now, to be sure, this shocking judgment is not given in a vacuum, either political, literary, or theological. In the person and tradition of Jeremiah, this statement rests on an acute moral analysis and on a poetic deposit, which is poignant in its anger, anguish, and eloquence. The conclusion repeated so often comes at the end of a career of urging repentance, exposing falseness, and symbolizing failure. But the conclusion is there nonetheless. It attests Jeremiah's certainty that poetic speech has to do with public reality, and his disclosing word concerns precisely the realities of Judah's life.

Perhaps the most staggering statement about this public judgment linking YHWH's resolute will and the public realities of Judah is the specific speech about Nebuchadrezzar. Much of Jeremiah's dismal anticipation is expressed in quite elusive, impressionistic language. We have seen, however, that it is not elusive but incisive in the judgment made about Babylon. Now we can see the most concrete affirmation for Jeremiah is that Nebuchadrezzar is YHWH's servant, an alien ruler commissioned for YHWH's purpose (25:9; 27:6; 43:10).[36] In saying this, Jeremiah is of course in the prophetic tradition of Isaiah who speaks similarly about Assyria, though not specifically about Sennacherib (Isa. 10:5), and of Second Isaiah who refers to Cyrus as "my shepherd, his anointed" (44:28; 45:1).

The theological import of such a designation is the unspoken conclusion that the king in Judah is no longer YHWH's servant, shepherd, anointed. The king has forfeited his role, and therefore the linkage of YHWH and Judah is jeopardized if not broken.

Finally we may observe one other exchange remembered about Jeremiah in 44:11-30. Jeremiah is remembered as frequently being in conflict with the Egyptian sympathizers, reflecting his "Babylonian decision." In this concluding episode he challenges the Judeans to true faith against religious practices commensurate with their Egyptian inclination (vv. 11-14). His opponents present a tight case against him of a quite syllogistic kind (vv. 17-18):

> We served the queen of heaven and prospered.
> We stopped serving the queen of heaven and lacked everything.

That is pretty convincing! Jeremiah's response (vv. 22-23, 24-30) shows that his judgment is theological and not pragmatic or political. He does not seek to refute the syllogism of vv. 17-18. He ignores it. He overrides it in his moral passion. Instead of an answer, he asserts once more that the sovereign rule of YHWH has moral implications that are simply unarguable, the evidence to the contrary notwithstanding. Jeremiah is perhaps Israel's supreme embodiment of the ability to subordinate both personal inclination and political reality to the sovereignty of YHWH. Any attempt to discern his person must reckon with that reality.

The portrayal given us shows that Jeremiah is in every way *a man of intense dispute.* His calling, his passion, his moral-political judgments, his poetic imaginative power all set him on a course of inevitable dispute. Thus he characterizes himself as "a man of strife and contention to the whole land" (15:10). In pondering the prophetic role, we note that the dispute is not accidental or incidental, because of wrong strategy or insensitivity. Nor is the dispute about marginal matters about which he might as well have compromised. As we have it, dispute is definitional to his call. The promise linked to his call is that he will be "against the whole land, against the kings of Judah, its princes, its priests, and the people of the land. They will fight against you . . ." (1:18, 19a). The conflict is there because he has been given a vision of and a word about reality that is deeply at odds with the vision of it held by his contemporaries; these two visions can in no way be accommodated to each other. Jeremiah witnesses to, speaks from, and hopes for an alternative world that his contemporaries could not understand or accept. It is this reality that governs the entire portrait and brings Jeremiah into conflict.[37]

On one hand, his dispute was with the public leaders and world-definers of his day. He insisted that the reality they thought they governed was a lie. He insisted on articulating as the real world the world he knew to be true.

Clearly he stood in conflict with *the royal apparatus*. This is most dramatically clear in the showdown of chapter 36, in which Jehoiachim finds Jeremiah's words intolerable. That confrontation then leads to the abuse and harassment that follow. That opposition is more poignantly expressed in 22:13-30, which addresses the wickedness of Jehoiachim, soon to be punished, and the hopelessness of Jehoiachin. The end of the poem (v. 30) seems to anticipate an end to the dynastic succession (see the inverse theme of kingship in 23:1-8).

Jeremiah is in conflict with *his prophetic counterparts*, who tend to support the political establishment and to speak assurances based on present policy. Again the most dramatic statement is in the exchange with Hananiah (27–28), in which Jeremiah displays a wistfulness that Hananiah should be right about his good news, even though Jeremiah knows he is not right (28:6). The more poetic articulation of the same issue is in 23:9-22, in which all such established prophets are dismissed as fakers.

Though difficult to assess, there is evidence of Jeremiah's conflict *with his own family and kinspeople from Anathoth* (11:21). It could be that the "Anathoth connection" (cf. 32:6-15) relates Jeremiah to the old priestly tradition of Abiathar.[38] Whether that can be sustained or not, there is a suggestion that Jeremiah is alienated from his own rootage. Indeed the poem of 8:8-13 pictures him in deep conflict with every element of leadership and he indicts everyone.

We should not, however, overstate the leadership conflict. Many oracles and poems of Jeremiah are not so specific. Most of them are undifferentiated, having a most general aim for the whole people. Jeremiah does not believe that it is a wrong decision by a judge or a wrong policy act by a king that needs to be righted. Rather it is the whole people who in their long history with YHWH have been recalcitrant and obstinate (2:13, 20; 18:12).

It is for that reason that the lawsuit language of indictment and sentence (even though handled with freedom and imagination) is the dominant mode of speech. Jeremiah is convinced that Judah is against YHWH and against covenant in its most fundamental claims.[39]

The disputedness of Jeremiah's life is more even than that. The so-called confessions show that Jeremiah is also in deep dispute with YHWH. While he publicly proclaims YHWH's will with passion and authority, these texts show that Jeremiah has also resisted the disclosures and in his own life has not found YHWH to be his "best friend" or special support. We may single out two motifs that disclose this man in his strife with YHWH. On the one hand, he hopes for *retaliation and vengeance* (11:20; 12:3; 15:15; 17:18; 18:21; 20:11). He keeps a long enemy list, and he dares to presume that his enemies are the enemies of YHWH (cf. Ps. 139:21). He yearns to see them done in. He has cast his lot with YHWH against the others, and he counts on his ally.[40] His other motif in these texts is his sense that he is *betrayed*, *deceived*, and *abandoned*, if not by YHWH, then in general. After he has cast his lot with YHWH, forsaking all others and being rejected, he concludes that the God who promised to be with him (1:19) is not. From YHWH's side, that is perhaps a statement that none may draw close to YHWH in his sovereignty, not even his called prophet. From Jeremiah's side, that is experienced as fickleness, and at no point do we see any clear resolution. This sense of estrangement belongs to his character, perhaps to the prophetic role more generally.

Thus these factors may be nuanced differently, but I think they cannot be resisted: (1) Jeremiah is overwhelmingly God's man. (2) Jeremiah is a speaker with poetic passion and stunning imagination. (3) Jeremiah is profoundly engaged in public events. (4) Jeremiah is a man of indignation and excruciating dispute. That peculiar configuration of characteristics permits one concluding judgment: Jeremiah is seen to *be a man who speaks the truth into a world of falsehood and self-deception.* By drawing this conclusion, I mean to make two points: (a) We should not be so fascinated with Jeremiah's person that we minimize his historic role as a bearer of truth into his situation.[41] (b) I submit that these four marks may be the indispensable basis for a truth speaker in the public arena. He could not have spoken the truth if he were not overwhelmingly *God's man*, if he were without *poetic imagination*, if he were not engaged in *public events*, and if he were not in *deep dispute*. And that is because, as this tradition knows, (1) truth is not our autonomous judgment, but comes only from God (cf. 23:18-22); (2) truth is not given in prose, but in poetry, which allows for God's freedom; (3) truth is not private, apart from public events; (4) truth is not without dispute in such a world of deception.

Jeremiah's truth is not eternal truth. He did not announce grand principles or abstract meanings. His truth was always as poignant and dangerous and timely as his moment. His truth from God for Judah is about "plucking up and breaking down," about "building and planting" (1:10).

Jeremiah's word borne in Israel concerns *the end of the known world,* the world presided over by the kings and priests of this age, who imagine themselves secure and stable and safe. Jeremiah must assert that that world, organized against God's covenantal faithfulness, will and must end, perhaps by the hand of Babylon. Such a terrible ending is always thought to be "too hard" (impossible) for YHWH (32:27). But YHWH can do it; life is forfeited if it tries YHWH too long.

Jeremiah's word borne among Judah's exiles is about the *beginning of a new world* wrought only by the mercy and freedom of God. This is a new possibility judged by hopeless former rulers to be impossible. They believe that there can be no new thing. Such a new world with a new David (23:5-6), a new covenant (31:31-34), a new healing (30:17) is always thought to be "too hard" (impossible) for YHWH (32:17). But YHWH can do it. Life is given again when YHWH is known to be the giver of newness.[42]

Jeremiah, the man *and his truth,* is time-bound. He belongs to his time and place, deeply in love with his people, deeply in hate with them also. So he spoke his truth to his time, and not more than that. The community around him has discerned that his words have futures within them, and so his passionate, painful way in the world continues to spill over into worlds coming after him. On the one hand, *the generation of exiles* immediately after him found his words still to have authority and power,[43] and that is why we have an ongoing Deuteronomic trajectory out of Jeremiah, which continues to present echoes of his words.

On the other hand, Jeremiah as the person who suffers and hopes most in ancient Israel continues as a powerful presence *into the New Testament.* The suffering of Jeremiah and the end of Israel, which he embodies, the hope of Judah and the new Israel he articulates have become modes for understanding Jesus, the one who can be destroyed and raised up (John 2:19). Jeremiah had led faithful people to listen for the weeping of death (Jer. 31:15; Matt. 2:18), and to live in hope of newness (Jer. 31:31-34; Heb. 8:8-12; 10:16-17). The words linger with power. This speaker in whom they are rooted continues as an agent of hard, hopeful truth.

CHAPTER TWO

The Book of Jeremiah

Meditation upon the Abyss

The book of Jeremiah is exceedingly complex and difficult to read. The standard historical-critical consensus about the book—established through the work of Bernhard Duhm and Sigmund Mowinckel—reflected the primary assumptions of that method: The book is constituted by the poetic oracles of the historical person Jeremiah (termed source A); subsequently, the poetic oracles of the prophet were supplemented by the prose narrative of his secretary Baruch, especially in the narrative of chapters 37–45 (source B); imposed upon these materials were the interpretative sections reflective of Deuteronomic theology (source C).[1] As was characteristic of that mode of scholarship, the poetic oracles assigned to the person of Jeremiah were taken to be the most important material, not only because of their poetic power, but because they were judged to be the earliest and most "authentic" and most readily assigned to the nameable person Jeremiah, who was evidently a religious genius. Negatively, the prose materials were judged to be later and second rate and, because later, degenerate and unimportant, at best a detraction from the "authentic" materials of the prophet Jeremiah. Consequently, the relationship of prose and poetic text has constituted one of the most vexing issues in Jeremiah studies.

From Person to Book

As with much of Old Testament studies, there has been a radical revolution in Jeremiah studies in the last two decades.[2] The profound change in interpretation has turned away from the person of Jeremiah to the book of Jeremiah. It is now widely concluded that any historical person of Jeremiah is in any case unrecoverable and that what we likely have in the text is an imaginative literary construct of the person and the prophet presented for interpretive reasons.[3] The turn from the person of Jeremiah also signifies a departure from nineteenth-century romantic fascination with the great person who is the carrier of spiritual genius to the interpretive work of an ongoing community that shaped the literature. Conversely, attention to the book of Jeremiah *as a book* is representative of a general perspective that views a book of the Bible not as an accidental collection of diffuse materials but as an intentionally constituted corpus that may reflect a sustained interpretive agenda. This shift from person to book underlies most of the new interpretive possibilities in Jeremiah studies.

Theology or Ideology

This shift from person to book was accomplished by two quite contrasted interpretive projects. From a *theological perspective* it has been suggested that the book of Jeremiah is a literary-editorial achievement designed to make a normative theological statement. Brevard Childs, consistent with this more general canonical approach, has suggested that the book of Jeremiah is roughly organized around themes of judgment and deliverance that correlate extensively with the old sources A and C; the poetic passages commonly assigned to the historical Jeremiah are statements of judgment, and the Deuteronomic passages characteristically speak of repentance as a foundation for new possibility.[4] Childs has not worked out this observation in any detail, but the direction of that argument is clear enough.

Ronald Clements (who has devoted a great deal of energy to the book of Jeremiah) had earlier suggested that the several books of the prophets have been systematically organized to be shaped according to the themes of judgment and deliverance.[5] This thematic organization is most obvious in the book of Ezekiel (chapters 1–24 as judgment, chapters 25–48 as deliverance), and, in a different way, the book of Isaiah with the development of what has been termed First, Second, and Third Isaiah. That editorial pattern is not as clear in the shape of the book of Jeremiah, but the point is evident with a focus on chapters 29–33 where promissory materials have been gathered together. In a closer study of chapters 1–25, Clements has quite stunningly made the case that the primary theological accents of Deuteronomic theology have shaped this material that appears to be diffuse; it is suggested, moreover, that Deuteronomic interpretation is a theological perspective designed to open the way for the emergence of postexilic Judaism.[6] In the perspective of Childs and Clements, the material serves as a quite intentional vehicle for the theological accents upon YHWH's judgment and grace; thus a theological effort of the first order.

In a quite different idiom and for a quite different purpose, Robert Carroll—the most influential Jeremiah interpreter of recent time—has also focused on the *book* of Jeremiah.[7] Carroll has little positive appreciation for any intentional theological interpretation that may be found in the book and prefers to use the term *ideology* for such interpretive moves. Though his use of the term *ideological* is not everywhere consistent, his more pejorative usage suggests editorial manipulation of the tradition within the book to make claims of meaning under the guise of literary presentation. Carroll argues that the book of Jeremiah is shot through with ideology, which means that the book is neither an innocent rendering of the historical Jeremiah nor a random collection of old materials, but it is put together, albeit awkwardly, to make an interpretive argument in a more or less sustained way.

It is quite remarkable—and in my judgment more than a little amusing—that Childs and Clements on the one hand and Carroll on the other come to quite parallel judgments about the book of Jeremiah, though with very different perspectives and intentions. Where the final form of the text is termed to be theological in a positive way or ideological in a polemical way, these scholars are agreed that the book of Jeremiah is reflective of a quite intentional interpretive agenda. It is important to pause to reflect on how far this now commonly shared perspective is removed from the source analysis of Duhm and Mowinckel, an analysis that never entertained a thought about the interpretive coherence of the book.

A Coherent Interpretation

If, in the wake of Childs, Clements, Carroll, and a host of other scholars, it is agreed that the book of Jeremiah reflects something of a coherent interpretive intentionality, then it is important to try to identify the interpretive engine that shaped the book of Jeremiah in its final form. While Childs is wont to speak (sometimes mysteriously) of "canonical forces," Carroll is more concrete in his suggestion, which seems to me to have great merit.

1. It is most plausible that the editorial hand that shaped the whole is that of the *Deuteronomists*. This term, now much used in the field, refers

(according to hypothesis) to a powerful body of interpreters that persisted over several generations and was informed by the covenantal-theological accents of the book of Deuteronomy. They continued in their imaginative interpretation in order to extrapolate from Deuteronomy for the sake of the ongoing life and faith of the community of faith in and through the exile. The proposal that the Deuteronomists shaped the book of Jeremiah suggests that they took up the remembered poems of "historical Jeremiah"—a character now lost to us—and shaped, arranged, and interpreted these materials, inserting among them their own work in prose in order to create a pattern of interpretation. Louis Stulman has given great attention to the decisive interpretive force of the great prose chapters in the book of Jeremiah, notably chapters 1, 7, 11, 26, and 36.[8] This claim of interpretive initiative for the Deuteronomists (through the prose) has the dramatic effect of transferring the weight of significance from early to late texts and from poetry to prose, so that the poetry is placed in the service of the prose, a move that would have scandalized Duhm and Mowinckel!

2. More specifically, one can notice in the book of Jeremiah the importance of scribes, learned men with writing skills who, in and through the exile, emerged as the primal fashioners and interpreters of Judaism.[9] In the book of Jeremiah, the scribe Baruch occupies a decisive role in the production of the "scroll" of Jeremiah, so that we may imagine that we witness in chapter 36 a signal that the prophetic has now passed into the custodial care of the scribal.[10] This may be indicated by chapter 36, whatever one makes of its historical claims. In a second instance, the scribe Seraiah is given a peculiar mandate by the prophet, and his anticipated activity is given dramatic location in the book of Jeremiah, namely, to assert the effective demise of Babylon (51:59-64). Thus the scribes seem to have left their signature on the book of Jeremiah, and these references to scribes in the book likely give clues to those who formed, valued, and cared for the emerging book of Jeremiah, long after the disappearance of the historical Jeremiah.[11] Following the lead of Moshe Weinfeld, we may plausibly posit a connection between the Deuteronomists, whose theological intentionality is evident, and the scribes, so that the scribes become the "book men" who give canonical force to the Deuteronomic theological program.[12]

3. If we look more closely, we may notice that Shaphan, his son Ahikam, and Gemariah, son of Ahikam, occupy conspicuous places in the prose materials of the book (Jer. 26:24; 36:10-12, 25; 39:14; 40:5-16; 41:1-6, 10, 16,

18; 43:6; see 2 Kgs. 22:3-14).[13] This suggests that the family of Shaphan constituted a major political force in Jerusalem (that was, after all, a small political economy) and perhaps a major political force in the production of the Deuteronomic-scribal book of Jeremiah. It seems likely, given the attentive support of this family for Jeremiah and his scroll, that the family was representative of and voice for a powerful political opinion in Jerusalem that opposed the royal policies of resistance to Babylon. The prose passages in the book present Jeremiah with "a word from the Lord" that it was YHWH's will that Jerusalem should surrender to Babylon, rather than to be destroyed by that ruthless empire (37:11-21; 38:1-6, 17-24). If Jeremiah's theological word is also reflective of a considered political opinion, then it may be that the edited book of Jeremiah is a product of Deuteronomic-scribal circles of Shaphan that decided and urged (on theological-*cum*-pragmatic grounds) that surrender to the empire was a responsible policy in the face of sure destruction. Thus the book of Jeremiah may represent a theological-political teaching against the royal policies that brought about the destruction of Jerusalem—politically and militarily at the hands of Babylon and theologically at the hands of YHWH. The work may be both a reflection of the actual dispute in Jerusalem and a durable testimony after the fact to the folly of the monarchy.[14]

4. If this body of tenacious theological-political opinion in Jerusalem is so convinced of its judgment and so powerful that it could accomplish the canonical rendering of its judgment, we may consider its continuing significance after 587. The Cold War slogan "Better Red than Dead" (in order that the community may live for another day) is a latter-day indicator that we need not imagine that the interpretive community of Jeremiah and the book it produced are necessarily fixed solely upon the loss of 587; rather they are concerned to generate futures of a certain kind beyond 587 and beyond the ignoble domination of Babylon.[15] That is, the book of Jeremiah as a "rolling corpus" moves beyond prejudgment of 587 to produce a ground for what becomes the reformation of the community of faith, now without monarchy, without a significant temple, without a safe city.[16] Thus the book of Jeremiah came to full expression in the scribal-Torah movement around Ezra, a movement already anticipated in the Deuteronomic-scribal work of the book of Jeremiah that was a remarkable combination of theological passion and political acumen.[17]

Looking beyond Judgment

Indications that the completed book of Jeremiah looks to a future beyond justly deserved judgment in the deportation of 587 are abundant:

- The appeal to "return" in the final form of the text is likely an appeal to the exilic community because the preexilic community in the book of Jeremiah was well past any "point of no return" (3:12-14; 8:4-7).
- The protocanonical scroll of Jeremiah 36 is, not unlike Isaiah 8:16, a resolve to leave testimony that there had been serious resistance to the destructive policies of the monarchy. The text stands as witness that there could have been another pattern of conduct and policy in Jerusalem that would have led to a very different future.
- The signature references to the scribes cited above indicate a recognition that leadership has now passed beyond king and prophet to the new mode of book men, of whom the quintessential example is Ezra, well beyond the judgment and exile.
- The defeat of Babylon, as the culmination of the oracles against the nations in Jeremiah 50–51, and the narrative rendition of the "sign" in 51:59-64 indicate that the book of Jeremiah looks beyond Babylonian brutality, an acknowledgment that the anguish of Psalm 137 has been embraced but will be overcome. The oracle of Jeremiah 50–51, moreover, is reinforced by the proto-apocalyptic oracle of Jeremiah 25 that anticipates the defeat and humiliation of Babylon.[18]
- The narrative account of trouble in postmonarchical Judah under Gedeliah is a harbinger of the political parties in emerging Judaism, including those who anticipate the restoration of monarchy (Jer. 40–41).[19]

All of these indications draw our attention to the later part of the book, consisting of what are judged to be later texts. In these texts the horizon of interpretation moves away from 587 and judgment to the prospects for what is yet to come after judgment. Most especially the promissory passages of chapters 29–33 (and especially the "Book of Comfort" in chapters 30–31) are a programmatic anticipation of restoration to the land. Best known in this corpus, of course, is the "new covenant" passage of 31:31-34 that asserts YHWH's readiness to restore the relation of Sinai with this chosen people, an old covenant now reconstituted on new grounds.

Pluck Up and Pull Down, Build and Plant

The decisive marker of 1:10 indicates that, in the end, the book of Jeremiah is preoccupied with emerging Judaism. This mandate to the prophet, which we may take as a thematic for the entire book, comes as "the words of Jeremiah . . . to whom the word of the LORD came" (1:1-2):

> See, today I appoint you over nations and over kingdoms,
>> to pluck up and to pull down,
>> to destroy and to overthrow,
>> to build and to plant. (1:10)

Of these six verbs in three pairs, the second pair, "destroy and overthrow," is not much echoed in the book, so attention is first of all given to the first and third pairs.

The verbs "pluck up and pull down" concern the destruction of Jerusalem that is to be accomplished through the words of Jeremiah. The prophetic literature is concerned with how the world is uttered to death and to new life. In the corpus of Jeremiah, we may see this "plucking up and pulling down" in several rhetorical strategies:

- The prophetic lawsuit that punishes Judah on the basis of indictment, for which Jeremiah 2:4-13 is the most commonly cited example;[20]
- The lamentations of Jeremiah, surely personal laments but here used to voice the grief of the community over the loss of all that the community cherishes (11:18; 12:6; 15:10-21; 17:14-18; 18:18-23; 20:7-8);[21]
- The metaphor of wound and sickness, especially utilized to voice the certitude that Judah is terminally ill, beyond healing (8:18; 9:3; 30:12-17);[22] and
- The familial relationships of husband and wife, parent and child, employed to bespeak the anguish, pathos, and cost that are involved for YHWH in the recalcitrance of Judah and the necessary response of YHWH in judgment (2:2-3; 3:1-5, 19-20; 31:20).[23]

Together, these passages constitute a remarkable rhetorical assault upon the illusionary certainties of Jerusalem and evidence the ways in which prophetic utterance, with remarkable imaginative force, subverts what had seemed settled and established. The rhetoric "troubles" Judah to death, a striking example of the way in which prophetic utterance leads historical reality in the canonical imagination of Israel.

It is, however, stunning that at the very outset of the edited book of Jeremiah, which is so preoccupied with exile (see 1:3), the Deuteronomic-scribal community of interpreters can anticipate the destruction of Babylon and the restoration of Jerusalem, in the word pair "plant and build." Nothing is denied of the harsh and complete judgment of "pluck up and pull down." That destruction, in the rhetoric of Jeremiah is, all the way to the bottom, the production of an abyss that is historical, political, economic, and theological, as voiced in the rhetorical. The mandate of 1:10, however, continues—in, through, and beyond the abyss—to speak an utterance to bring Jews through that unutterable abyss by proclaiming the newness that is a gift of the God who "has torn and who will heal" (Hos. 6:1; see Job 5:18).

The final form of the book of Jeremiah, designed to walk Jews into, through, and beyond the reality of destruction and exile, is indeed a sustained meditation upon the abyss caused by destruction and enacted through Babylon, an abyss about which Judaism has never ceased to reflect. While the interpretive community employs many diverse materials to provide a script for restoration and hope, it never strays far from the thematic line of the four principal verbs in 1:10.

- In 18:7-10, the prose passage speaks of "a nation," clearly Judah, that is subject to YHWH's decree, but is able by obedience or disobedience to alter even the resolve of YHWH for the future. This statement would suggest that YHWH's verdict on Israel is not a blind, fixed decree, but a judgment impinged upon by and responsive to Judah's conduct. Thus the passage asserts a remarkable zone of historical freedom whereby Israel—even in the wake of destruction—may choose for itself a different future (see Ezek. 18:14-18).
- Jeremiah 24:6-7 is clearly addressed to exiles who have already received the effect of the negative verbs. The accent is upon the positive verbs, plant and build, addressed precisely to those who "return."
- In 31:28, the two negative verbs have already been enacted, and now comes the news of YHWH's goodness in a "second watch" that constitutes the future of Israel.

- In 45:4, the negative verbs prevail, suggesting that here Baruch is presented as a device for judgment. That wholesale negation is qualified only by verse 5 that promises exemption for Baruch, a representative of the scribal group that constitutes the remnant community of Judaism.[24] Thus even the wholesale negation of Jerusalem is qualified with a promised survival of the remnant into the future (see 39:15-18).

Future Readings of Jeremiah

There remain, to be sure, elements of the book of Jeremiah that defy any inquiry about coherence. Still, there is enough coherence in the theological (Childs, Clements) and ideological (Carroll) unity of the book to suggest that it makes a deliberate statement in a way that does not rely upon any scissors-and-paste editorial explanation. More recent scholarship invites us to read the Bible with greater alertness to the evidence that something intentional is being done with and through the text that is not innocent reportage.

Such recognition of theological-ideological intentionality in the book itself suggests that the reader of the book of Jeremiah is authorized by the book to continue the work of theological intentionality. As the Deuteronomic-scribal commitment was free and empowered to "roll the corpus" forward to serve new needs in a subsequent generation of the faithful, so we may watch as the corpus continues its interpretive "roll." I will suggest two futures to this theologically-ideologically formed, dynamic scroll.

First, the four verbs—and their capacity to utter Jerusalem into the abyss of 587 and the exile and then to utter Jerusalem out of the abyss— have as their *derivative counterpoint in Christian tradition the crucifixion and resurrection of Jesus.* (A specific connection is made in John 1:19-22.) That is, in the story of Jesus, the Friday crucifixion is the "plucking up and pulling down" of conventional messianic possibility; the Sunday resurrection is the "planting and building" of messianic claim in splendor and power. Of course, I do not suggest that the Christian presentation of Jesus through these same themes should displace the Jewish abyss of city, king, and temple. That Christian act of interpretive imagination, however, is not unlike that committed in the book itself. *Mutatis mutandis,* Christian readers are also invited to ponder the abyss wherein is the truth of our life. Canonically—beyond historically—the book of Jeremiah offers an act of paradigmatic imagination whereby God is always terminating what is most treasured and then giving again beyond explanation.

In a second extrapolation, if we think of the four verbs and the invitation to meditate on the abyss, the book of Jeremiah is a useful script for the performance of abyss in the contemporary world. I believe that the great pastoral reality for the church in the United States is that we are watching the termination of the world we have loved too long and lost—a world of Western, white, male, heterosexual domination, privilege, and certitude. It has evaporated before our very eyes. Its loss creates acres of rage and anxiety.[25] That loss, moreover, may be like the loss of Jerusalem—according to the text of Jeremiah, a judgment of God on a power arrangement too long recalcitrant. The two positive verbs of Jeremiah may script hope for the newness that God is giving, a newness that we cannot see clearly and that may come in forms we do not prefer.

It is my judgment that the great pastoral opportunity among us is to utter faithful folk into the abyss too long denied, and to utter faithful folk through the abyss to newness, a difficult move given the despair among us. It occurs to me that the book of Jeremiah, given its interpretive intentionality, intends precisely this double uttering in the sixth and fifth centuries B.C.E. Because the canonical book of Jeremiah has not ceased to speak in its imaginative way, it may still yield a double utterance of judgment that contradicts denial and hope that overrides despair.

Imagine how it would have been in the days of the abyss if there had been no book of Jeremiah; no text to utter Israel into the truth of its loss so that Hananiah's phony hope might have prevailed (Jeremiah 28); no text to utter Jews into possibilities beyond the deportation.

Our society is mostly like that, lacking an adequate script for truth-telling about the abyss, the loss, and the possibility. Without the script, the victims and the perpetrators of abyss engage in denial that does not face reality or in despair that does not hope. The book of Jeremiah, however, invites other utterances. The script of Jeremiah invites other performances. There is a word from the Lord given us by these amazing scrollmakers. The ones entrusted with the scroll—Jews and Christians—are exactly the ones for truth-telling. At the center of that truth to be told is exactly the God who delights in steadfast love, justice, and righteousness (9:23-24). Without a new performance of that script, we may settle for "wisdom, might, wealth."[26] There need not be such a deathly settlement, however, because the script awaits new performance. No wonder Paul's great pondering of the cross ends with allusion to Jeremiah:

> He is the source of your life in Christ Jesus, who became for us wisdom from God, and righteousness and sanctification and redemption, in order that, as it is written, "Let the one who boasts, boast in the Lord." (1 Cor. 1:30-31)

It is often observed that the book of Jeremiah is unreadable. That judgment, however, refers to our conventional rationality through which the book of Jeremiah makes no sense. If, however, we see that the book is a meditation upon the abyss, into it and out of it, then we can see that the book is indeed readable. What is in fact unreadable is the abyss for which we have no ready categories. The abyss is unreadable, moreover, because the God who presides over the abyss will not be read through our central categories. Once we face that unreadable God who acts in freedom and faithfulness, then the abyss becomes readable and the book of Jeremiah as a script for performing abyss makes sense of an odd but compelling kind.

CHAPTER THREE

Recent Scholarship

Intense Criticism, Thin Interpretation

The year 1986 was an extraordinary year in Jeremiah studies, for we saw the appearance of three major critical commentaries on Jeremiah in one year. The Jeremiah contributions of 1986 are especially important because Jeremiah no doubt has peculiar poignancy for our contemporary situation of faith in Western culture. The publication of these commentaries is an invitation to every preacher, teacher, and interpreter to make a major investment of energy in the book of Jeremiah.

The three commentaries on which I shall comment are those by Robert P. Carroll,[1] William McKane,[2] and William L. Holladay.[3] To these will be added in our discussion a fourth work, by Ronald E. Clements.[4] The first three are major critical efforts reflecting an enormous amount of work, energy, and discerning judgment. They are certain to shape and determine Jeremiah studies for a long time to come. Clements's work will be dealt with separately because it is of another genre, being intentionally an expository presentation. At the outset I express my sense of awe, amazement, and gratitude for these commentaries, each of which embodies many years of careful work. My critical comments are in the context of that appreciation.

I

The first three commentaries together reflect the shape and limits of current critical study. The central critical issue of the book of Jeremiah is that there is a body of powerful poetry in the book that lives in an odd relation to a more verbose, very different, theologically tendentious prose. Clearly the book of Jeremiah, as it stands, had a long complicated history of formation.[5] The book of Jeremiah is held to contain a core of Jeremiah's work, which has been subsequently expanded, reshaped, and reinterpreted to meet later needs. The book of Jeremiah is the record and residue of that long process of redaction in the interest of ongoing contemporaneity.

This scholarly legacy from Bernhard Duhm and Sigmund Mowinckel has led scholarship to focus on two closely related questions: (1) What is early and what is late? and (2) What is genuine and what is addition? That is, the recognizable literary enigmas of the book have been shaped as historical questions to see when and in what context each piece of literature was created. It is characteristically assumed that the historical context provides the clue to the intention of the text. This preoccupation with historical approach to the literature has set the direction and, I believe, the severe limitation of much Jeremiah study.

II

This conventional way of posing questions about Jeremiah, for better or worse, is still dominant in these commentaries.

Holladay is much informed by the methods of Helga Weippert, and his commentary follows the older line of focusing on the historical Jeremiah.[6] Holladay's governing presupposition about the historical Jeremiah leads him to date the material as precisely as possible according to a presumed chronology of the prophet.[7] Holladay claims for the prophet not only the great poetry, which is generally conceded, but also much of the prose, which he considers to be a recasting of the poetry by Jeremiah. Holladay's emphasis focuses on the person, life, ministry, and speech of Jeremiah. Thus his argument largely revolves around historical questions and seeks a match between the text and the context in which it must have been uttered. In my judgment, Holladay becomes embarrassingly specific about different verses in a unit being assigned to different times. Such a procedure holds the imagination of the text-creators hostage to historical experience, as though the writer-speaker could not imagine beyond concrete, identifiable experience. The logic of such a view is to require imagination to live within the limits of known historical experience, obviously an inadequate way of receiving such evocative literature.

The commentary by Carroll forms a significant contrast with Holladay's work. Indeed Carroll's book is a bold, inventive proposal for a major break with the dominant critical tradition. Much informed by Winfried Thiel,

Carroll regards the present form of the book of Jeremiah as an intentionally redactive work of the sixth-century exile. That redactional work used
existing materials from the time of Jeremiah; but the recasting has been
complete, to serve the religious needs of the exilic communities.

An important implication of Carroll's work is that any access to the
historical Jeremiah is impossible. The book does not intend or purport to
offer data about the historical Jeremiah, and the pursuit of such a question is wrong-headed and should be abandoned. It may seem that Carroll
has emancipated interpretation from the deep grip of historical questions
that so much preoccupy Holladay. In fact, Carroll is as much preoccupied
with dating as is Holladay, with determining what is early and what late,
and in an odd sort of negative way, what is authentic and what is not. The
difference is that while Holladay seeks to recover the historical Jeremiah,
Carroll seeks to portray the Deuteronomic Jeremiah. Carroll's effort, however, still seeks a historical placement of the text, reflective of a conviction
that the historical location provides the decisive clue to literary intention.
I do not believe Carroll's approach represents any serious departure from
a long-standing historical focus. Moreover I do not believe the difference
argued by Carroll is much of a gain for interpretation, as long as the literature must always be submitted to the norm of history.

Carroll's work lives at the edge of a defiant pugilism that keeps the
book interesting but also distracts from the interpretation. My sense is
that Carroll has a negative, abrasive relation to the literature with which
he has lived for so long. On the one hand, he concludes we have no access
to the historical Jeremiah because the material has been massively recast.
On the other hand, he seems to regard the Deuteronomist (to whom he
assigns much of the book) as a heavy-handed ideologue who is uncritical,
unthinking, and intolerant. Carroll also considers such theological passion, as reflected by the Deuteronomist, as dishonest and fundamentally
unacceptable.

It is disconcerting that Carroll is impatient with (or dismissive of) both
literary and theological claims. On the one hand, the magnificent literary
efforts reflected in the text are regularly dismissed by Carroll as rhetoric,
metaphor, or hyperbole, without paying any attention to the strategic and
decisive function of such literary uses.[8] As a result, the choicest elements in
the text are mostly dismissed as irrelevant and unimportant. On the other
hand, theological claims are generally bracketed under the word *ideology*.
More curious is the fact that the same word, *ideology*, is used both for the

"YHWH-only" party in the literature[9] and for the contemporary feminist interpretation toward which Carroll has pronounced antipathy.[10] His use of *ideology* for the second matter (feminist interpretation) makes one wonder about the first use of the term, when it is directed toward the claims of the text itself. Much of the time Carroll's comment is a polemical argument that does not always contribute to our understanding of the literature.

The commentary by McKane is the sort of volume that one would expect in the International Critical Commentary (ICC) series. It is loaded with textual detail in the most ponderous way. It reflects the close, disciplined, exhaustive, tenacious reading of the text associated with the high days of textual criticism at the turn of the nineteenth century.

All three commentaries reflect erudition, but from that perspective, McKane is the most astonishing. He has worked closely with the versions and has paid careful attention to the classical rabbinic exegesis. There is a wealth of detailed information for those who have the patience to dig through it. McKane is at his best in solving some of the seemingly unsolvable riddles of the obscure texts by his patient sorting out of the linguistic evidence.

McKane believes that Weippert has taken on an impossible and unconvincing task of connecting the prose to the person of Jeremiah, and that Thiel is so consistent as to be reductionist in his conclusion about a Deuteronomic editing. McKane provides a painstaking report on all the places where he has either appealed to or critiqued Weippert and Thiel.[11]

McKane's own theory of the formation of the book is less doctrinaire and straitjacketed. He proposes that there was a "rolling corpus" in which texts were handled, transmitted, and repeatedly recast to keep the text live.[12] He has no grand theory about the formation of the book and is content to work a text at a time.[13]

McKane's book is exceedingly hardgoing, and my first impression is of its density. Indeed, it is nearly unreadable except for a specialist who is willing and able to follow the detailed contours of the technical work. That is partly the nature of McKane's argument and field of investigation; but beyond that, the format of the book makes his work nearly inaccessible. In the end, the problem may be McKane's propensity to avoid interpretive judgments, so that sometimes one is not sure what he thinks the text means. His avoidance of interpretive judgments on all but the closest technical matters is, I assume, grounded in his observation that the claim that this is the "word of the Lord" is a claim not to be followed in a commentary because "all language is human language."[14] Well, yes, but the literature makes another kind of claim. The interpreter, in my judgment, cannot simply dismiss the claim of the text but must see what the claim means. Moreover one need not embrace a high theology of the text's authority to admit theological interpretation as a part of the task of comment.

While these three commentaries go about their work in very different ways, and from very different perspectives, one is impressed that this is, in all three cases, intense criticism. These commentaries are marvelous exhibits of what critical scholarship can do and do well.

III

That, however, leaves us with the question, what should a commentary seek to do? Many different answers will be given to that question, and Carroll has the good grace to urge his readers to read all the commentaries and not settle for his or for any one.[15] Readers of commentaries, however, will characteristically have a broadly identifiable expectation. In a consideration of that question, Bernhard Anderson has suggested that a good commentary should do the following:

1. Be reflective of and responsive to the history of interpretation.
2. Be reflective of a "double loyalty" to the scholarly community and the community of faith.
3. Provide necessary information "without becoming tediously detailed or burdensomely lengthy."
4. Take a firm stand on current hermeneutical debate.
5. Draw the reader into the world of the text without being didactic or moralistic.[16]

Anderson's criteria reflect a generally shared expectation.

We are bound to say that on the first point of "history of interpretation" these commentaries are on the whole well done. They tend to be preoccupied with recent "guild interpretation," though McKane pays attention to the rabbis and Holladay attends to the Reformers.

On the other criteria, these commentaries are not concerned with interpretive issues of the contemporary faith community, whether Jewish or Christian. On the whole, Carroll seems resistant to the possibility of attention to the faith community and, for McKane, that horizon is not operational. For Holladay this dimension is only incidental and not seriously intentional. While these commentaries are long on critical questions, the interpretive outcome is characteristically thin.

Hermeneutical issues that move from "meant" to "means" are largely lacking in these commentaries. The model uniformly pursued is that of a detached, objective observer who plays no role in the interpretive process. The issue is not raised of how or in what way these texts might be "true."[17] There is no hint of a second loyalty to a community of faith that looks to these texts, of a probe about how the issues of truth and faith might impinge on such a community, or even an awareness of a human community that yearns for authorizing interpretation. The domination of the historical questions means that pertinence to the context of the contemporary writer or reader is completely eliminated.

The methods utilized in these commentaries uniformly guarantee a bracketing out of interpretive questions. The conventional approaches of the scholarly community are historical and linguistic. An imaginative hermeneutic requires utilization of literary criticism that pays attention to the function of words, phrases, sounds, images, metaphors, and tensions in evoking for the listener (ancient and contemporary) a different reading of one's own social experience. Moreover careful attention to the intentional, evocative power of language and rhetoric spills over into theological surplus.[18] In such an imaginative literary process the theological questions are raised and theological decisions are not just permitted but required.

Consider an extreme example from Carroll. He writes, concerning 3:1-5, "Now there may be the basis for a theology of the pain of God here, but cuckoldry is more a matter for ribaldry than a serious foundation for doing theology."[19] Is this not to dismiss the evident intention of the text itself? Carroll continues, by drawing his own theological conclusions: "He [i.e., YHWH], like an outraged cuckolded husband, can only retaliate by smashing up the place and destroying everything (cf. 4:5—6:26)." Carroll concludes that the "incompatibility" in the text between the absolute rejection of Judah and the yearning for a return can be dismissed with a theological judgment, impossible from a human, legal point of view yet possible with God; "but that is to fail to grasp the absoluteness of the divine rejection of Judah spelled out so categorically in 2:5-37."[20] We must ask from where Carroll has arrived at the conclusion that the incompatibility is no basis for theology, when his own draconian literary criticism dissolves the very claim that stands at the center of the text. The problem is not in the subtle theologizing done in the text but in the antiseptic notion of theology that governs the commentator's field of perception, albeit in the name of objectivity. Such a presupposition, which is incongruous with the text under consideration, in fact robs the text of its capacity to have an alternative say. The text is more radical than the commentator is prepared to have it be.

How is it that criticism and interpretation have become such embarrassed and awkward partners? What of criticism that does not better serve interpretation? From where will the faith community do its interpretation if it receives such lean help from criticism?

My expectation, of course, is that these distinguished commentaries, in the most distinguished series now underway, should prize critical, objective, scientific scholarship. That is what they set out to do. Yet what kind of objectivity is it when Holladay and Carroll can draw such antithetical conclusions? Or what scientific scholarship is it that dismisses a text that claims to be "the word of the Lord" with the external judgment that "all language is human language," so that the commentary dismisses the central affirmation of the commented-upon text without any hermeneutical uneasiness? I conclude that such an interpretive posture is not objective, but it is in fact quite subjective. It is, however, the subjectivity that has been sanctioned and authorized by the critical guild. Probably it is accurate to say that the stance taken uniformly in these commentaries is not objective but detached, that is, staying distant from the dangerous, evocative claims of the text itself. When the method used resists the claim and character of the text studied, we likely have distancing that is detached, in order (wittingly or not) to escape the terrible and wondrous claim of the text.

The commentary by Clements is an important and successful departure from the preoccupation of the commentaries just mentioned. While Clements is fully conversant with the critical issues, he has set out to do interpretation that moves beyond conventional critical questions. He has succeeded largely because of his willingness to focus on the theological issues, and because of the pastoral empathy he manifests toward the text and toward the people moving in and through the text.

While he is no ideologue about canon criticism, Clements is prepared to look at the book of Jeremiah whole and to consider the parts in relation to the larger aim of the book. Without getting bogged down in the historical questions that so preoccupy Holladay and Carroll, Clements sees the book as a study of and meditation about the crisis of exile, its theological significance, its pastoral dangers and potentialities. Readers of Clements will find serious and sustained wrestling with issues that have important analogues in our own pastoral-theological situation.

We may cite three cases as examples of Clements's perspective:

1. Clements proposes that the "Book of Comfort" and the surrounding "hope passages" in chapters 30–33 form the pivotal center of the book. That is, these chapters are not simply another element in a miscellaneous collection but are an interpretive clue to the sense and intention of the whole. At the center of the literature is a profound trust in God, who will rule over and overrule the situation of despair that is the fulcrum of the book.

2. Clements boldly suggests that the whole book struggles with the question of theodicy. That issue, however, is not a speculative matter but one raised from inside of faith by those who wonder about the tenuous, vexing relationship between historical circumstances and the reality of God. In his treatment, Clements makes clear why commentaries that are stuck in historical questions never get to the theological issues that create the power and dynamic of the book. Finally, the dating and context of the text do not matter much if the battle for faith is not the focus of our reading.

3. In discussing the "oracles against the nations" (chapters 46–51), Clements quickly moves past the usual critical dismissal of these poems to see in them rumination on God's cosmic sovereignty. The nations imagine they are autonomous but are finally called to account according to God's purpose.

Two things are clear in such powerful interpretation. First, Clements has not violated critical convention in his treatment; it is nevertheless abundantly clear that matters of dating and authorship are not much help or hindrance to serious interpretation. The real issue is the willingness to ask a different kind of question. Second, focus on such issues as hope, theodicy, and sovereignty makes the text quickly conversant with the recurrence of just those issues in our own time. The interpretive work to which Clements calls us requires not only critical sophistication but also a readiness to be boldly theological, recognizing that faith issues are real issues, even in the Bible. Clements has not done our interpretive work for us, but he has opened the way for our better work, inviting us to the same courage and empathy he exhibits so effectively.

IV

My reflection on these commentaries is not as an outsider to the guild but as an insider who shares the work, problems, and presuppositions of these scholars, even if not all their vast skills. The question pressed upon me as an insider is, How do we comment in a social situation of such urgency as ours? If we grant even the most general claim of the text that this is a live authorizing word that continues to have power to liberate imagination for obedience and daring, then we are bound to ask what the text *continues to say* that matters, how we *listen with availability*, and how in our interpretation *the continued saying* and the *available listening* are brought together. In trying to make a move from criticism to interpretation, my sense is that the first three commentaries give little attention either to the "continued say" or the "available listening" that belongs to taking the text with seriousness.

A Jeremiah commentary might ask, What in this powerful literature could usefully and faithfully redescribe the world?[21] To redescribe, I submit, is urgent. It cannot be done from our private imaginings, which are too weak and domesticated, but only from an authorizing text. How could it be that the text of Jeremiah might redescribe our human life to permit new perceptions, new actions, new compassions, new obedience, new hopes? A partial agenda might be the following:

Are *prayers about injustice* (*theodicy*) any longer capable of being uttered, and is an answer imaginable or hearable?

Can *the royal-temple complex* work its powerful will toward death through an ideology of greed and anxiety, or will it finally succumb to a larger, inscrutable power that will out?

Is a "*YHWH-alone*" passion simply an omniscient imagination of self, or is there a moral coherence to our common life?[22]

What of *the daily manufacture of exiles*? Are such people fated to be despised and dismissed, or is there hope?[23]

Is there *a word from the Lord* or is the sky empty; is reality shaped only in the narrow perimeters of realpolitik; can the powerful finally have their way, or is there a transcendent answerability?[24]

Is there *a rending of a cosmic heart* when pain ushers in care that outruns
anger? Or is such a thought merely wishful rhetoric?

The "continued say" of the Jeremiah tradition concerns a strong critique
of the world of power politics, moral indifference, economic cynicism, and
historical displacement. It dares to say in the context of the evident world
that:

Justice questions have not been and cannot be bracketed out.
Large concentrations of cynical power—political and/or religious—can
never be ultimate, but "they have their day and cease to be."
There is a moral coherence to the world (in Israel articulated as Torah)
that will not be mocked.
Exiles—refugees, hostages, marginal ones—cannot be written off and
finally forgotten.
There is an odd, inscrutable, concrete word of assurance and demand
that is at work in the poem and the repeated dictum, "Thus says
the Lord."
This cuckolded husband, yearning mother, betrayed father, enraged
potter, ambushing lion of a God struggles with rage, rejection, and
passion, and sometimes embraces "a more excellent way."

These claims, which I believe to be central to the Jeremiah literature,
are not ordinary claims. Indeed they are highly unconventional, radical,
subversive, affrontive, outrageous, and unsettling. They cannot therefore
be articulated in ordinary ways. The voice who dares to speak in such ways
(whether that voice is named Jeremiah or the Deuteronomist or simply B)
must find outraged, pathetic, intrusive, buoyant speech with which to say
such things. Interpretation requires attention to the "continued say" of the
text and the struggle of the text to find extraordinary ways to speak these
extraordinary descriptions of reality.

The "continued say" of the Jeremiah text was unwelcome before the
collapse because it was too hard. It was unwelcome in light of the collapse
because it smacked of propaganda and seemed to promise more than was
permitted by convention and the reasonableness of the dominant ideology. Yet the "say" has powerfully continued until that very "say" has arrived
at canonization. We have before us a canonized "say" that continues to
demand our attentiveness and our attention.

Our "available listening" is as astonishing as the "continued say." We can be available for listening only in our own context, nowhere else. Our particular context of interpretation suggests that:

> The power of violence and brutality is so large among us that the question of theodicy seems almost silly.
>
> The royal-temple ideology is so all-consuming, we can scarcely make a discernment outside its comprehensiveness.
>
> Our emotive individualism is so compelling that any ". . . -alone" claim is in immediate jeopardy.[25]
>
> The manufacture of exiles as the necessary by-product of large, self-serving concentrations of power happens on so many fronts, it is hard to imagine exiles who will not finally be scuttled and forgotten.[26]
>
> The dominant offers of "absolutes" among us seem so fated as to make a "rendered cosmic heart" unthinkable.

In light of these realities, how would it be possible to be available for listening to this "continued say" in our situation? This is the challenge we face as critical interpreters. Obviously such a challenge requires great learning as reflected in these commentaries. It also demands consummate artistry and nervy passion for a construal that has theological substance and courage.

We linger so long and so persistently over these texts of Jeremiah because we have a hunch that they hold a prospect of redescribing the world, that the world need not be seen through the tired eyes and heard through the uncircumcised ears of the ideology of brutality and anxiety. It need not, but it will be seen and heard only in that way, unless interpretation offers an alternative.

It is the disproportion of intense criticism and thin interpretation in these commentaries that has led my thinking in this direction. These masterful commentators (Holladay, Carroll, McKane) of course know all about these matters that I have mentioned. This is, thus, not a critique of their work. It is rather a reflection on our curious situation as scholars and interpreters in our season of urgency.

The classical models of critical interpretation practiced so well in these commentaries have been so keen on distance that intentional interpretive linkages are often perceived as too risky and illegitimate. The problem, however, is the kind of distance that is maintained between the text and our situation. On the whole we are still committed to a *historical distance* in which the text belongs to a time and place and is held there and cannot move toward us.[27] There may, however, also be an *artistic distance* that of course does not rush to intimacy with our time but mediates, processes, hints, and finally discloses a different world to us. That disclosing has the character of revelation. The text is finally revelatory because its odd utterance is uttered in such unavoidable and compelling ways.

It is difficult to write about these books in the context of a commitment to the hermeneutical enterprise. In another context, it would be sufficient to say these are splendid, competent studies. But that commitment requires that these commentaries be reviewed not only in the environs of the scholarly community but in the presence of the church and synagogue, and with a yearning, frightened eye on our world that is collapsing. In the very long run, one wonders if a verdict will be given about us, that we let the text have its powerful say in ways that mediated faithful human options in our time; or if we will be judged to have kept the text at such a distance that the larger questions from these texts were not permitted and the daring hints of resolution were not made available.

ITEM CHARGED

P.Barcode:

Due Date: 11/11/2019 04:30 PM

Title: Like fire in the bones : listening
for the prophetic word in
Jeremiah / Walter Brueggemann ;
edited by Patrick D. Miller.

Author: Brueggemann, Walter
CallNo.: BS1525.52 .B78 2006
Enum.:
Chron.:
Copy: 1
I.Barcode:

CHAPTER FOUR

Theology in Jeremiah

Creatio in Extremis

The book of Jeremiah offers a clear test case and model for the shift in scholarly paradigms in Old Testament study. In the "history of traditions" perspective dominated by Gerhard von Rad, the tradition of Jeremiah is firmly situated in the exodus and Sinai-covenant traditions of Moses, but with some engagement with the David-messianic traditions as well.[1] This entire phase of scholarship has resulted in a lopsided emphasis upon the traditio-historical background of the book.

We may notice, however, an addendum to von Rad's perspective that has controlled Jeremiah studies. Because of the three-source theory of Bernhard Duhm and Sigmund Mowinckel, the Deuteronomic redaction of the book and the so-called Baruch document left the way open to discerning evidence of sapiential influence in the literature.[2] On the one hand, Moshe Weinfeld has urged a linkage between wisdom and the traditions of Deuteronomy.[3] On the other hand, James Muilenburg has explored the scribal role of Baruch and has linked scribal activity to the more general category of wisdom.[4] Thus it is possible to see a development in the Jeremiah traditions toward wisdom influence that in turn suggests an openness to creation. This possibility, however, has been a quite subordinate point in the interpretive models that situated Jeremiah in the Mosaic-covenantal-levitical matrix reflected in the Deuteronomists and voiced in the tradition of Hosea.[5]

I

The important shift in interpretive models permits us to pay much more sustained attention to creation themes in the tradition of Jeremiah.[6] While it is clear that "creation" is an ill-defined rubric and therefore may include many diverse elements, and while there is at the moment a temptation to pancreationism (like an earlier pancovenantalism), it is unmistakable that this general perspective on Yahwism pervades the book of Jeremiah, a pervasion mostly denied and kept invisible by the once dominant history-of-traditions perspective.

Leo Perdue has provided a convenient overview of "creation theology in Jeremiah" in terms of (a) creation and history, (b) creation and the destiny of the individual, and (c) wisdom and creation.[7] Of particular interest is his discussion of the "chaos tradition" concerning the divine warrior that shows up both in the so-called Scythian Songs and in the Oracles against the Nations.[8] It is telling that this theme, especially in light of the work of Frank Cross, Patrick Miller, and Paul Hanson, can be understood in terms of "creation-chaos," whereas von Rad linked these same texts to a holy war, a clear illustration of how particular methodological assumptions mandate and preclude certain readings.[9]

We may list some of the rich variety of creation motifs evident in the Jeremiah traditions, in part informed by Perdue's exposition:

- An emphasis upon *land* can be understood in terms of Moses-Joshua historical tradition but can also be seen as the space for life willed and maintained by the creator God (2:7; 3:19; 4:3; 33:12; 45:4)[10] and made possible by YHWH's guarantee of *fertility* (8:13, 20; 22:6; 31:5).
- Fertility in turn is made possible by the assurance of *rain*, a matter of great significance in a marginal, arid climate (2:1-3; 3:2-3; 5:24; 14:4, 22).
- Focus upon land, fertility, and rain is also confirmed by the utilization of concrete "metaphors of nature," for example, horses and birds (8:6-7), plants and wild animals (1:11; 5:6; 12:9; 24:1), and grain, wine, and oil (31:12). Such imagery saturates the poetry.
- More generally we notice, along with Perdue, linkages to wisdom, that is, regular, orderly patterns of reality (8:7; 15:14; 17:11).
- Perhaps most interesting is the claim of 5:22 that YHWH's ordering of the sand of the seashore creates a boundary and a limit to chaos, thus providing a safe, viable, fruitful place for human habitation.

This listing is only representative. It is sufficient nonetheless to indicate that the tradition of Jeremiah places YHWH on a wide, panoramic screen, as wide as all creation, and situates Judah in its theopolitical crisis amid the guarantees and threats that are as large as all creation. Because it is not possible to explore all such uses, I want to focus only on three cases that I take to be "limit expressions" of the "limit experiences" of Judah living in a creation that is fully dependent upon YHWH and fully open to YHWH's singular guarantee of life.[11]

II

In any consideration of creation themes in Jeremiah, an important reference point is 4:24-29, which is situated in a series of poetic units concerned with foreign invasion.[12] Historically this poetic unit refers to the threat of a foreign invader (apparently Babylon) who will at the behest of YHWH terminate life in the world and, consequently, life in Jerusalem. Canonically this text and the themes it presents function as *judgment* in a two-stage "final form" text of *judgment and hope*.[13] Special attention may be paid to this text, both because it is an epitome of the ominous quality of life in jeopardy from YHWH and because of its wondrously symmetrical mode of articulation.[14]

The poem proceeds in four parallel lines, together with a fifth line naming YHWH as the sole agent of the dismantling of creation, even as YHWH had been the sole agent of creation. The first four lines are introduced by *rā'îtî*, the report of an observer who anticipates the destruction, accented in each line by *hinneh*, bespeaking the surprise, intensity, and extremity of the destruction. The lines proceed from the most general (heavens and earth) to the landscape of earth (mountains and hills), to the inhabitants (human and birds), and finally to the specific land of well-being (*karmel*) that YHWH has guaranteed and that Judah now inhabits. These elements of creation are matched and trumped by the terms of negation, "waste and void" (*tōhû wābōhû*) at the outset, "quaking and moving" as signs of elemental instability, and a double negation, *'ên*.[15] Every line except the first summarizes with "all"—all hills, all birds, all cities—nothing spared, nothing held back, nothing protected, nothing guaranteed.

It is unmistakable that the dismantling described here witnesses in calibrated ways to the creation strategy of Genesis 1. Jeremiah 4:24-26 is a step-by-step subtraction from the "very good" creation upon which Israel has counted and in which its own life is lived. It is of course sensible to say with Perdue that such rhetoric of "the cataclysmic upheaval of nature is obvious hyperbole."[16] Such a verdict, however, misses the cumulative intent of the rhetoric, which is to imagine and invite the listener of the poem to host a scenario in which nothing reliable or life-sustaining is left. Creation theology here functions to voice a complete, unreserved, elemental negation of all that makes life livable, a negation that could hardly be uttered without such large language. Conversely the rhetoric makes the theological point that YHWH is fully capable of termination, and in this circumstance ready to terminate an awesome, sublime articulation of sovereignty. Those addressed are pressed to discern themselves in a moment of radical rejection, more radical and wholesale than any "historical tradition" could possibly voice. This is the most imaginable discontinuity that could be uttered. When the text is seen as an articulation of limit designed to lead Judah beyond its conventional imagination, there is nothing hyperbolic about it. This is the real thing for YHWH the creator, the real thing for creation that has no autonomous existence, and unmistakably the real thing for Judean listeners.

III

Given this intense portrayal of demolition, we cannot be emotionally or cognitively prepared for the assurance of 31:35-36, 37, which I take to be an antithesis to 4:23-26. These two brief oracles in chapter 31 appeal to the stability and reliability of creation as a ground from which to assert the stability and reliability of YHWH's promise of durability to "the offspring" of Israel. Whereas 4:23-26 voices YHWH's destruction of creation, these oracles assure that such demolition is precluded, prohibited, and made impossible in the economy of YHWH.

This oracle that stands in penultimate position in the "Book of Comfort" (chs. 30–31) makes what may be regarded as the most extreme guarantee of well-being in creation theology. It is viewed by contemporary scholarship as a later part of the "rolling corpus" of the Jeremiah tradition.[17] The oracles may be treated as distinct, isolated units or as confirmation of the promise of new covenant in 31:31-34.

In any case, each oracle, termed by Herbert Huffmon as an "impossible promise," is organized around an "if" of impossibility (in each case an impossibility for creation) and taken as an assurance of the impossibility of the cessation or rejection of "the offspring" of Israel.[18] In the first oracle, the authorization formula (v. 35a) is supported by the doxology (v. 35bc), and reinforced by a reiteration of the divine name (v. 35d). The doxology consists of two participial verbs, the first concerning sun, moon, and stars together with the crucial term "fixed order" (*ḥuqqôt*), the second concerning the sea (see Ps. 146:6). The four elements of creation here mean to comprehend the entire scope of creation. The whole of v. 35 only certifies who it is who speaks, the one with power to resolve, to initiate, sustain, and guarantee the created order.

It is this one who speaks the "if . . . then" of v. 36. The "if" that is taken to be "not possible" is the cessation of these "fixed orders" from before the face of YHWH.[19] On the basis of the fixed order of creation that cannot cease, the "then" is the equally impossible thought that Israel will cease; Israel is grounded in the bottom-line claim concerning the indelible sureness of creation.

The same structure pertains in the oracle of v. 37, presented as it is, sandwiched between two formulas of authorization. Here the impossible "if" is the measuring and exploration of unfathomable creation that is beyond all human measurement. It is the creation impossibility that provides the ground for the "then," the impossibility of the ending of Israel's existence. The power of these assurances, unlike either vv. 31-34 or vv. 38-40, is the wonder of the "natural order," a wonder of regularity and dependability that would seem to be nourished and noticed in something like wisdom teaching.

The juxtaposition of 4:23-26 and 31:35-37 suggests the extreme interpretive possibilities of creation theology hosted within the tradition of Jeremiah. It is likely that 4:23-26 is authentic to the prophetic person and is surely early, concerned with *judgment* upon a recalcitrant community; it is probable that 31:35-37 is a later utterance from a subsequent generation, designed to offer *hope* to an exilic or postexilic community when the very existence of that community is unmistakably in jeopardy.

Thus the two texts reflect chronologically a movement from early to late, together with very different circumstances. Canonically they move from judgment to assurance. Something like a two-stage understanding of life with YHWH is surely indicated.[20] If, however, we take a synchronic view of the tradition and see the two accents together in the final form of the text, then an unrelieved "tension between present misery and future property" is evident in the book, as noted by Robert P. Carroll.[21] The juxtaposition of these two "limit expressions" of utter demolition (4:23-26) and total assurance (31:35-37) suggests that neither the demolition nor the assurance is the proper focus of creation theology in the tradition of Jeremiah. Rather both claims are instrumental and point beyond themselves to the one who speaks, YHWH, the one who presides over creation and over the destiny of Judah. These two extremes of expression, therefore, bear witness to the theological claim that finally Israel must come to terms with YHWH upon whom its future well-being solely depends. Both the coming destruction and the subsequent assurance are functions of YHWH's sovereign governance that Israel cannot evade and without which it cannot live.[22]

IV

In the context of these two most extreme statements, we may now consider one other recurring hymnic assertion of creation theology that will call attention to three texts (10:12; 32:17; 51:15). I take up these three texts because they roughly echo the same cadences of what must have been a more or less stylized doxological assertion. The subject of that stylized assertion is clearly creation in its linkage to the Creator, and the matrix of the recurring formulation is clearly sapiential.[23]

Thus if we are to look for the natural habitat of this rhetorical pattern, we will likely find it in wisdom materials that are at the same time instructional and liturgical. It is not our purpose to trace the antecedents of the uses of Jeremiah, except to contend that the doxological articulation is an older formulation situated outside conventional "prophetic" discourse that revolves around speeches of judgment and promise. One such reference point for such antecedent sapiential articulation is in Proverbs 3:19-20:

> The LORD by wisdom founded the earth;
> by understanding he established the heavens;
> by his knowledge the deeps broke open,
> and the clouds drop down the dew.

This formulation begins with the naming of YHWH and identifies three agencies whereby YHWH creates wisdom, understanding, and knowledge. Beyond the triad of agents, the third portion of the statement (v. 20) departs from the parallelism of the first two lines in two ways. First, the third statement of agency (knowledge) includes two objects in parallel lines (deeps, clouds), so that the match of agent and object in the first two lines (wisdom-earth, understanding-heavens) is violated. Second, the verbs in v. 20 have the created objects as their subjects, and not YHWH, as in the first two lines. Thus the third element of the unit breaks what seems be the natural cadence by greater variation.

This small textual unit is regarded by R. Norman Whybray as a part of a second larger expansion in the development of Proverbs 1–9.[24] More importantly, William McKane, along with Whybray, observes that the purpose of the unit is to link wisdom to YHWH, so that YHWH is seen to be the agent of the reliable, dazzling order of creation.[25] McKane, moreover, suggests that these verses belong to an editorial piece closely connected to Proverbs 8:22-31. And because Proverbs 8:22-31 figures large in any theological assessment of sapiential tradition, we are able to suggest that Proverbs 3:19-20 articulates a pivotal theological claim.

In Proverbs 8:22-31, wisdom is reckoned to be an intimate of YHWH in the work of creation. In Proverbs 3:19-20, the same claim is made, except that "wisdom," not yet "personified," is here richly expressed by three agencies, wisdom and the two parallel terms. These two verses, then, make a primal statement about lived reality as creation and provide the baseline for thinking theologically and ethically about cosmic and social reality with its orderliness, its uncompromising requirements, and its unfathomable gifts.[26]

V

It is clear that the Jeremiah tradition takes up this doxological, sapiential claim that redefines the world as creation and asserts the connection between YHWH and the world through the verbs and agents of creation. It is clear that while the Jeremiah tradition recontextualizes such a sapiential formulation, it is no longer intended simply as a doxological baseline. Rather the rhetoric is drawn into sociopolitical crisis with which the Jeremiah tradition is preoccupied. The first such use of this doxological formula is found in 10:12:

> It is he who made the earth by his power,
>> who established the world by his wisdom,
>> and by his understanding stretched out the heavens.

The larger unit of 10:1-6 is peculiar in its context, offering a deeply polemical and doxological contrast between the idols (who are powerless, false, and merit no attention) and YHWH (who is incomparable, true, living and powerful). The polemic against idols (cf. Pss. 115, 135; Isa. 44:9-20) is not usual in traditions as early as Jeremiah, and the weight of scholarly opinion has been against the authenticity of the passage. Be that as it may, the final assertion of v. 16 draws even the religious polemic into a Jeremianic matrix.[27]

More specifically, vv. 12-15 sharply contrasts YHWH and the idols. In vv. 12-13, YHWH is the creator God who works with immense power through all creation. Indeed the large rhetorical claims here correspond to facets of the Joban speeches of the whirlwind. The counterassertion of vv. 14-15 is a stark contrast made with an inventory of negatives: stupid, without knowledge, shame, false, without breath, worthless, and delusion. The contrast is detailed, absolute, and sustained.

The precise doxology of v. 12 is more consistent in form than is the sapiential model cited from Proverbs 3:19-20. Our verse in Hebrew lacks the divine name (present in LXX as in Prov. 3:19), but there can be no doubt who, in context, is asserted as the living, true God. It is this God who acts through three agents: power, wisdom, and discernment. Two of these elements are parallel to those of Proverbs 3:19-20, but here "power" displaces "knowledge" as the third agent. Moreover this articulation has three verbs, of which YHWH is the subject—"makes," "establishes," "stretched out"—so that only the middle verb, *kûn*, is parallel to Proverbs 3:19-20. The structure of this verse features three well-delineated parts. The third line, unlike that of Proverbs 3:19-20, stays closely parallel to the first two lines and has only one object, thus yielding a triad of objects— earth, world, heavens—to stay congruent with the three verbs and the three agents.

The claim of the whole is that the world, and therefore the world of Israel, and therefore the world of Jeremiah's seventh-century crisis, is completely at the behest of YHWH, who is the subject of all the verbs. It is indeed the decisive governing capacity of YHWH that is featured, though in the poem we are given no tilt toward either demolition (as in 4:23-26) or guarantee (as in 31:35-37), for both demolition and guarantee are free choices for the living God.

It is evident that the poem, in its doxology and its polemic, takes a curious turn in v. 16. It is possible to regard this verse as an addendum for the sake of tribal chauvinism. It is also possible, however, to see v. 16 as the climactic point of the entire poem. The specialness of Israel to YHWH is clear; but the double claim for Jacob—YHWH as *Jacob's portion*, Israel as *YHWH's inheritance*—is intertwined with more "creation" claims: "YHWH of Hosts" has "formed all," thus echoing the great doxological claims linked to YHWH's power and authority as creator.[28] The claims made for the creator in v. 16 are completely congruent with the doxology of v. 12, thus making YHWH's attentiveness to Israel not a belated "election" but a factor in the very fabric of creation. Because the verbs of v. 12 are all positive, with no hint of negation or destruction, the purpose is to assure Israel of YHWH's reliable attentiveness in all of his vitality and power. The poem, of course, is a bid for loyalty to YHWH and an insistent warning against idols that perish, but the ground for appeal to loyalty to YHWH is not threat but guarantee. The doxological affirmation of YHWH as creator is here voiced as the ground for Israel's steadfast reliance upon YHWH, a ground that is intrinsic to the primal work of the creator.

VI

It is discerned by scholars that 10:12-16 is reiterated in 51:15-19.[29] The entire corpus of the Oracles against the Nations (chs. 46–51) has a problematic linkage to the Jeremiah tradition, particularly chapters 50–51 concerning Babylon. Nonetheless it is clear that 51:15-19 is a peculiar feature in this extended oracle.[30] The weight of the entire oracle is the devastation of Babylon; the counter theme here is the enduring commitment of YHWH to Israel in v. 19.

The opening verse (v. 15) reiterates 10:12. Again YHWH's name is lacking; again three verbs with three agents and three objects are present. Together they constitute the sum of all creation. The larger unit of vv. 15-19 again divides into an affirmation of YHWH (vv. 15-16), an attack on alternative loyalties (vv. 17-18), and an affirmation of Jacob-Israel as the peculiar object of the creator God (v. 19).

In 51:15-19, the verses of 10:12-16 are set in the oracles against Babylon. The horizon of the oracle is very large, anticipating the demolition of the hegemonic power of the time. At the threshold of the oracle, more reticent than Second Isaiah, is the anticipation of the coming Persians who will do the work of destruction. In the prose of v. 11, it is the coming "Medes"; in vv. 12-14, it is the invading empire that will come with troops; and in vv. 20-23, "you" (unspecified) will fight for Israel. The title "Lord of hosts" sounded in 51:19 and in 10:16 is also voiced in v. 14.

The unit makes clear that the creator God is larger, stronger, and more determined than even this awesome, brutalizing superpower. The doxological and polemical rhetoric of the oracle must find a way to affirm YHWH as more absolute than the seemingly absolute superpower, and the only way to do that is to seize upon the creation themes of wisdom that are not tamed by historical references to YHWH. Of course, vv. 19 and 20 refer to Israel, thus drawing the doxological tradition close to the crisis of exile. All of the powers of the creator are mobilized for the sake of Israel, for Israel before the might of Babylon has no alternative way to the future.

The relationship between the uses of the creation doxology in 10:12-16 and in 51:15-19 is not obvious. In the first usage, the assurance is offered as a basis for exclusive loyalty to YHWH against all alternative possibilities, together with a summons. In the second usage, the assurance is offered without any such summons to loyalty, as a ground of hope and a resistance against despair and docile submission to the empire. It is possible and perhaps likely that the doxology of 10:12-16 is simply taken up later and reused by a subsequent poet. Alternatively, William McKane, following Bernard Duhm, suggests that the redactors of 51:15-19 "did not know that it had appeared at chapter 10."[31] The question of the relationship between the two uses is beyond resolution. What is clear is that in making its sweeping Yahwistic claim, the tradition finds a way of pushing behind any historical possibility to the Creator, who is the only source of comfort and strength, a source found by these voices to be adequate in more than one crisis.

VII

A third, truncated use of the same doxological formula is found in 32:17, in the narrative that stands amid the poems of hope in the Book of Comfort (chs. 30–31) and the collection of promises in chapter 33. Chapter 32 is organized around the narrative concerning land entitlement in vv. 1-15 that yields the reiterated summons of v. 25 and the promise of v. 44.[32] Within the specific, anticipated land transaction, the chapter offers a prayer (vv. 16-25) and an oracle (vv. 26-41) that express both the extremity of destruction and the extremity of new possibility. Given both extremities, it is asserted that "Nothing is too hard for you," first as an affirmation (v. 17) and then as a question that implies affirmation (v. 27). This material thus ponders YHWH's extreme possibilities in the depths of the exile, including the possibility of YHWH abandoning his people (a termination of the assurances in 10:12; 51:15) and the possibility of YHWH regathering his scattered people.[33] This long prose unit is indeed a limit expression required to voice the limit experience of Israel in the sixth century.

I suggest that 32:17 is a pivot point in this meditation upon YHWH's extremities: "Ah Lord GOD! It is you who made the heavens and the earth by your great power and by your outstretched arm! Nothing is too hard for you." This verse is uttered at the beginning of Jeremiah's prayer, which voices a recital of Israel's past with YHWH (vv. 18-23a), a speech of judgment (vv. 23b-24), and a reiteration of YHWH's promise (v. 25). The function of the opening doxology appears to be a motivation, linked to the promise of v. 25.[34] That is, the concrete historical promise of v. 25 would appear to be impossible, but the creator God is the one who does the impossible. The prayer reaches outside historical possibility to move YHWH into the larger arena of the possible.

Thus creation itself is a sign and measure of YHWH's capacity to do beyond what the world thinks is possible. In the doxological formulations, the opening is more focused and more powerful than those already cited in 10:12 and 51:15. YHWH is addressed with the title *'adonai*. This usage of the doxological formula is cast as a prayer; therefore, direct address is especially appropriate. The address is reinforced by the attention-getter *hinneh*. The substance of what is to be said to YHWH is introduced by the emphatic pronoun *'attâ* followed by a perfect verb.[35] The doxological affirmation has only one verb and two objects, heaven and earth. Moreover the agents (great power and outstretched arm) are different from the other uses, except that "power" is also an agent in 51:15.[36] The formulation, therefore, is quite different, but the structure of the utterance is close enough to be considered in the same thematic field. The point here is not simply an assurance (as in 51:15-19) or an assurance with summons (as in 10:12-16). Because of the form of address, the purpose is to remind YHWH of his capacity to do something.

The motivation of this truncated doxology is reinforced by the second half of the sentence: YHWH does impossibilities! The impossibility celebrated in this verse is the powerful action of the creation of heaven and earth; the impossibility in which Israel now lives is "these disasters," the end of Jerusalem and the ensuing exile. The impossibility anticipated here is restoration:

> Yet you, O Lord God, have said to me, "Buy the field for money and get witnesses." (32:25a)

> Just as I have brought all this great disaster upon this people, so I will bring upon them all the good fortune that I now promise them. Fields shall be bought in this land. . . . (vv. 42-43)

The impossibility for which petition is made flies in the face of the concessive clause ("though") of v. 25b: "though the city has been given into the hand of the Chaldeans." The impossibility and the petition for it constitute a counterreality, counter to the exile, countered only on the ground of the power of the creator.

The rhetoric that stretches from v. 17 to v. 25 has the force of voicing the hope of rehabilitation in the land as a miracle commensurate with the act of creation. Appeal is made to the one as ground for the other, ground out of which Israel hopes and out of which YHWH may act.

VIII

While it is clear that the Jeremiah tradition in many incidental ways (as mentioned above) appeals to creation thought, the most important point is that creation themes are of structural importance to the theological accents of judgment and hope in the final form of the text. Four conclusions may be drawn in that regard.

1. It is clear that the tradition of Jeremiah is familiar with and knows how to use effectively available themes and images of creation thought. It is now clear in biblical scholarship that Old Testament theology through the twentieth century and beyond, largely propelled by Gerhard von Rad's determinative essay of 1936, stands in need of a major correction. In the battle of the German Church with National Socialism, von Rad had linked creation theology with fertility religion, as it was manifested in the "Blood and Soil" ideology regnant in Germany. In response to that crucial church crisis, von Rad drew an important theological conclusion about the Old Testament:

> Our main thesis was that in genuinely Yahwistic belief the doctrine of creation never attained to the stature of a relevant, independent doctrine. We found it invariably related, and indeed subordinated, to

soteriological considerations . . . because of the exclusive commitment
of Israel's faith to historical salvation, the doctrine of creation was
never able to attain independent existence in its own right.[37]

In retrospect it is evident that von Rad overstated the distinction between
creation and soteriology.[38] And in the United States the same judgment
was forcefully made by G. Ernest Wright.[39] That judgment, for several
generations, has caused scholars to overlook the appeal to creation in biblical literature.

At the same time, if cautiously construed, von Rad's judgment has
merit. It is clear in the texts we have considered that creation is "invariably
related" to Israel's place in YHWH's economy. It is surely true that "the
doctrine of creation was never able to attain to independent existence in
its own right." It is not clear, however, that such thought is subordinated to
soteriology. I should argue rather that it is subordinated to the claim that
YHWH is the governor of all of reality, both what we have come to call
history and what we call creation. That is, creation theology is an instance
of the theonomous character and quality of all of reality, including the
reality of Israel's life.

2. In the tradition of Jeremiah, there is no doubt that the core themes
are demolition and rehabilitation. Creation themes in Jeremiah, I suggest,
are designed to affirm that the experience and reality of demolition, while
serious, is *only penultimate*. Similarly, the prospect of return and restoration
is also real and serious, but *also penultimate*. Undermining the ultimacy of
both demolition and rehabilitation is the more extreme claim of YHWH
the creator, who can do the impossible by dismantling creation (and Israel's
life) and who can do the equally impossible act of revamping creation (and
Israel's life). All of life is referred to the creator God, who is not restrained
or restricted by any "given" of either creation or history. Thus the doxologies we have cited counter the absolute autonomy of Israel, the absolute
despair of Israel, and the absolute hegemony of Babylon. Nothing is absolute, except the "Thou" who occupies the transformative verbs of power.

3. It is important that the theological claim not be separated from the
rhetorical act. The doxologies may be about the Creator and creation, but
they are said, sung, and spoken acts. The deabsolutizing of the penultimate
realities of demolition and rehabilitation takes place through an extreme
statement of wonder. The rhetoric may strike us as so familiar and conventional that we do not notice. In fact, the claims are extreme. In 4:23-26, it is

extreme to say "behold" four times to dismantling. In 31:35-37, it is extreme to speak an "if-then" assurance that rates the durability of Israel with the durability of creation. It is extreme when the claim for YHWH subverts the alternative of idols (10:1-16), when the claim of YHWH overrides the landless present tense of the exiles (32:17), and when the claim of YHWH trumps the hegemony of Babylon (51:15-19). It is an extremity of rhetoric in which the tradition asserts what the world cannot reasonably entertain.

The rhetoric must be so extreme, however, because the tradition offers *speech* that matches *experience*. The extremity of expression is required in order to make available the extremity of experience, which in Judah is the loss of a safe world and the prospect of a new world.[40] With this rhetoric it is possible to make available the loss and the future prospect. Such expression makes the density of the experience inescapable. The enduring effect of such rhetoric is to press the listening community to face its own lived life, to ensure YHWH as the pivotal player in that lived life, and to certify to coming generations that lived reality presided over by YHWH is a reliable lens through which to engage other crises that have the same world-ending and world-making scope. Indeed it is the richness of the limit expression that causes this Jeremiah to be canonically perceived as revelatory.

4. It is important to recognize the odd, subversive world given in this extreme rhetoric. It is unmistakable that YHWH the creator is the subject of every verb. Heaven and earth, like Israel, are always on the receiving end of that activity, always the object acted upon. The most extreme form of rhetoric is that of creation, in which all imaginable reality is object. It does not surprise us, in this context, that Judah and Jerusalem are objects in the same way.

Such a view of reality contends against the conventional Enlightenment notion of autonomy that perhaps echoes the ancient anti-YHWH claims. In a splendid articulation of the grammar of Enlightenment, Nelida Pinon urges:

> You must know who is the object and who is the subject of a sentence in order to know if you are the object or subject of history. If you can't control a sentence, you don't know how to put yourself into history, to trace your own origin in the country, to vocalize, to use voice.[41]

Here one can hear echoes of Karl Marx's urging that human persons must become subjects of their own history!

I happen to agree with that human mandate. However, the covenantal traditions of Judaism and Christianity, voiced in the magisterial I-Thou of Martin Buber and more recently in the "religion of the face" in Emmanuel Levinas, insist that beneath that emancipated autonomy there is an inescapable Holy Other.[42] The creation theology of Jeremiah attends to the Holy Other, who ends every dysfunctional effort at autonomy only to authorize again an emancipated, rehabilitated history, which gives great play to the voiced subject beloved by the inscrutable Thou. It is a reality Israel mostly refuses, learning again and again that this reality is the only source of comfort and hope, a reality in which the Creator offers the only possibility for creation.[43]

Next Steps
in Jeremiah Studies

The essays in *Troubling Jeremiah*, published in 1999, exhibit the fact that Jeremiah studies are off in new directions with a great deal of vigor and energy.[1] It is a commonplace that the three great commentaries of 1986 provide a key marker in the turn of Jeremiah studies. While the work of William Holladay does not figure greatly in newer methods and approaches, his prodigious effort serves the important purpose of pushing historical-critical study as far as can now be imagined.[2] While few would now go that route, Holladay has provided a reliable and stable baseline and foil for newer ventures. It is the important merit of Robert Carroll that he has irreversibly introduced the category of ideology into Jeremiah studies, so that neither historical-critical nor innocently theological interpretation is credible any longer.[3] Carroll's move in that direction has now become a usage at the center of our common work. It appears to be a major contribution of William McKane, without neglecting his important and dense textual work, to provide the notion of a "rolling corpus" as a way of understanding the thematic constancy of the book of Jeremiah together with what appears to be its disjunctive development.[4] The present conversation draws heavily upon these commentaries, though it is of course informed as well by the larger interpretive currents that are at work in Old Testament studies, most especially a move away from an innocent positivism to what is conventionally termed a postmodern perspective.

The rich and supple interpretive possibilities are evident in the valuable summary of options in theological exposition by Leo Perdue.[5] Along with attention to the major scholarly ventures and emerging new models for biblical theology, Perdue's study has the special merit of illustrating those large possibilities by particular reference to what may be done in Jeremiah interpretation. Perdue's focus upon Jeremiah indicates that Jeremiah is not only a fruitful focus for scholarship but a pivotal point of dispute in interpretive matters, and likely also to be a principle datum for biblical theology at the beginning of the twenty-first century. In the final section of this essay, I will consider some reasons why and how this may be so.

I

It is not news any longer that scholarship has moved decisively from *diachronic* to *synchronic* ways of reading. And while some scholars may be polemical about the matter, most are inclined to adopt something of a both/and approach.[6] The reason for this is simple. While sympathies are characteristically in a synchronic direction, it is obvious to everyone that the voices sounded in the book of Jeremiah are profoundly in touch with real historical realities in the seventh and/or sixth centuries, so that one cannot be purely synchronic, as though the book floated in the air. It is of course not clear about the extent or character of the contact points between this literary piece and historical reality, but one cannot proceed without an awareness of the large context of emergency in which the literature is set.

Leo Perdue, first in his book *The Collapse of History* and now in his essay in *Troubling Jeremiah*, has performed an especially important service in reviewing, summarizing, and assessing the important critical issues related to the question of *diachronic* and *synchronic*. He makes it clear that this general rubric (that revolves around the vexed question of "history") generates a host of problems, a variety of approaches, and rich possibilities for interpretation that were not available in the old monolithic approach of historical criticism. Specifically issues of (a) ideology and interpretive stance and (b) pluralism are deeply at stake in our new interpretive environment. As the responses to Perdue by Lawrence Boadt, Dennis Olson, and Thomas Overholt in *Troubling Jeremiah* make clear, we still have hard work in front of us that as of now admits no consensus.

I have come to the conclusion that while the deep interpretive crisis present in Jeremiah studies and in theological interpretation more generally can be characterized as the vexed relation between modern and postmodern perspectives, the reality of how scholars work is very different from that. The direction taken by a scholar of interpretive work depends upon a *felt threat* and a *felt need* that are quite personal, subjective, and existential, even if they are presented in more erudite fashion. (This is perhaps indicated by the way in which seemingly scholarly questions can generate adrenalin and acrimony that seem oddly disproportionate to the question.) On the one hand, if the felt threat is taken to be *fragmentation* of interpretation (as seems to be the case for Perdue), then the felt need is for some coherence that yields a modernist perspective and that sustains something of a core of interpretive stability. If, on the other hand, the felt threat is *reductionism* (as seems to be the case for Burke Long), then the felt need is for openness and freedom in interpretation that embraces postmodern pluralism as a way of keeping the process open. While Perdue suggests his own propensity in this regard, the great merit and gain of his work is to lay out with clarity the taxonomy of current interpretation. It seems important, in my judgment, that while different scholars, out of particular felt threats and felt needs, focus upon a certain direction of interpretation, we keep before us the map of the entire enterprise, entertaining the thought that we may learn from each other and in the meantime act attentively and with respect toward one other.

At the moment, the future of scholarship is clearly in a synchronic direction. There is nonetheless still a great deal unsettled about what that means. Earlier studies by Kathleen O'Connor, Pete Diamond, and Mark Smith are enormously suggestive about the synchronic shape of Jeremiah 11–20, and the intentional placement of the so-called "Confessions" in a grid of the larger text.[7] More recently, Ronald Clements has extended such reflections concerning the theological grid of the entire unit of chapters 1–25.[8] It remains of course to see how such arguments can be further extended.

The most influential advocate of synchronic interpretation is Robert Carroll, who has not paid primary attention to the niceties and symmetries of the synchronic but has been mainly concerned to show that any access to the historical is impossible. That is, the final form of the text is a literary-rhetorical-imaginative constant that stands at an important distance from anything we might regard as history. When Carroll pursues this notion of rhetorical distance plus his accent on ideology, he concludes that the text characteristically is axe-grinding in ways that heretofore have been regarded as theological, though Carroll tends to reduce such to sociopolitical tendentiousness.

In *Troubling Jeremiah*, Diamond has considered the theoretical inadequacy of historical critical study to address the problems of the text it has helped us to see.[9] Synchronic contributions include that of Stulman on chapters 1–25, Holt on chapters 37–44, and Wells on chapters 40–44.[10] The discussion of Diamond and O'Connor, though not preoccupied with synchronic method, clearly appeals to such a perspective.[11] All of these seek to read without reference to conventional historical considerations.

In a very different way from that of Carroll, with a theological interest Carroll would eschew, Brevard Childs purposes that the book of Jeremiah concerns a theology of God's word that issues variously in assertions of *judgment* for rejection of the word and a summons to repentance and *promise* what "was part of the divine plan from the outset."[12] In a way with more nuance, Ronald Clements argued some time ago that the prophetic literature has been edited to focus primarily upon themes of judgment and promise:

> It is rather precisely the element of connectedness between the prophets, and the conviction that they were referring to a single theme of Israel's destruction and renewal, which has facilitated the ascription to each of them of the message of hope which some of their number had proclaimed after 587 B.C.[13]

Clements's more recent discussion shows how the accents of Deuteronomic theology have shaped Jeremiah, a theology in its own way concerned with judgment and promise.[14]

It is clear that *synchronic reading* and *canonical interpretation* are not to be equated. Nonetheless an important convergence may be seen in these approaches. One important accent in synchronic approaches is a negative one, namely, to loosen the text from history. But once it is loosened from history as a principle of explanation, one is driven to "intentional meaning," whether Childs's "theological" or Carroll's "ideological." Thus I suggest that we may see something of a general agreement about the synchronic, even if it receives different scholarly valuations. In a recent brief note to me, Carroll has suggested that in fact the "earlier" material of "judgment" is further removed from the actual voices of the text (the text being later) and so the "later" material of "hope" is to be taken as a more reliable and exact claim of the text. This is an important move in the direction of the theological calculations of Childs and Clements. The conclusion I draw is that once a move is made to the synchronic, it is almost inevitable that the material will be taken as statements of intentional memory in some larger pattern of meaning, whether that larger meaning is taken to be theology or ideology.

II

The move from diachronic to synchronic is marked by a move from *historical analysis* to *rhetorical study*. Attention to *synchronic interpretation* and *rhetorical analysis* overlap, but they are not the same. And therefore it is important to recognize that we are only at the beginning of rhetorical analysis. Perhaps it is correct to observe that synchronic perspectives tend to deal in larger units and ask about the interface and interaction between texts or larger collections of texts that seem to be disjunctive.

By contrast rhetorical criticism tends to focus on smaller units and to ask about the intentional operation of the text. There is no doubt that James Muilenburg is the progenitor of such an approach, and the unavailability of his draft of a Jeremiah commentary continues to be an aggrieved loss to us all. Here I wish to make only a single point about the character of rhetoric, particularly as it is practiced in ancient Israelite-Jewish materials such as Jeremiah. This rhetoric is endlessly pluri-vocal, subversive, and deconstructive.[15] It does not admit of a single meaning and evokes ongoing interpretation that is never finally settled. In part, this is the character of poetry and thus pertains especially to the poetic sections of the material. In part, it has to do with the elusive quality and character of Hebrew articulation that is evocative and venturesome but seldom conclusive. And in part, so far as Jerusalem is concerned, the literature is a reflection within a community that must speak, but must speak about an unutterable *Tremendum*.

I have been helped by the juxtaposition Philip Fisher makes between *myth* and *rhetoric*:

> *Myth* . . . is always singular, *rhetorics* is always plural. Myth is a fixed, satisfying, and stable story that is used again and again to normalize our account of social life. By means of myth, novelty is tamed by being seen as the repetition or, at most, the variation of a known and valuable pattern. . . . Rhetoric, in contrast, is a tactic within the open questions of culture. It reveals interests and exclusions. . . . Rhetoric is the place where language is engaged in cultural work, and such work can be done on, with, or in spite of another group within society. Rhetorics are plural because they are part of what is uncertain or potential within culture. They are servants of one or another politics of experience. Where there is nothing openly contested, no cultural work to be done, we do not find the simplification into one and only one rhetoric. Instead we find

the absence of the particular inflammation and repetition that rhetoric always marks. We find no rhetoric at all, only the ceremonial contentment of myth.[16]

I find this statement illuminating of Jeremiah. There is clearly cultural work to be done, both in response to enormous displacement and in response to contested and competing futures.

To be sure, in Jeremiah studies we do not use the term *myth*, but it occurs to me that our term *ideology* comes close to what Fisher means by myth. Indeed Fisher continues to say about myth and rhetoric:

> Within the term *ideology* we are right to hear a combination of calculation, cynicism about social truth, a schoolteacher's relation to the pupils, indoctrination, and propaganda. Whether as reality or hope, ideology implies that one part of the legitimacy of authority is a monopoly on representation, and this is exactly the condition in which rhetorics become irrelevant.[17]

It appears to me that much talk about ideology (myth!) in Jeremiah studies is premature, precisely because there is no monopoly of representation, and surely rhetoric is not yet irrelevant. It is precisely the contested character of the future in Judah, as Christopher Seitz has best explicated, that precludes our flattening the rhetoric into ideology or myth.[18] There is no doubt that the Jeremiah tradition inherits and utilizes mythic material, for example, the broken marriage, the foe from the north, God as patron of the city. But these standard thematics are handled in the Jeremiah tradition in supple ways with imagination and freedom. Thus what is mythic is made into rhetoric that remains open in interpretation. It is important to attend to this suppleness and not impose a closure that belongs to the reader and not to the text. Evidently Jeremiah is not yet beyond "the particular inflammation and repetition" that rhetoric always marks. To be sure, such advocacies as we have in the material might wish they had become "fixed, satisfying, and stable" but they had not,

- because things were not settled;
- because the community is endlessly contentious; and
- because the several advocacies claim to appeal to a "Holy One" whom even they know cannot be reduced to fixity.

We may therefore expect and exercise close attentiveness to rhetoric in the recognition that settlements are elusive, and what we have at best are bids and not conclusions.[19] We may welcome the essays in *Troubling Jeremiah*, focused on rhetorical analysis, including those of Diamond and O'Connor, Nancy Lee, Alice Ogden Bellis and Marvin Sweeney, even though Sweeney's discussion parses the rhetoric with some attention to redactional development.[20]

III

Such a contrast between rhetoric and myth, or alternatively rhetoric and ideology, leads us naturally to consider the role of *ideology* in Jeremiah studies. Carroll's introduction of the term into our common work is to insist, surely rightly, that the several advocacies in the text, including "God-advocacies," are not innocent, but are highly tendentious, intentional, and characteristically self-serving. It is Carroll's intention, in substituting ideology for theology, to bring God-claims in the text into social-scientific confines and so to nullify the privilege of God talk.

It is of course well known that ideology may be understood simply in a Marxian sense as *distortion*, or in a non-Marxian way, as in Clifford Geertz, as an attempt to state a communal, shared *meaning*, an affirmation that contains no pejorative or polemical intent.[21] When we are all on our good behavior, we may intentionally accept "ideology" in this second way, as simply a sober, fair-minded recognition that a communal shared meaning is offered. In such a usage, ideology is not more than a mode of "social construction of reality."[22] And in the book of Jeremiah, we may imagine that the Deuteronomic teaching that is prominent in the final form of the text is a social construction of reality that especially prizes Torah obedience, that takes seriously the God who is said to authorize the Torah and to summon obedience, and to acknowledge the obedience of a particular segment of the community. So far so good.

I have come to think, however, that in strongly felt interpretive situations like that of Jeremiah studies where we interpreters seem as passionate as our forebears in the literature, it is impossible to adhere to a non-Marxian usage, because there is always ready at hand a bootlegging of "distortion" in a polemical way. Even in his present essay that is greatly refined from his initial use in the commentary, Carroll's non-Marxian usage cannot finally refrain from "a power group over the rest of the community" concerning "who controls past and future."[23]

None of this is problematic except to notice that such usage of the term *ideology* is gratuitously reductive. The trade-off of *ideology* for *theology* of course reduces "YHWH" simply to a cipher for a greedy, intentional program of land acquisition. In *Troubling Jeremiah*, the essay by Wells makes a comparable and well-said argument. What happens is that YHWH is reduced in the most extreme Feuerbachian way. That may indeed be correct. Except that such flatness will never permit us to understand what the voices in Jeremiah intend to be saying or doing. It is my impression that Geertz and other anthropologists resolved to try to understand cultures on their own terms as much as possible, rather than on modernist scientific terms that can easily show such cultures to be "silly." One cannot, I suggest, simply reduce YHWH to a social function in an Israelite text and eliminate YHWH as agent and yet hope to understand what is being done and said.

I have no wish to polemicize against Carroll and have participated enough in that. Carroll is surely right in his polemic against excessive privilege for theological claims. But an easy move to ideology is not very effective because a non-Marxian ideology would need to accept YHWH as a key factor in meaning, YHWH understood as more than illusion or projection. My point is that there is no easy or innocent settlement of categories of ideology and theology, and to project one's own reservations of certain categories of utterance (or one's own enthusiasms) is hardly helpful or scholarly. I suspect we shall continue to banter about this matter. Those who prefer theology cannot expect privileged claims. Those who prefer ideology cannot pretend scientific detachment when the usage is reductionist. We must make sure that we offer arguments based in the text and not simply dismissive name-calling driven by current resentments. It may well be that we need yet to find a better word that is free of the accumulated freight of time.

IV

The larger categories of *rhetoric* and *ideology* invite a distinct comment concerning feminist interpretation in Jeremiah studies. As in every aspect of our field, feminist undertakings have not had a smooth entry into Jeremiah studies. At the outset of this phase of scholarship, Carroll applied the term *ideology* in a catchall usage concerning such advocacy positions, with special reference to the work of Phyllis Trible. Since that time, of course, we have learned a great deal and refined the categories of both *ideology* and *feminist*.

It seems unmistakable that we have a great deal of work remaining to be done in this regard, especially in the poetic materials where the use of metaphor and image is not only elusive but also enormously venturesome. The several studies of Kathleen O'Connor, following the lead of Trible, suggest ways in which materials can now be read afresh to great advantage.[24] Our concern is not simply with the role of women in the literature, but the ways in which feminist imagery in the text permits the most elemental, painful, and wondrous of interactions to be voiced beneath conventional modes of reportage. Here I may mention three lines of investigation that will be of great benefit in time to come:

1. Gale Yee, with reference to Hosea, has considered how feminine imagery not only reflects patriarchy but also in important ways subverts the very claims of patriarchy that it reflects.[25]

2. Renita Weems has shown how violent sexual imagery is in substance a social practice of violence that may indeed evoke violent human practice, reflective of the rhetoric of divine abusiveness.[26] There is no doubt a great deal more of this to pursue in the traditions of Jeremiah, as Angela Bauer's essay in *Troubling Jeremiah* makes clear.

3. Most important, so it seems to me, is the notion of "antilanguage" on the part of William Domeris (see *Troubling Jeremiah*). If, as seems likely, the dominant rhetoric of ancient Israel in the seventh–sixth centuries is patriarchal, then the risky sexual metaphors that pay attention to female-Israel may indeed be seen as antilanguage that gives voice to counterreality, or in the terms of Domeris, antireality. If that is so, moreover, then the old and intractable problem of relating poetry to prose becomes substantively urgent, for that interface becomes an interface between *rhetoric on its way to ideology* (Dtr) and *anti-utterance* in the poetry that Deuteronomic editing did not nullify but preserved. Such antilanguage, apparently valued by would-be ideologues, testifies to the quite provisional claims of would-be ideology, a provisional quality perhaps dictated both by the ambiguity of circumstance and by the elusiveness of the Key Player in this ideological-theological articulation. Such antilanguage that pervades the tradition warns us against taking the final form of the text as too settled or stable. Whether the use of such antilanguage is happenstance or intentional, it bespeaks an openness that no amount of loudness or firmness can easily overcome.

V

There is a great deal of evidence now to suggest that the book of Jeremiah in final form is a literature that is intensely *future oriented*. By that I do not mean that we can substantively identify eschatological themes, for that is a much too cognitive approach. Rather the shape and texture and character of the text intends to be generative into the next generations of text-preservers and text-readers and text-hearers.

If, as seems clear, there is a movement from early to late, at least ostensively from pre-587 to post-587, as the Jeremiah tradition keeps growing and being restated after the demise of Jerusalem and after the demise of the lifetime of the prophet and after the displacement of leading citizens, then it does not surprise that the movement of the text toward "final form" is indeed generative and is itself a practice and a product of such ongoing generativity.

While matters are not yet sorted out, it seems clear that the pivotal role of chapter 25,[27] the corpus of Oracles against the Nations that anticipates the overthrow of the nations, the particular narrative enactment of 51:59-64 concerning the "sinking" of Babylon, and the prose addendum of chapter 52 with particular reference to 52:31-34 all indicate that the process of the book continues to ponder how to end, and in light of a literary ending to wonder what comes next. It is not yet clear, if it ever will be, how this convoluted material is internally related, nor can it be said that there is an agreed-upon ending for the future, even in the MT, without reference to the different arrangement of the Greek version. Rather the literature and its framers are restless about what comes next and care greatly about it.

What seems important to me in this regard is that McKane's "rolling corpus" is not rolling aimlessly and without direction. Rather the "roll" of the tradition is on a steady trajectory toward new possibility. It is altogether possible that the "roll" toward new futures may be understood (a) *geopolitically*, as exilic Israel moves into the Persian defeat of Babylon that in turn permits some rehabilitation of the community; (b) *ideologically*, as the Babylonian community of Jews asserts hegemony in reshaping Jerusalem; or (c) *theologically*, as YHWH is reckoned to be a God of fidelity. I do not imagine that these dimensions of the future are mutually exclusive, but rather that the shapers of the book of Jeremiah—geopolitically, ideologically, theologically—cannot and will not believe that termination is the final fact. Carroll's suggestion, that the promise is in fact closer to the lived reality of the final form than the judgment, is an important acknowledgment of that remarkable affirmation about the future. It is not at all necessary (or possible) to distinguish the pragmatic and fideistic elements in that decision, but only to notice that the bracketing of "captivity" (1:3) and "captivity" (51:28-30, 31-34) contains within it a remarkable resolve that "captivity" is indeed provisional. And so the scroll keeps rolling.

VI

In the end, the book of Jeremiah is an effort to construe and imagine the defining emergency of Israel-Judaism with reference to YHWH as the agent of both judgment and possibility. Having recognized that the terms *theology* and *ideology* are in their different ways problematic, it seems important to me, in the end, to recognize as well that the book of Jeremiah, without reference to YHWH, is no book at all, and that its sustained act of imagination is emptied of any force if YHWH is flattened out to be only a code-term for aggressive land acquisition. Thus I finish with the anticipation that our future work in Jeremiah inevitably will be in some way theological, if we take the material of the book seriously.

The reference to YHWH in the book seems to be pervasive and indispensable. We do not know how naive, innocent, or fideistic the framers of the book were, but given their sophistication about other matters, we may imagine that they were not simpletons about uttering the name of YHWH. They meant by the utterance to point to the inscrutable mystery at the center of public life that would not be tamed but that may in some important way be known by reference to antecedent experiences and articulations. It is a commonplace to say that in that ancient world "atheism" was no real option, but that "idolatry" is an endless agenda, by which I mean a dispute about what is true and reliable and what is false and fickle about the intransigent mystery that pervades human, public life.

Whether a belated modernist or postmodernist reader happens to agree with this naming of that Holy Intransigence seems to me of almost no interest or merit. Of course there is a temptation in some circles to want with excessive eagerness to subscribe to what the text seems to affirm or even press it further so that the God voiced in this material becomes the more established God of the orthodox, hegemonic Western tradition. Such a domestication and familiarity predictably evokes an adamant skepticism, seeming to be most acute among those nurtured in authoritarian fundamentalism who readily spot authoritarianism wherever it surfaces in interpretation and wherever it seems present in the text. Such belated fideism and complementary skepticism seem to me beside the point and inadmissible in our study, for our work is not to impose or to expose, but to hear what is here imagined. The proper procedure, so it seems to me, is to explicate the claims of the tradition as best we can, without reference to our own readiness or resistance, and then, only then, at the end, to assess our own engagement with or distance from these claims. I understand of course that such attentiveness to the claims of the tradition is never innocent or pure. But a proximate effort can be made that does not begin in either exuberant embrace or polemical rejection. Without denying interest and bias, it is important that they are not, at the outset, given completely free rein. A premature certification or dismissal of claims seems only to block our capacity to entertain the material.

It is commonly remarked that the book of Jeremiah is "unreadable," that it is so filled with disjunction that it makes no coherent sense. But then, the judgment of unreadability is a common judgment made in Greek reading of Jewish texts that proceed by a different voice.[28] The judgment of unreadable may be more a judgment on the reader than on the material.

I wonder then if it could be that "unreadability" is not a profound *problem* in the book of Jeremiah but rather a *core datum* to be attended to as a crucial part of the book's *testimony*.[29] It occurs to me that "unreadability" may reflect that

1. *the experienced Tremendum* of history, the loss of treasured, guaranteeing Jerusalem and the ensuing displacement that required a disjunctive voicing;[30]
2. *the contested shape of life and faith* and the competing claims of vying communities that means that no voice can effect a smooth hegemony, but that the political interpretive situation of necessity is a cacophony of claims and counterclaims;
3. the experience of the *Tremendum* and the political contestation together may be witnesses, so that they attest to the *disjunctive character of YHWH*, the one who defeated the city, authorized the empire, and summoned the interpreters. It is this Holy One, so the material suggests, who legitimated the political and literary practice of disjunction. The book cannot be made "readable," perhaps, without violating this Holy One who refuses conformity to such contained sense-making;

4. those of us who practice Jeremiah interpretation as a goodly company, I propose, cannot spend all our energy on our intraguild disputes, important and interesting as they are to us. Thus I suggest that Jeremiah studies has a special public responsibility not only to popularize our research but also to permit this "unreadable" material to be an opening for the "unreadable" quality of our own time and place.

Somewhere Elie Wiesel has commented that Jeremiah is a part of the Bible that we now need to be reading. He does not specify why that is so. It takes no great imagination, however, to suggest what he may mean. Specifically, the barbarity of the twentieth century—with special but not exactly exclusive reference to the Shoah—might suggest that the *Tremendum* of sixth-century Israel has an analogue in our time. More generally, one might ponder the collapse of the "known world" of the West at the end of the twentieth century to be a parallel to that primal collapse of Israelite life and faith shadowed in the book of Jeremiah. Cultural analogues and parallels, however, are not an adequate access point for our contemporary reading of Jeremiah. In the end, we finally must push beyond cultural issues to theological wonderment. Here I may identify three facets of the question of God in that ancient text that in contemporary life, in my judgment, belong to the serious reading of Jeremiah:

1. As much as anyone, Wiesel has insisted that the only valid form of knowledge that counts in deep human emergency is testimony, whereby exposed human agents, without institutional credibility or authority, give an account of human reality that attests to the reality of God. Testimony is a lean mode of knowledge, but may indeed be the only serious offer of meaning and hope in an environment like that of the sixth century or our own. Whatever may be said of the person of Jeremiah and whatever may be said historically about Jeremiah 36, the book of Jeremiah is indeed offered as testimony to a rereading of reality at the behest of God.[31] In a social environment wherein conventional positivism has failed—the positivism of science or of theology—ours may be a moment of reading that is left with only testimony. And if so, Jeremiah constitutes a witness of great durability and generativity.

2. The God given in this text, and offered by testimony from that text to our context, is indeed an elusive, holy figure who will not be captured,

caught, domesticated, or reduced by way of our explanations. The quality of YHWH is nicely voiced in 23:23-24:

> Am I a God near by, says the LORD, and not a God far off? Who can hide in secret places so that I cannot see them? says the LORD. Do I not fill heaven and earth? says the LORD.

This is a God from whom no secret can be kept, but a God who may be kept secret. I take it that the elusive language of the book is because YHWH is not directly and fully available by utterance or in any other way.[32] In that text and in our context, perhaps, the Holy One inhabits but also haunts in ways past inhabiting. And while conventional theo-ideology may want the habitation, what is most given here is the haunting. The haunting God among this haunted people is sure to be unreadable, precisely the proper God for an unreadable time like ours.

3. But there is more here than holy elusiveness. As Abraham Heschel has seen best, the God who haunts is the God who is uttered and given in deep pathos, so that sovereignty comes as generative suffering.[33] It is exceedingly important that this recognition of suffering is not projected backward by Christians from the cross of Jesus, but receives its best voicing from that quintessential Jewish voice of Heschel. As he has seen, the suffering of the poet and the poet's preservers echoes and embodies the suffering of YHWH. And were Heschel doing his study today, he would surely say that some presence-in-suffering is the primary claim, practice, and assurance of the book of Jeremiah that might now claim our attention.

Our time, like that time, is seduced by deep denial (6:14; 8:11):

- We imagine certitudes better than risky testimony.
- We imagine holiness available in tamed categories.
- We imagine sure scriptings free of suffering.

But of course none of this is given. This script keeps insisting otherwise, in censoring and in generative ways. If this book now is not read, the book is not damaged. It is rather the unreading time that is diminished . . . and it need not be so.

I am aware of the hazards of theological contemporaneity in appropriating a text. I share the common reluctance of our discipline about easy connections and I propose none. In my judgment, Carroll is right in his insistence on responsible, contemporary reading that depends on two conditions:

> For those prepared to do the hard work entailed, and who live in circumstances out of which such a project naturally arises, there is material in Jeremiah which may be beneficial for our time.[34]

Carroll's reference is to Czechoslovakia post-1968. I do not romanticize, but given the crisis of Western culture, many folk qualify, in my judgment, for the right circumstance where hard work may be usefully done. The issue in that ancient text and in our present context, so it seems to me, is that of *relinquishing* what is being ended by holiness and the even more demanding work of *receiving* what is being given in suffering love.

In the end, the contemporary public question is: What kind of material is this in the book of Jeremiah? Some time ago I gently chided colleagues who were keen on criticism but thin on interpretation.[35] Since I wrote that, I am helped greatly by distinctions already made in 1979 by George Steiner, who distinguishes *critic* and *reader*. He observes that the critic rightly engages in a *distancing* process whereby one may arrive at objective meaning.

But the reader, unlike the critic, has a different stance. The reader

> inhabits the provisional—in which manifold term he recognizes as relevant the notions of "gift," of "that which serves vision," and of that which "nourishes" indispensably. . . . The reader proceeds *as if* the text was the housing of forces and meanings, of meanings of meaning, whose lodging within the executive verbal form was one of "incarnation." . . . As lived by the true reader, the text is irreducible to, inexhaustible by, even the most penetratively diagnostic, explicative visions—be they linguistic, grammatological, semiotic, historicist, sociological, "deconstructive," or what you will.[36]

In the end Steiner observes:

> The critic prescribes a syllabus; the reader is answerable to and internalizes a canon.[37]

I have no resistance about our work of prescribing a syllabus; it is our proper critical work. If, however, that is all, we shall have missed the scroll. The "canon" here is not the rigid, reductionist "canonical" to which Childs is obligated. The term here, I take it, means a normative script invested with presence. Our work is to move, I propose, through and beyond syllabus, when syllabus is well done, to canon, to a normalizing voice that refuses to be "readable" precisely because readability produces domestication.

One other phrase from Steiner instructs me: "A syllabus is taught; a canon is lived."[38] Canon is the embrace of a generative text beyond the regime of thought and analysis to where the claims must be faced and lived. Jeremiah as canon is an authorization to live in lean testimony to a holy, pathos-filled presence. The aim of such scholarship that is demanded by the material, in my judgment, is to move through the paces of criticism so that this unreadable script may rescript our unreadable lived reality.

The outcome of such reading-living is the emergence of an anti-community, or we might better say a countercommunity, counter in good times to *self-deception*, counter in lean times to *despair*. Such a stance of "anti" is a tough one—whether in Jerusalem or in Babylon. It may issue in doxology (20:13) that shades immediately to despair (20:14-18). Or it may be weeping (31:15) that culminates in mercy (31:20). Either way, an "anti" stance studies the syllabus carefully, and then moves to subversive authorization, in jeopardy, everywhere accompanied.

II.

Listening for the
Prophetic Word in History

CHAPTER SIX

The Prophetic Word
of God and History

The claim that "God acts in history" is not compatible with our
Enlightenment notions of control, reason, objectivity, and technique.[1]
Indeed, if one begins with the assumptions of modernity, history can only
be thought of as a bare story of power, in which the God of the Bible can
never make a significant appearance. The claim that "God acts in history,"
that God's word impinges upon the human process, requires a very different beginning point. In fact, this claim ultimately becomes a counterclaim
and bypasses the common debate concerning whether history is a tale of
either raw power or the blind faith of supernaturalism.[2] In reality, this
claim rejects both of these options.

I

A prophetic understanding of history must assert itself against two com-
petitors. First, there are the temptations of modernity, which have perhaps
been embodied in the "doctrine" of Henry Kissinger.[3] This view assumes
that history is an essentially closed process in which one must manage the
available pieces as best one can because there will be no new pieces. This view
empties the historical process of inscrutability and mystery and endeavors
to eradicate ambiguity. It concludes that "might makes right," that "history
is written by the winners," and that history is simply "the story of the state,"
that is, the story of power concentrated in the hands of those who deserve
it, who can manage it well, and who benefit from it. This view of history is
powerful, reflecting our fear of, and our sense of, our cosmic homelessness;
this view drives the arms races and ends in a despair that brutalizes, either
in the name of the state or against the claims of the state.

Second, and in odd alliance with the first view, is an older, religious view of the historical process. This view affirms that all of life is in the hands of the gods (or God), that humankind may propose but God disposes, and that, in the end, human choice does not matter. This kind of supernaturalism, which eventuates in fatalism and is manifested in astrology, leads to an abdication of human responsibility and human freedom. It invites despair on the one hand and recklessness on the other because it is God who will finally decide.

I submit that the first of these views is the one most powerful among us and that the second holds little attraction if it is spelled out with any precision. In truth, however, these two views converge in a massive verdict of despair. Whereas the former insists that human power is everything, the latter maintains that, in the final analysis, human power and effort are futile. Together, these two views envisage a historical process that is essentially fated, in which there are no important possibilities that lie beyond our several necessities. In the case of the one, we are fated to terrible power and, in the case of the other, fated to miserable helplessness; still, either way, we are fated. For those struggling for faith in our society, these two views constitute the greatest, most visible, and available options open to them.

II

The theme "Prophetic Word of God and History" begins at a different point, in a different mode of discourse, and uses a very different epistemology.[4] It resists the modernist reduction that reduces history to power; it likewise resists the religious temptation of supernaturalism. It begins with astonished, unjustified, unargued speech of affirmation and celebration that asserts and testifies to the intrusion, surprise, discontinuity, gifts, judgment, newness, and ambiguity that are present in the midst of the human process. In other words, this theme insists on speaking precisely about those matters that the other two views of history want to deny, namely, the notion that astonished, unjustified, unargued speech is human speech, filled with daring chutzpah and focused on scandalous particularity. This speech is so daring as to specify concrete places where the presence, purpose, and reality of God's "otherness" make decisive inroads on the human process in either friendly or hostile ways. It names the places where intrusion, gift, ambiguity, and newness are present, and it gives to those happenings the name of holiness, either holy graciousness or holy judgment.

There is no way to understand prophetic speech (or prophetic ministry) without going back to the very old, very deep, very odd Jewish rootage of such speech. Indeed "prophetic" is a mode of dangerous Jewishness in a safety-seeking world of imperial certitude; it raises the claim that history does not begin in power plays or in "natural" origins but in miracles that are discerned, construed, celebrated, and confessed in astonished faith.

1. A test case is the conversation of Abraham, Sarah, and the three messengers in Genesis 18:1-15.[5] The visitors announce that Sarah will have a baby in her old age. In disbelief, Sarah snickers. As a rebuke to Sarah, one of the visitors responds, "Is anything too difficult for God?" The word *difficult* (or too hard, too wondrous, impossible) is the Hebrew word *pela'*. The means whereby Abraham and Sarah receive an inexplicable future is through a *pela'*, through an emergent occurrence that they and their world defined as impossible. History (that is, the transactions of human freedom and human possibility) does not begin through human initiatives or acts of courage or cleverness but in an inexplicable turn that prophetic faith confesses to be the work of God, a work that stands outside the expectation, prediction, and horizon of human control. Indeed one can argue that human history persists because this God who visited Abraham and Sarah and who worked a *pela'* continued to keep open historical, human possibilities beyond all human expectation. While our fearful human inclination is to close down this historical prospect, it is the work of this God and the speech of this God that can keep the historical horizon open.

2. This narrative speech of Genesis 18:1-15 concerning a miracle secures its focus for ancient Israel in the narrative of Exodus 1–15, which is the world's primal *pela'*. In this event (regularly reenacted in passover liturgy), the tight birth control exercised by the Egyptian empire is broken (cf. Exod. 1:15-22) and a new people is formed within the world of empires, a people with no clear historical antecedents.[6] Out of the promissory word of God, this people appears as a *novum* in the history of the world and is freed for covenantal relations and obedience to the Torah, which is a charter for human equity, justice, and dignity. Martin Buber has said of the inexplicable event of the exodus that it is a miracle marked by "abiding astonishment,"[7] which is to say that the exodus is a known happening that continues to give off power and to claim attention and allegiance. Indeed the exodus continues to astonish and keep the world open. It denies

the closed definitions of what is possible, definitions that are coercively imposed by the empires of the world. Michael Walzer has shown that this *pela'* of the exodus has continued to be a remarkable engine for revolutionary newness in the world, continuing to enliven and authorize subversive futures against every status quo.[8]

Observe that this originary event—the generation of a new community in the world—is opposed to modernity's reduction of history to power, for Pharaoh had all the power on his side and could not prevail. Observe that this originary event is also opposed to an easy supernaturalism, for it is essentially a human act whereby Moses (and Aaron) confront Pharaoh and lead a "long march" to freedom.[9] Clearly, the decisive show of God's power in this event is mediated through the actions and speech of Moses. It is this convergence of holy resolve and human courage that initiates a newness the empire can neither understand nor resist.

3. The prophetic tradition of Israel is the offspring of both the narrative that tells of the "newness" bestowed on Abraham and Sarah and the Mosaic event of liberation. In Israel there arose a series of human speakers, prophets, who were emboldened by holiness and who conceived of scenarios of possibility that "the rulers of this age" had declared to be impossible. On the one hand, these prophets dared to envision a terrible impossibility, namely, that God's own people would answer for their cynical, willful disobedience and come to a suffering end. On the other hand, these prophets dared to imagine a totally new beginning, whereby God would re-form God's people in exile so as to create, as there had not been before, a people after God's own heart. These prophets dared to speak of "plucking up and tearing down, of planting and building." They dared to speak what their contemporaries regarded as either craziness (cf. Hos. 9:7) or treason (cf. Jer. 38:4). They dared to voice what imperial power had nullified and fate had settled. And in their speaking, they worked a newness.

4. It is through this tradition of new possibilities that the early church understood Jesus. In him, it saw wonders worked and impossibilities enacted. Power for newness swirled about him that establishment authority could neither resist nor nullify. Through his presence, the lame walked, the deaf heard, the lepers were cleansed, the dead were raised, and the poor had their debts canceled (Luke 7:22-23). In the end, the church was persuaded and confessed that even death could not hold him (Acts 2:24).

It seems clear that lying at the foundation of the church is the claim that Jesus is a full embodiment of the prophetic tradition of the Old Testament.

Jesus speaks and enacts the holy word of God in ways that "pluck up and tear down," that "plant and build." It is equally clear that the church's discernment and story of Jesus do not stop with this characteristically Jewish understanding. The church has gone further, to confess that Jesus is not only an *utterer* of the word but is himself the *uttered* word. Jesus' own person is God's word of life that shatters all idolatrous forms of life and makes new community possible.

The church crystallized its understanding of Jesus, which is radically Jewish yet moves beyond Jewish prophetic categories, through the formula "word becomes flesh" or, in its more metaphysical affirmation, "two natures in one person." Even such a formulation as the latter, however, does not depart from our primary assertion that prophetic speech is *human utterance of holy word.* Accordingly, Christians affirm that Jesus' life is indeed a human utterance, an utterance of the very word, will, purpose, and intent of God. The recurring temptation of the Christian tradition is to remove this word from the public process, either into privatistic spirituality or into theological ontology away from public issues. Such temptations misread both Jesus as the church experienced him and the Jewish tradition that is decisive for understanding him. It is the claim of prophetic Christology (as it is of Jewish prophetic faith) that God's abiding intention for creation becomes operative precisely in the midst of suffering and visible primarily in the hope-filled emergence of public newness.

I do not argue that Jewish prophecy must come to a Christological conclusion. Rather I assert simply that Jesus of Nazareth cannot be understood except in terms of the rhetoric and epistemology of Jewish prophecy, which does not admit of escapist reductionisms, either into privatism or ontology, and which attends to scandalous newness wrought by the power of God.

III

The courage and burden of these prophets of scandalous impossibility was to find speech that is adequate for the character of God. There would be no prophets (as here understood) without this God who is the subject of their speech, and there would be no prophetic word were God not a God of whom it can be said, "Thus says the Lord"; to put it succinctly, human utterance sounds holy speech. Accordingly, for all our interest in sociology and politics, the theme we strike is theological in nature and has to do with the character of God and the courage to bring this God to speech.[10] What the prophets assert is that human processes and policies are, apart from this God, wrongly construed. I suggest three ways of speaking about this God who keeps human history open to possibility. The character of this God who does wonders (*pela'*) is described one oracle at a time, one crisis at a time, one possibility at a time:

1. This God, unlike other gods, is *holy,* brooking no rivals, utterly unapproachable. There is at the center of the historical process a force and a will that cannot be harnessed, domesticated, manipulated, or bought off.

2. This God, unlike other gods, is a *"lover of justice"* (Ps. 99:4), intolerant of injustice, mightily at work in the public processes of history, allied with the powerless, critical of the greedy powerful, intervening with a "preferential option for the marginal."

3. This God, unlike other gods, because holy and because just, is a *dangerous, subversive God,* unsettling every status quo that offends holiness and that mocks justice. This God, unlike any other, is one who subverts, ending what is cherished and beginning what we little expect, in order that the world may receive and enact its proper life as God's creation.

The prophetic word in history is human utterance about this God, unintimidated by modernity, unimpressed by excessive religion, nonnegotiable about rhetoric, nondefensive about its epistemology, daring to insist that this God who works wonders in the historical process is still at large, liberating and healing.

IV

Speech about this God, speech that is daringly human and embarrassingly particular, regularly sounds themes that demand attention and require a revisioning of the human process. I should like to identify five such themes that are characteristic of the prophets, though many others might be cited.

1. Out of God's unaccommodating holiness, the prophetic word is *against idols,* and consequently against self-serving, self-deceiving ideology.[11] Idolatry and its twin, ideology, always want to absolutize some

arrangement of power and knowledge so that we may bow down to the work of our hands. Against such an absolutizing pretension, the holiness of God critiques, exposes, and assaults every phony absolute since all such absolutes of nation, race, party, or sex will end in death.

2. This holy God *refuses, then, to absolutize the present*, any present. This holy God drives always toward a new unsettling, unsettled future, which is not yet visible, when God's purpose will be accomplished and God's regime fully established. This threatening, promising future, which lives on the lips of prophets, warns against taking the present with excessive seriousness, even if it is a present that we happen to value inordinately.

3. Out of God's justice, prophetic speech characteristically speaks about *human suffering*. It takes human suffering as a definitional datum of the human, historical process. Thus, already in the exodus narrative, when Israel cries out, God sees, God hears, God knows, God remembers, and God intervenes (Exod. 2:23-25; 3:7-14).[12] It is the utterance of hurt that moves God to newness. The powers of modernity want not to notice human suffering; they want to define suffering as a legitimate and necessary cost of well-being or as an inexplicable given of human history. Prophetic speech demystifies pain and sees clearly that much pain is principally caused by the manipulation of economic and political access whereby the strong regularly destroy the weak. Such suffering is not a legitimate, bearable cost; and it is not inexplicable. Instead, social pain is a product of social relationships that can be transformed. Prophetic speech focused in hurt speaks against any tidy administration of social relations that crushes human reality in the interest of order, progress, profit, or "the common good."

4. Out of God's justice, prophetic speech characteristically takes *a critical posture over against established power*. Established power, in predictable ways, always manages to legitimate itself until it drives every other factor out of the social equation and history comes to equal not only the play of power but finally the embrace of this particular arrangement of power.

Prophetic speech refuses such a seductive domestication of the historical process. Prophetic speech not only insists that the raw use of power is wrong and must pay heed to human reality but also makes the more difficult claim that, in the end, raw power cannot succeed and is not the final datum of human history. Prophetic speech is realistic in knowing that massive power matters enormously; it is equally insistent that massive power does not matter ultimately as regards the outcome or significance of the human process. This view of power is not an obscurantist super-naturalism that bails out with reference to God. Rather it is the studied conclusion that there simply is not enough power in the long run to sustain itself in the face of human restlessness among those who refuse to be eradicated as an inconvenience. Moreover this human restlessness that refuses eradication is rooted in God's own resolve for the world.

5. Prophetic speech, finally, is not an act of criticism. It is rather *an act of relentless hope that refuses to despair* and that refuses to believe that the world is closed off in patterns of exploitation and oppression.[13] It stands against a closed present tense that is either excessively complacent about social relations or excessively despairing about an unbearable present tense. This speech knows that such closed-off life inevitably produces brutality, the child of despair, either out of strident control or out of hopelessness. It dares to assert in any and every circumstance the conviction known since Abraham and Sarah and Moses and Aaron, namely, that there is a God who can and will make all things new, even in the face of our most closed-down, self-satisfied present tense. This is what the text means when it asserts that God works an impossibility in order that "all the earth may know that there is a God in Israel" (1 Sam. 17:46).

V

It is obvious that our theme cannot be grasped by questions about ancient prophetic rhetoric. Instead this theme, in its powerful contemporane-ity, is focused on a very present-tense question: Can this prophetic faith, rooted in old treasured texts, be credible in our situation? Can it be credible against dominant theories of raw power and against current practices of pious abdication? This question is a difficult one, and I provide no easy answer. I can, however, suggest four elements in an affirmative answer that may permit our embrace of the prophetic tradition to be viable and credible.

1. First of all, the question is not, "Is God's word powerful in the historical process?" To answer this question would be to engage in a metaphysical speculation that can issue in no clear answer. Rather I suggest a very proximate question that in some ways is easier and in some ways more demanding. I pose the question this way: "Can the synagogue and the church, the communities committed to this prophetic claim, do the hard, demanding, intellectual, rhetorical work that will construe the world according to this

memory and this discourse?" The question, then, is not about God but about our courage and imagination. It is not a question of speculation but of practice. Can these communities of faith (and their ordained leaders) find tongues and ears and the will to embrace, articulate, and enact an odd, particular, scandalous mode of reality against the powerful reductionism all around us?

Thus I submit that the crisis of "word and history" is not that God has become obsolete or discredited with the rise of modernity but that these communities of odd discourse, entrusted with such speech, have compromised their vision and domesticated their passion. Where such speaking stops, the word ends its intrusive say in human history. The pastoral task, then, is the recovery of such discourse in quite concrete ways. Note well that the issue is not that of heroic courage by pastor or rabbi but of an entire community of circumcised/baptized believers that trusts its own way of speech. The issue of such peculiarity is not unlike the maintenance of Jewish discourse in a world of Hellenism; there is now a struggle for discourse that besets both Jews and Christians in an intellectually leveling, particularity-denying culture.[14]

2. The odd moment in which the world finds itself cannot be taken as "proof" that the word of God governs history. Proof is neither sought nor offered on such an issue and is indeed a misleading category. Indeed that category is a product of modernity. Nonetheless events in Eastern Europe and South Africa since the late 1980s make unmistakably clear that there are public possibilities that emerge and erupt well beyond any option entertained by established power. Moreover it is astonishing that the word—on the lips of poets and novelists and visionaries—has characteristically played such a crucial role in these turns of human affairs. We have witnessed the odd reality that the word has turned out to be more compelling and powerful than tanks or guns or secret police. Wherever that happens, it is a miracle, that is, a happening that contains "abiding astonishment."[15] We do not understand how such a happening can occur; we only notice that it does happen. It becomes unmistakably evident that such brutalizing, despairing concentrations of power in terms of secret police, tanks, and guns do not possess the means of coercion or intimidation to stay the holy power of justice that subverts all dehumanizing status quo. It takes no great imagination, in these specific cases, to see that daring speech can and does cause the fall and rise of public order. Indeed in the case of the dramatic changes in Eastern Europe and South Africa over the

last fifteen years, it takes enormous resolve to read such events apart from an affirmation of the word impinging upon history. Thus I suggest that the events of our recent past do indeed constitute evidence that all our powerful technique has not and cannot banish the powerful, holy word uttered by human lips in the matrix of suffering and hope. Ancient Israel is the one who first enacted such odd power where there was the convergence of holy resolve and human utterance.

3. Of course most of us are not placed by God to live and believe in Eastern Europe or in South Africa. Ours is a more difficult place, and we are always tempted to imagine that were we somewhere else, things would be more obvious and compelling. It may be that the ethos and lack of serious discourse in the cultural matrix of the United States make ours a most difficult environment in which to utter such holy words. Despite all our talk about "freedom of speech," serious human discourse has, in reality, all but disappeared among us. Issues are not much joined. Serious hope is scarcely practiced. Deep hurt is largely unacknowledged. Ours is a most coopted climate for humanness, besot as we are with power, arrogant in our greed, confident in our technology, still belatedly determined to work our powerful will in the world, characteristically on the side of brutalizing power. It is ironic indeed that, in this society so impressed with "freedom of speech," holy speech of abiding astonishment can apparently be completely obliterated by technique.[16] The cost of such "progress" is enormous, even if little noticed. This cost comes in the disappearance of a human infrastructure, in the erosion of public institutions of justice, health, and education, and in the emergence of a permanent and growing underclass; the ultimate cost, however, is an absence of political will to match resource to need. Indeed the drastic separation of resource from need in our society is done almost with the arrogance of virtue, the virtue of a nullified compassion. The outcome of such a procedure is the breakdown of persons, families, communities, and institutions, the near disappearance of what is humanness.

If one asks how this destructive process in our society can be countered or subverted, the answer is that it will not happen, in the first instance, by great programs or strategies but by utterance, unafraid speech that brings holiness back into history, that lets justice sound in the presence of power, that owns suffering even in a climate of apathy, that voices hope in the midst of despair, and refuses brutality in the name of the coming rule of God. Thus, for us, called to faith and life here, our theme is not an interesting intellectual question but an issue of our vocation and our common future. The prophetic tradition, however, has always surfaced with speech in the most difficult of contexts—and this is our "most difficult context."

4. The issue of a history-making word is not an intellectual question about whether modern people can believe ancient claims. It is a political question of what kind of power has power for life.[17] It is a question of rhetoric: Can concrete speech that utters the sounds of human passion have a hearing in the midst of technological speech? Most of all, it is an intellectual question about the premises of human life that are to prevail among us.

The technological effort to silence and overcome awkward human-holy speech is not a neutral, value-free, modest proposal.[18] It is a deeply partisan enterprise. What passes for objectivity is, in fact, a massive ideological claim that need not be respected as objective but critiqued as a false ideological proposal for reality.[19]

I suspect that prophetic speech—history-making, human-holy speech about hurt and hope—has disappeared because we have accepted the pretensions of technological silence.[20] Our proper task is, in the tradition of Israel's prophets, not excessive respect for the silence of technique but exposure of that silence for what it is, a surreptitious, determined resolve to end the rhetorical-political process that makes human life possible, that lets God be present and effective among us. Practitioners of this Jewish, prophetic tradition are in a polemical situation that requires naming the destructive option, now so powerful, and providing a serious, positive alternative.[21]

Clearly the main body of the church and synagogue little suspects the critical situation of faith in which we find ourselves. The outcome of the struggle between *prophetic utterance,* which enlivens, and *technological silence,* which censures, depends upon those who care to join the fray so as to help the faithful see that our God-given humanness will not last long beyond, or outside of, this dangerous tradition of speech. Where such rhetoric is stilled, our humanness is increasingly nullified. The intellectual challenge is not to provide a rhetorical addendum to our technological orientation but to counter it from the ground up.

Conclusion

In the face of the collapse of Soviet Communism, Francis Fukuyama has proclaimed the "end of history."[22] By this, he suggests that democratic capitalism has established a permanent ideological hegemony in the world. Such an assertion is, on the face of it, false, dangerous, even absurd. It is an ideological claim farcically masquerading as nonideology in order to banish the reality of class from political consideration. Such an "end of history" happens only when holy-human speech is lost. I submit that the prophetic word of God is the unending, resilient minority insistence that power cannot finally drive out human hurt and human hope. Note well, I do not suggest that prophetic speech constitutes some grand supernaturalism that invites theological obscurantism; nor does it consist in making predictions; nor is it "social action."

Prophetic speech (that is, the way God's word impinges upon human history) is concrete talk in particular circumstances where the great purposes of God for the human enterprise come down to particulars of hurt and healing, of despair and hope.[23] The synagogue and church have this demanding, awkward task of claiming much more than can be explained. What we have to say is rooted in textual memory and is driven by present pain. This speech insists that the processes of public power, where such speech is nullified, are a false reality that cannot endure. We bear witness that what we know and utter is not only dangerous and subversive but also life-giving. About the riddle of power, truth, and holiness, we echo the odd conclusion of the book of Proverbs, so evident in the world where history has not ended:

> No wisdom, no understanding, no counsel
>> can avail against the LORD.
> The horse is made ready for the day of battle,
>> but the victory belongs to the LORD (21:30-31).[24]

An Ending
That Does Not End

The book of Jeremiah is occasionally judged by critical scholarship to be "unreadable," that it lacks coherence and is so marked by disjunction that it cannot be seen whole.[1] What is meant, of course, is that it cannot be read sensibly according to our Western habits of coherent literature that make a single, sustained affirmation.[2] The book of Jeremiah is indeed unreadable unless one can allow for the plurality of voices that are shrill, disjunctive, and in conflict with one another, for that is what is given us in the book.[3]

I

The book of Jeremiah is "unreadable," it seems clear enough, because it is a commentary on, a reflection about, and an engagement with an "unreadable" lived experience. Without facing all the complexities and uncertainties of critical history, it is clear that something decisive happened in and to Jerusalem with the Babylonian assault, culminating in the destruction and deportation of 587 B.C.E.[4] The community of deportees, along with other communities of displaced and/or bewildered Jews, had a long time to reflect on that strange event that we may, for convenience, peg at 587. That reflection, however, was not clear, singular, or coherent, for it was marked by a host of uncertainties that precluded a "readable" commentary.

The obliqueness of the event is in part political. Jerusalem before 587 and several interpretive communities after 587 were filled with disputatious opinion that in some large part served vested interests. The questions of what went wrong and whom to blame are preliminaries to the seizure of initiative and the assertion of legitimacy for the future (as in ch. 24).[5] That is, every reflection is in some measure a positioning for the future.

Along with such political bewilderment and posturing, these lived events evoked serious and imaginative theological reflection. Characteristically, Israelite interpreters proceeded with the assumption that YHWH was a key and decisive player in these events, and therefore "prophetic" discernment—voices that claim to speak on behalf of YHWH—was in play. The role and purpose of YHWH in these events, however, were not obvious. For that reason, bewilderment and dispute were the order of the day, theologically as well as politically. It is a theological debate or quarrel about a historical experience, the meaning of which is unclear, that lies behind the unreadability of the book of Jeremiah.

The interplay of competing interpretations is in part a function of long-standing competing traditions—Mosaic, Davidic, and Zionist, among others. Beyond that, the interplay of competing interpretations arises because it is clear in some quarters that none of the old traditions are adequate for this moment, and something new, different, and venturesome must be said here in a wholly new circumstance. Underneath that, moreover, we may imagine that the practice of such lived interpretation is done by discerning people who themselves are *not sure* what they are witnessing and living through and therefore *not sure* what is to be said.

II

The theme for reflection seems to be given in the events themselves. It is an *end*—what happened in 587 is an end of the royal line, the end of a certain kind of temple practice, the end of a certain social cohesion and coherence. Beyond that, not much is certain, and it depends on how deeply the communities want to go about the end.[6] Is it the end of the community of Jerusalem as a viable cult operation? A viable political entity? Is it the end of faith? Is it the end of YHWH's attentiveness and fidelity? Or is there more yet, and if so, on what basis?

It requires no great imagination to see that different interpreters and different commentators rooted in different interpretive traditions, situated in different circumstances, and given different personal inclinations with different social status at stake will judge the matter differently. This capacity to hold together such differences in comment and reflection without reconciling them or without privileging any of them is definitional for "unreadability" and surely qualifies as "postmodern." Indeed one can make the claim that 587 ended a certain form of Jerusalem's modernity that operated with a single set of claims that ensured certainty and privilege.[7] Unreadability may reflect twentieth-century contemporary interpreters, well-schooled in modernity and accustomed to reading texts "modernly," standing in the face of a postmodern text as bewildered as were the framers of that text.

III

It is not necessary to specify the many poignant ways in which the poetic vision of the book of Jeremiah anticipates and imagines the end in material conventionally judged "early and genuine."[8] The imaginative entry into the *finality* of life with YHWH is enacted in rich and daring symbolization such as, for example, that of a broken marriage that culminates in "abandonment" (3:1—4:4) and terminal illness (8:18-22; 30:12-15).[9] That material, familiar to us and explicated most sensitively by Abraham Heschel, offers the most powerful and elemental truth of suffering that "the end" produces, which can only be voiced in poetry.[10]

Of that "ending," I wish to specify only some uses of the verb *kalah* that anticipate a complete termination:

> You have struck them,
> > but they felt no anguish;
> you have consumed them [*klh*],
> > but they refused to take correction. (5:3)[11]

> I will scatter them . . .;
> and I will send the sword after them, until I have consumed [*klh*] them.
> (9:15; Eng. v. 16)

> They shall perish (*klh*) by the sword and by famine, and their dead bodies shall become food . . . (16:4)

In these three cases, the verb *klh* bespeaks a decisive ending. In 5:3, the statement is on the lips of the poet, in 9:15 and 16:4 it is a divine oracle in prose.

These three uses are matched by a negative use of *'ahar* in 5:31:

> . . . what will you do when the end [*le'aharîthâ*] comes?

In 10:25, moreover, the verb *klh* is used, only here the end is at the hands of the nations and not the direct work of YHWH:

> They have devoured (*'kl*) Jacob;
>> they have devoured (*'kl*) him and consumed (*klh*) him,
>> and have laid waste (*šmm*) his habitation.[12]

That much is commonplace. The statements fit our usual assumption about prophetic judgment in general and Jeremiah in particular. It strikes us as conventionally appropriate for what might be said, either in anticipation of 587 or in reflection on it by the prophetic materials that are "early and genuine."

IV

What interests us, however, is that this rather straightforward conclusion about the loss of 587 is held with great unease in the tradition, unease that contributes precisely to the unreadability of the text. I will comment in particular on three texts that are situated in what is commonly regarded as "early and authentic" poetry from the prophet.

In a context of savage anticipation of the undoing of creation (4:23-26) and a conclusion that asserts YHWH's resolve not to relent or turn back from a determination to destroy (vs. 28), comes 4:27:

> For thus says the Lord: The whole land shall be a desolation; yet I will not make a full end [*klh*].

The verse is clearly at deep odds with those around it and contradicts the characteristic announcement of the end. Indeed the two parts of the prose verse itself are at odds, for the first phrase ends with "a desolation." There have been, of course, various strategies to comment on the last line in ways that contribute to readability. Perhaps the verse is a prose insert, as the NRSV seems to suggest. Or the negative *lo'* can be converted to *lah* ("to her"). Or with William Holladay, one may revocalize to "and none of it."[13] Obviously, all these efforts are to find a way out of a statement that is unambiguous but does not fit the main claim of the lines around it.

The same "problem" is evident in 5:10. The small textual unit of 5:10-13 has the characteristic elements of a speech of judgment. The indictment is that Israel and Judah have "been utterly faithless" and "have spoken falsely." The sentence is "destroy" and "strip." The lines conclude with a statement of deep resolve to destroy, not unlike the final line of 4:28.

In the midst of that speech of judgment, and just after the verb *destroy* (*sḥt*) comes our verb:

> . . . but do not make a full end [*klh*]. (v. 10)

Again the verse is problematic for a single reading. Here the preferred strategy simply deletes the negative in order to "correct" the "inconcinnity" and bring the line into conformity with the context.[14]

Our third text, 5:18, is again situated in a context of massive, relentless destruction. Verse 17, speaking of the "enduring nation" that will destroy, is dominated by the verb *devour* (*'kl*).

> They shall eat up [*'kl*] your harvest and your food;
>   they shall eat up [*'kl*] your sons and your daughters;
>   they shall eat up [*'kl*] your flocks and your herds;
>   they shall eat up [*'kl*] your vines and your fig trees.

The verse culminates with a different verb for "destroy" (*yrš*). Verse 19 is commonly judged to be in prose, but clearly refers to the wholesale destruction, again with marks of a speech of judgment:

> *Indictment*: You have forsaken me and served foreign gods in your land,
> *Sentence*:   You shall serve strangers in a land that is not yours.[15]

The justification for destruction in Jerusalem (v. 17) and deportation (v. 19) is unambiguous. Then, in the midst of this clarity about the end, comes verse 18:

> But even in those days, says the LORD, I will not make a full end (*klh*) of you.

The prose character of the verse plus the introductory phrase likely marks this verse as an "intrusion."[16]

In all three texts, 4:27, 5:10 and 5:18, explanations can readily be given about why this utterance ("not an end") does not belong where it is or does not mean what it says. Studied and conventional critical strategies easily dispose of the texts that do not "fit." These critical maneuvers are examples of the standard ways in which criticism serves to make the text readable.

It is worth observing, of course, that these critical "corrections" are not required or mandated by the text itself, but are judged to be necessary by the critical commentator, he or she having decided beforehand what the text must say (or cannot say). The critical commentator characteristically has decided beforehand that the text must speak with one voice that is the dominant voice, so a lesser, challenging, conflicting, competing voice in the very same text is untenable and must either be silenced or made to conform. Note well, I do not say that such a reader has decided substantively ahead of time what must be said, that is, that this is an ending; rather, such a reader has decided "modernly" ahead of time that there can be only one voice and that here this one, characteristic voice is the voice of an end. Thus the dominant voice, by critical maneuver, is given complete hegemony in the text. The substantive outcome that is likely incidental to such a maneuver is an unqualified, unmitigated assertion of an end, no voice to the contrary. Thus the text three times says:

I will not make a full end (4:27),

Do not make a full end (5:10),

I will not make a full end of you (5:18).

The text undoubtedly says that three times. But it must not and cannot say that, and so when we finish, it does not! By now the text has become readable.

Our work here, however, is to consider postmodern rejection of such readability that refuses the text's own terms. In this context, I take our postmodern responsibility to be to refuse such a flattened, hegemonic reading and to pay heed to the lesser voice that seems odd in this conversation. That is, our work is to see what this strange, disruptive utterance might intend, rather than to silence or distort it. In these three cases, we must wonder why the final form of the text would say "not a full end" in such a way as to speak against the "end speech" of the dominant strain.

The lived outcomes of 587 were never clear. The meaning of the "end" was not given in the "facts" themselves, but awaited interpretive utterance.[17] No one knew what happened in 587 until what happened was "said," until it was given some construal. It did not take great imagination to see an end in the events, even though what was *seen* was *said* imaginatively in the poetic traditions of the prophets (2 Kgs. 21:12). The remaining issue, after the utterance of an end, is whether such an utterance has fully exhausted what has happened. These three modest statements that I have cited assert a conviction that there is more in the event that remains to be said. It is easiest to conclude, as critical scholarship has characteristically done, that these are later judgments, reflecting a subsequent experience of the community that had in fact not ended, that found new signs and measures of YHWH's fidelity. That is what is meant by the dismissive and conventional label "gloss."

It occurs to me, however, that already closer to the event itself, not necessarily late and without waiting generations for new data in new context, some might have made this disquieting utterance/counterconstrual. Perhaps "not a full end" is simply an emotional refusal or inability to see what is there; such a thought, moreover, permits the counterthought that perhaps the conviction of an end, so fully stated in the Jeremiah tradition, was an ideological effort to see more than was there, because it was not an end. That is, we cannot simply assume that the "speech of end" is correct while the contrary speech is not. Perhaps "not a full end" is wishful thinking, such a deep cherishing of what was that its end was unthinkable and therefore, finally, unspeakable. Or perhaps "not a full end" is a doggedly determined theological affirmation and that while the political, economic apparatus had ended, YHWH is no quitter and that YHWH's faithful passion is not coterminous with visible arrangements. Or perhaps it is not resistance or wishful thinking or determined faith, but simply a vacillation before unclear evidence, vacillation designed precisely to keep things open against the dominant judgment, not because the end could not be faced, but because it is not known yet what might constitute compelling evidence of an end. In this alternate opinion, "not a full end" is to be taken as deliberately dialectical and dialogical with "a full end," not wanting to nullify the other opinion but wanting to keep open that for which not enough is known to give certain closure.[18]

It is entirely possible to probe what might have been intended in these statements as I have done—or at least to report how they strike this reader—without attributing too much authorial intention to the options.[19] I judge that the major responsibility of this discussion in any case is not to consider primarily the text but to consider our interpretive habits. Our critical habits are mostly intolerant of minority views and counterconvictions. Our habit is to give no privilege to mystery, bewilderment, or unresolve, precisely so that there can be a single reading, either a single reading to be taken up by a believer or a single reading to provide a "grain" against which an academic skeptic can read.[20] What these utterances recognize, however, is that lived reality is not so single, neat, or obvious as to permit single, unchallenged construal. Such a text as these invites living with unresolve that may, in this case, be a God-given, God-enacted unresolve.[21] It could be, if we engage a second naiveté that is genuinely naive, that the God who enacted 587 did not know, could not see, had not yet decided if this was an end—too soon to say, because this God is capable of twists and turns that defy our usual readability.[22]

V

It turns out that these three utterances did indeed speak the truth, for the identifiable community of Israel as YHWH's people did not end and indeed "Jerusalem" did not end. This truth-telling may be understood as the belated conviction of another generation that subsequently produced emerging Judaism. This belated conviction could be expressed as William McKane's "rolling corpus," so that what was decisive and resolved eventuated otherwise against the "early" judgment.[23] But even if that is the case, the three statements turn out to be telling the truth and protesting against the single-minded harshness of the "speech of end." That this is not an end can be understood *historically* as Judaism emerges. That it is not an end can be understood *literarily* as the scroll "unrolls." That it is not an end can be understood *theologically* in terms of the One who plucks up and tears down being the same One who plants and builds, the One who will not be fully contained in or caught completely in the "speech of end."

Given the openness that our three utterances maintain against closure, we may consider several extrapolations from "not an end." Among these is, most importantly, 30:11 (emphasis added):

> For I am with you, says the LORD, to save you;
> I will *make an end* of all nations

among which I scattered you,
but of you I will *not make an end*,
I will chastise you in just measure,
and I will by no means leave you unpunished.

Now this utterance is in the "Book of Comfort," where such a statement is no longer objectionable, as it has been judged to be in the three earlier cases. The dominant verb is *save* (*yš'*) and no longer *destroy*. That dominant verb permits the statement "not a full end," though the chastisement and punishment can now be kept on schedule. What interests us is that the negative statement—"not a full end" (not "corrected" here by any critical scholar)—is matched by a positive use of the same verb: "I will make an end [*klh*] of all the nations." The poetic tradition is indeed capable of saying this directly when that is what is intended, without any correcting assistance from criticism. Now that great claim can be said directly, unambiguously, "an end to all the nations," surely meaning Babylon and all its allies and functionaries. Indeed such an end is required if Israel is to have "not an end," for it is the end of Babylon that makes "not an end" a reality for Jerusalem.

This same rhetoric that apparently applies to Babylon in 30:11 is twice used, in very different contexts and genres, with reference to Egypt. In the Oracles against the Nations, it is particularly with reference to Egypt that our phrasing is used in the context of a salvation oracle for Israel:

As for you, have no fear, my servant Jacob, says the LORD,
for I am with you.
I will make an end [*klh*] of all the nations
among which I have banished you,
but I will not make an end [*klh*] of you!
I will chastise you in just measure,
and I will by no means leave you unpunished. (46:28)

Even though this verse is in the long chapter concerning Egypt, the assertion here is a positive one concerning Jacob/Israel. There is to be *no fear* because there is *no end* of Jacob/Israel. The verse closely parallels 30:11. The "not an end" is again matched, as in 30:11, with an "end" for the threatening superpower that challenges the will and authority of YHWH. There is to be an ending, but not for Jacob/Israel!

In slightly different rhetoric, the polemic against Egypt occurs at the end of the final prose denunciation of Egypt, or more specifically "all you Judeans who live in the land of Egypt":

> I am going to watch over them for harm and not for good; all the people of Judah who are in the land of Egypt shall perish [*klh*] by the sword and by famine, until not one is left. (44:27)

Now there is to be a Jewish ending, and it is not here corrected or modified by criticism, as in the three earlier cases I have cited. This final polemic would seem to be on the lips either of Jews who remained in Jerusalem or, more likely, Jews who were in Babylon and became the dominant voice of emerging Judaism. In either case, there is no dissenting voice here to suggest that the end pronounced over Egyptian Jews is "not an end." Except that we should notice that this is a Jerusalem or Babylonian text.

Perhaps in a text of Egyptian Jews (that we do not have), there might have been a whimsical, hopeful utterance, "not an end." Or if not such a text or even such an utterance, perhaps an unheard prayer or an unrecorded affirmation or an unuttered wish. We have seen how criticism may belatedly silence such yearning or determination. Perhaps there were other devices for silencing to make sure that this Jewish community in Egypt heard only an imposed finality. After 30:11, which may pertain to *Babylon* and after 46:28 on *Egypt* and 44:27 on *Jews in Egypt*, we may also note finality voiced toward Babylon that is the ground of Jeremianic hope expressed as realpolitik. Babylon must end for these to be "not an end" in Jerusalem:

> You who live by mighty waters,
>   rich in treasures,
> your end [*qets*] has come,
>   the thread of your life is cut. (51:13)

VI

In the end [*sic*], the issue is not only canon-making, or even competition between interpretive communities, it also concerns the force of newness that goes under the name of YHWH. Finally, the tension in the text is theological, even if that theological tension inevitably comes in historical and/or literary expression. "In the end," the book of Jeremiah honors these silenced utterances and affirms that 587 was indeed "not an end." Now, with a different term, there is indeed an "afterward" for this community-not-ended:

> In the latter [*aḥarth*] days you will understand it clearly. (23:20)

> For surely I know the plans I have for you, says the LORD, plans for your welfare and not for harm, to give you a future [*'aḥarth*] with hope. (29:11)

> In the latter [*aḥarth*] days you will understand this. (30:24)

> There is hope for your future [*'aḥarth*], says the LORD, your children shall come back to their own country. (31:17)

This is not an afterward that the community can describe. It is an afterward not in hand, not yet given. It is not-yet-lived history. It is, rather, passionate poetic conviction that requires utterance that moves past history and past uttered verdicts of closure, to say much more than is known, to imagine more than can be seen.

In many places, the book of Jeremiah has "a sense of ending."[24] The final form of the book is, however, unsure and restless with such a sense. Its sense of an ending is a historical judgment, but a historical judgment that floats in an ocean of freighted theological conviction. In the end, this restlessness refuses an ending, refuses to let observed data dictate the edges of faith. For that reason, apparently without a clear sense of an ending, no clear ending for the book of Jeremiah could be managed. There are, to be sure, efforts at such an ending, and they are not to be taken lightly; but they are, each one, provisional.[25]

1. The best-known ending, most obvious, is in the Hebrew text that persists in English translation in 52:31-34; it concerns the ongoing exile of King Jehoiachin, ongoing for thirty-seven years. But the discussion of Gerhard von Rad, Martin Noth, and Hans Walter Wolff evidences that this ending is not clear.[26] Perhaps this ending is designed exactly to reflect the conversation of "end/not end" that we have seen in our three texts, that is appropriate to this construal of reality with YHWH—not closed, but not known.

2. If for the moment we can take chapter 52 as an addendum borrowed from 2 Kings 25, we may consider 51:59-64 as an ending; clearly verse 64b has the cadence of a literary and intentional ending. Babylon is "sunk." That sinking creates space and possibility for Jerusalem. There is indeed an ending, but it is for the empire and not in Jerusalem. The ending is rather in Babylon, where Nebuchadrezzar had imagined that his domination would never end (see Isa. 47:10).

3. If we continue to bracket chapter 52 and, in addition, allow for the movement of the Oracles of the Nations (chs. 46–51) to chapter 25 along with LXX, then 45:5 becomes the ending.[27] Jeremiah 45:1-5 is an oracle that confirms a massive ending of "the whole land":

> "Thus says the LORD: I am going to break down what I have built, and pluck up what I have planted—that is, the whole land. And you, do you seek great things for yourself? Do not seek them; for I am going to bring disaster upon all flesh, says the LORD." (45:4-5a)

There is, however, a qualifier for Baruch:

> "But I will give you your life as a prize of war in every place to which you may go." (45:5b)

Baruch here is many things. He is the aide of the prophet who has been taken to Egypt (43:6). But he is also a cipher for the continuing faithful community of Jews who stayed close to the truth of Jeremiah, perhaps to the entire construal of the tradition of Deuteronomy. Baruch is also point man for scribalism that here becomes Torah teacher who assured new forms of faithfulness and well-being to Judaism.[28] He is all these; to him (them) is uttered an exception of well-being—not a final end.[29]

There are many endings to the book of Jeremiah. But there is no ending. Because there is "not a full end." All of this, the lack of an ending, will "be understood in the latter days," days perhaps not unlike our own (23:20; 30:24). For now, the "latter days" may be postmodern, when we refuse any reduction that makes matters simple and manageable. It occurred to me that the modernist passion for a single voice may be a mark of modernist despair that expects nothing. It is in the tensive conversations of disputed interpretation that newness comes. Thus "single reading" may be not only an intellectual commitment. It may also be a theological commitment to closure that expects nothing and will receive nothing. The modest counter-voice of 4:27, 5:10, and 5:18 refuses such closure. We do well to listen again, without silencing or distorting a faint alternative to ending.

CHAPTER EIGHT

A Second Reading
of Jeremiah
after the Dismantling

The internal dynamic of the book of Jeremiah is a two-stage development of the tradition that is decisive for the shape of the literature
and for its theological claim.

I

That two-stage development can be articulated in three ways:

1. In terms of *literature*, scholarship has made a distinction between the
actual work of the person of Jeremiah and extensive Deuteronomic extrapolations. The precise nature of the relation between the two is difficult and
there is no scholarly consensus.[1] But it does seem to be the case that there
are prose materials that are derivative from the poetry of Jeremiah. That
prose is cast in language reminiscent of the tradition of Deuteronomy, but
that derivation is probably not simply an alternative literary form. In all
likelihood the derived materials aim at another function than the original
poetic materials do.

2. In terms of *historical sequence*, there is no doubt that we can identify
materials that are placed before the destruction of 587 and after the destruction of 587, even though in many ways the first deportation of 597 posed
as an important point of reference for Jeremiah.[2] The distinction between
pre-587 and post-587 materials is not simply in the interest of chronology. The historical, sociological context of the community is very different
and therefore later materials have a quite different pastoral agenda. This is
reflected in E. W. Nicholson's title, *Preaching to the Exiles*.[3] His argument,
now followed by many scholars, is that the circumstances of the addressees

of the later literature is one of exile, very different from Jeremiah's prior addressees. A different message is therefore required.

3. In terms of a *theological concern*, one can distinguish between a literature of judgment and a literature of salvation. In his canonical analysis of the book of Jeremiah, Brevard Childs[4] argues that this shift from judgment to salvation is the overriding theological agenda of the book in its present canonical form.

These distinctions—literary, historical, theological—can be seen to be all of a piece. Thus we may suggest that in broad outline these various factors converge. In the canonical book of Jeremiah there is:

a. A literature that is from *Jeremiah*[5] that is *preexilic* and that is essentially a statement of judgment. It can hardly be disputed that Jeremiah's primary work is located before the destruction of the city. Moreover his persistent message is to assert God's judgment on the city and God's dispatch of "an enemy" from the north to work his destruction. Occasionally this leads to a summons to repentance, but most often it leads simply to a sad assertion of the end.

b. A literature commonly judged to be from *Deuteronomic redactors*, addressed to exiles and therefore *after 587*, which announces *hope* and God's resolve to work a new thing. One can note a change in style and certainly a change in substance, which make the conclusion of an alternative dating inescapable.

It is important, however, that these two stages of the literature of Jeremiah not be seen as completely distinct in all these aspects or as juxtaposed only artificially. If we are to take the literature seriously in its fixed canonical form, then we must presume that this literature has integrity and the two parts are in important ways related to each other. While we cannot be clear about the literary and historical connections, we can assume that theologically the assertions of judgment and hope hold together because they are the work of the same God addressed to the same community, albeit in different circumstances.

It follows from this that the two literatures (Jeremiah and Deuteronomistic),[6] from the two periods (pre- and post-587), with the two themes (judgment and hope), must not be confused with each other. But they also must not be separated from each other. The one follows the other and is shaped and informed and becomes poignant because of the other. Theological exegesis of the "second stage" must attend to the claim that it is the same God who destroys and works newness, who works newness precisely out of the destruction over which God has previously presided. Thus I regard the inclination to separate clearly the two moves of literature (as in the case of Robert Carroll, who acts as though these are simply distinct literatures) as missing the main theological point of the juxtaposition, that the God who judges to death is the very God who works new life.[7]

II

The present discussion considers the vision report of Jeremiah 24. The date of the text given in v. 1 is in the reign of Zedekiah, after the first deportation of 597, which included King Jehoiachin. It is a prose narrative, which, as we shall see, offers hope for exiles. Of the three pairs of categories we have established, two are clear:

1. The text is located in *exile*, not before.[8]
2. The text speaks both hope and judgment, but the stress point is on *hope*.

On the basis of these matters, plus its phraseology, a number of scholars regard chapter 24 as a Deuteronomic text, thus belonging to the "second stage" of Jeremaic literature. Scholars are not fully agreed, however, for Henning Graf Reventlow[9] makes the case that it is unnecessary to assign the material to the Deuteronomic process. It is not necessary for us to decide this matter, though I am inclined toward a Deuteronomic placement. It is enough to be clear that the text is *after judgment* both chronologically and theologically. That move to assertion of hope after judgment belong structurally and integrally to the book and faith of Jeremiah canonically understood (as Childs has discerned), regardless of its literary source.

We need not linger over the vision report itself (vv. 1-3). The secondary literature notes repeatedly that this vision report is formally consistent with the visions of chapter 1 of the book of Amos. Our purpose here is not to consider the phenomenological element of how visions occurred. Rather our interest is in the theological claim borne by the vision. Jeremiah saw something, was shown something by God, which permitted him to make an odd and unexpected theological judgment about the historical process. The vision permitted a historical judgment that was not necessary before 598 and indeed was not possible. The vision accompanied the new circumstance that had set Judah in an odd, unprecedented situation, which required a new reading and a new redescription of reality.[10]

The substance of the vision itself is not helpful to us. Indeed *the figs* as such seem irrelevant. Nothing is made of them in the chapter and no subsequent reference is made to them in the tradition of Jeremiah (except the parallel use of Jer. 29:17-19). In fact, the vision seems rather to want only to get the words "good" and "evil" in the purview of the prophet, and nothing more. Of course it would hardly be necessary to have a vision in order to surface these words. The historical process had done just that. The prophetic indictment has already established the evil of Judah, and the Babylonian invasion of 598 had sealed the case.

What is startling is that the oracle proposes that any figs are *good*. This is a new hint in the process of judgment. Any faithful reading of what happened could readily conclude that the *evil ones* had *received* evil (the exile).[11] Somewhat less compelling is judgment that the good ones had received the good of being left in the land. It is significant that any of the Judeans are regarded as good, in the face of both destruction and exile. But if any segment of the Judean community seems to have merit, it is those left in the land. If land is as crucial as the Deuteronomic tradition suggests,[12] then being left in the land should be *good*, and being taken from the land should be *evil*. The entire Deuteronomic tradition leads to that conclusion.

It is a truism of scholarship that the Babylonians took the cream of the crop from Judah in order to squelch further rebellion. Perhaps so. But that is a judgment made on the basis of critical political analysis. It is not an obvious conclusion that is reached on moral or theological grounds. The canonical judgment is that the doing of evil leads to evil consequences.

Thus a reliable formula of social retribution is sufficient for a conventional judgment. It is enough to see that some are rewarded by staying in the land and some are punished by exile. This must have been an obvious and convincing conclusion after 598, at least among those who remained in the land.

No vision is needed for that conclusion. Vision is needed only if the conventional reading of the day is to be contradicted and controverted. That is precisely how this vision functions, to counteract that rather obvious reading and to offer a counterreading that takes one by surprise.

III

The vision itself, verbalized in v. 3, contains no hint of its substantive message. It is the following interpretive word of vv. 4-10 that permits that vision to contradict the popular judgment, hence the messenger formula of v. 4. The assertion of v. 5 contains the main point of the vision, balanced negatively in v. 8. The entire positive judgment is vv. 5-7, but vv. 6-7 only elaborate the verdict of v. 5. What a stunning verdict it is! The vision and its rendering contradict the popular conclusion and reread the present circumstance of Judah in an astonishing unexpected way. The initial phrase "like these good figs" is not substantive but only links the oracle to the vision. The key assertion follows: "I will recognize for good."

This hiph'il verb *'akîr* places the stress on the agent, YHWH. Reventlow persuasively draws the conclusion that it is not the quality of the figs but the destiny of the figs wrought by YHWH's decision that is at issue and the point of the oracle.[13] As Reventlow understands it, there is nothing in the exilic group that evokes or warrants such a judgment, but only the decision of YHWH. If that reading is correct, then the verb *'akîr* carries weight not unlike *ḥāšāv* in Genesis 15:6, which means that the judgment is a free designation of YHWH without reference to the merit of the community.[14] The rereading of historical circumstance depends solely on YHWH's verdict. That the rereading depends on a verdict seems likely, though the verb *nkr* could conceivably contain the notion that the exiled group is "recognized" as good, not simply "declared" good. It could be that the verb intends precisely such an ambiguity, but that seems unlikely, and I believe Reventlow has made his point.[15] In any case the outcome is not in doubt. YHWH has designated this group to receive what is good—namely blessing (cf. "good" as blessing in Deut. 30:15, a text perhaps related to Jer. 24). "Good-evil" is used in three other places in the Jeremiah tradition to fix the destiny of the city or the people. In 39:16 and 44:27 (cf. Amos 9:4), the Egyptian exiles are set for evil and not for good. There is no doubt that this is YHWH's action and not the quality of the community, except in so far as evil begets evil. In 21:10, the same point is made concerning the city. In 29:11, in a variant form, the Babylonian exiles are addressed positively:

> I know the plans I have for you, says the LORD, plans for welfare and
> not for evil, to give you a future with hope.

The controlling word pair here is *šalôm-ra'â*, but the meaning is the same with *šalôm* as with *tôv*. Clearly we are dealing with YHWH's decision and not with Judah's merit. Interestingly the word *ḥāšāv* is used here not only as a noun but also as a participle. On the basis of the participial form, Reventlow's judgment is sustained. This participial usage makes a nice connection between *'akîr* in our passage and the decisive use of *ḥāšāv* in Genesis 15:6. The assignment of "good" to Judah is a free verdict of YHWH without merit on the part of the Babylonian exiles. The vision contradicts obvious popular judgment. That contradiction rests solely on YHWH's sovereign judgment given freely without cause and without explanation. That sovereign freedom contradicts the expected and common judgment. Thus v. 5 asserts an incredible "new thing."[16] The ones under *punishment* (exile) are now declared to be the bearers of *blessing*.

In 24:5 (as in 29:11) then, we are at the theological pivot point of the tradition of Jeremiah. We have said that the theological structure of the book of Jeremiah is "two-staged." But beyond the literary and historical arguments, the linkage between the two stages is difficult. It is not sufficient to state, as canonical criticism is inclined to do, that the two are simply there. That lacks the dynamic that is required to understand them.[17] In v. 5, we are given the clue to the theological linkage. The turn from judgment to hope, from exile to "good," is wrought by the assessment of the world.

The exposition of this counterverdict by God is articulated in vv. 6-7 in a series of first-person pronouns with active verbs to express YHWH's free, sovereign action. These statements in the mouth of YHWH contain a remarkable collection of formulae.

a. I will set my eyes on them for good (blessing).[18]
b. I will bring them back to the land.

The verb *šûv* is used here as in 29:14 where it occurs with both *qavaṣ* and the phrase *šûv ušĕvôt*. Restoration to land is clearly the resolution of exile and the full turn from judgment to hope. If there were not restoration to the land, then any other judgment would not be so dramatic or so compelling.

c. I will build up and not tear down,
    I will plant and not root up.

In v. 6, the dominant formula of the Jeremiah tradition is utilized. In 1:10, both positive and negative actions are evidences of YHWH's governance. The use of these verbs in 18:7-10; 31:28; 42:10; and 45:4 indicate the great flexibility of the formula.[19] Only here and in 31:27 are the positive verbs set in sequence *after* the negative ones. In 42:10 and 45:4, it is the negatives that are foremost. In 18:7-10, there is still a choice, though the choice seems forfeited already in v. 12. But here, as in 31:27, the negatives have already happened. God has no more tearing down and rooting up to do. The positive verbs, *plant* and *build*, are beyond the negatives, which are already implemented. Restoration is only to exiles and that restoration is founded only in YHWH's free assertion. The move from negatives to positives is not understood simply as a literary process of redaction nor simply as historical sequencing. It is understood as the free action of reversal that YHWH can do without explanation. Thus the oracle of vv. 5-7 concerns a free action of YHWH that goes against expectation and against popular judgment.

d. I will give them a heart.

Earlier (4:4), Jeremiah had hoped for a repentant heart, but that was before the deportation. Indeed Jeremiah had reached the judgment that Judah was not capable of changing heart (cf. 13:23). In a structure not unlike that of Ezekiel, the preexilic insistence is upon repentance (cf. Ezekiel 18), but exilic realism is that repentance is not possible. Only a free action of YHWH, which overrides the obduracy of Judah, makes a future relation possible. The gift of a new heart as a free act of YHWH is commensurate with the hopelessness of Israel to change at all (cf. Ezek. 36:26). The move from the possibility of 4:4 to this text is parallel with the move from Ezekiel 18 to Ezekiel 36. The exile makes clear that Judah is unable and unwilling to do the repentance that is required. Therefore, a new act on the part of YHWH is necessary if there is to be a future. It is that drastic move on the part of YHWH that is announced here.

The new heart is for the sake of acknowledging YHWH,[20] that is, for the renewal of the covenant.[21] The old people of that old heart, that is, before 598, did not "know" and could not know. From the new knowing comes the covenant formula, a fully reestablished covenant relationship. The outcome is a return with a whole heart, a new heart given by God, a heart prepared for obedience. To return with a whole heart is a theme sounded especially for exiles (cf. Deut. 4:30; Isa. 55:6). God is available precisely to exiles, as he refused to be available prior to exile (Jer. 7:16; 15:1-4).

It is clear that the exposition of the verdict of v. 5 in vv. 6-7 is an exceptionally strong passage that makes powerful appeal to the memory of Israel. It is a collage of the most formidable formulae that Israel has for hope and for new beginning. These are highly stylized statements. There is scarcely a word in these verses of assurance that falls outside the set formula. The future is rooted in what Judah knows best from its past. All of the formulae bear witness to a new beginning, when YHWH values precisely what has been sharply devalued.

IV

Verses 8-10 in chapter 24, which complete the unit, serve as a negative counterpart to vv. 4-7. One has the impression that the oracle report is not terribly interested in this part, but it is offered for completion of the case in symmetrical fashion.

The actual negative verdict is given in v. 8, which parallels v. 5. It is equally astonishing, only now we are prepared for it. The people who remained in the land must have reckoned themselves as blessed. They had watched the sorry events of 598 and had noticed that they were untouched. Public life continued to function for them. To have this negative judgment announced in that context must have been remarkably polemical. It is interesting that the verdict is not so delicately given. In v. 5, the goodness is "regarded." Here the statement is flat and one-dimensional. They are bad.[22] They are not reckoned as bad or declared to be bad. They are bad. Perhaps the verb indicates "handed over to evil," but even that is not parallel to ʾakîr. The rhetoric of the two matching verdicts (vv. 5, 8) is not equal. That is because the good verdict (v. 5) is an act of sovereign freedom whereas the negative verdict (v. 8) is a necessary one given the evidence. The difference in rhetoric calls attention to the power of the first verdict in v. 5.

The text groups together two communities, the Judean remnant and the Egyptian exiles. What the two have in common is that they are not in Babylon. The "Babylonian orientation" of the book of Jeremiah requires that every other group be critiqued and rejected as irrelevant for the future. No reason is offered for "bad." It is simply presumed and asserted.

This verdict is supported in vv. 8-10 by two well-established formulae. Both of them have to do with the consequence of the evil, not the ground of it. The first in v. 9 announces that the judged communities will be reduced to a humiliation in the eyes of the other nations:

> I will make them a horror, an evil thing, to all the kingdoms of the earth, to be a reproach, a byword, a taunt and a curse in all the places where I shall drive them. (My translation)

This abasement of Judah before the nations gathers together three elements of the tradition. First, it may be a public use of the fear of humiliation expressed in the Psalms of personal lament (e.g., Ps. 13:4). The same motif is now used for public purposes. Second, it surely is an inversion of the whole election tradition. The people that was to be the head (cf. Deut. 28:13, 45) has become the tail. Clearly God's special commitment here is terminated. Third, the verb pattern of the abasement formula appeals to and reiterates the formula concluding the call narrative in 1:10.

The actual wording of this judgment (24:6) in five members (horror, reproach, byword, taunt, curse) appears in a variety of configurations:

42:18   four members: execration, horror, curse, reproach
44:8   two members: curse, reproach
44:12   four members: execration, horror, curse, reproach
44:22   three members: desolation, horror, curse
49:13   four members (but it is not addressed to Judah):[23] horror, reproach, desolation, curse

In 1 Kings 9:7, which is clearly Deuteronomic, there are two members with an exposition in v. 8. In that passage the lawsuit is complete with the basis given in v. 9. The basis is absent from our passage but is, of course, presumed.

The other use of special interest to us is in the curse recital of Deuteronomy 28:25, 37 (cf. Lev. 26:32):

> You shall become an object of horror to all the kingdoms of the earth. . . .
> You shall become an object of horror, a proverb, and a byword among all the peoples where the LORD will lead you.

The redactional history of this chapter is complicated and unsure.[24] It cannot be certain that this is an old curse formula. Yet it is so highly stylized that it must be a fixed formula and surely is not freely composed in our context. So this very massive curse formula is used to negate the election tradition, for it concerns precisely Judah. It is noteworthy that our verse (Jer. 24:9) is the only judgment formula with five members, which means it is the most extreme of all uses. The ones in the land and the ones in Egypt are utterly rejected.

The second formula that exposits the negative verdict of v. 8 is the three-fold curse formula of v. 10. It is clear that we are dealing with a set formula that had important visibility in this period, though we cannot be sure of its antiquity.[25] The standard usage is the three-membered curse (14:12; 21:9; 27:8, 13; 38:2; 44:13), though it is also used with only two members (without pestilence, in 11:22; 16:4; 44:12, 18, 27). It can also be used with a fourth member to intensify the danger. In 15:2, the fourth member is exile and in Ezekiel 14, the fourth member is wild beasts. The formula in all uses indicates the covenant is fully negated (contrast Jer. 24:7) and the community is under a death sentence. The ones in the land and the ones in Egypt are bound to death.

The standard formulae in these various uses are given two different expositions that draw them closer to the historical reality of Jeremiah. On the one hand, the set list of curses is extended in various ways to speak about utter extermination. That may be implied in the list itself, but it is variously made explicit so that the point is not missed (this is so in our text and in 11:22; 27:8; 44:12, 17): "Until there is none left." On the other hand, Jeremiah's uses reflect his "Babylonian reading" of the historical crisis. He is convinced that his contemporaries have two choices and only two. The curse recital is not inevitable. An alternative that permits life is submission to Babylon (21:9; 27:13; 38:2). The reference to Babylon has the effect of breaking the finality and inevitability of the curse. But, of course, the Babylonian alternative in our passage is confined to the good figs in vv. 5-7. The bad figs in vv. 8-10 have already rejected the alternative and now have no option but death. In this way, the Jeremiah tradition links the *classic curse formula* to the *historical particularities of policy* in this specific moment. A liturgic formula is utilized in the interest of policy advocacy.

V

Thus far the rereading of Judah's history through a vision (vv. 1-3) has led to two message-statements. Both the positive affirmation (vv. 4-7) and the negative judgment (vv. 8-10) are a gathering together of a list of the most formidable and characteristic formulae available in the covenantal-Deuteronomic tradition. Every sentence is heavily styled. But what concerns us is that all of these formulae are in the service of a remarkable judgment (disclosure, revelation) concerning God's verdict and posture in the midst of the historical process. The fact that the formulae are pressed into service in this way means that the central claim is more important than any of the formulae. While we have attempted to explore the specific formulae, the claim of the oracle is greater than the sum of the parts consisting in formulae.[26] While critical study can help us to understand and locate each of the parts, it is the verdict of the entire unit that needs to concern us, but which most critical study may miss. That verdict is in fact a complete inversion of a natural, obvious reading of reality. The landed are for death, the exiles are for life and hope. The inversion is as decisive as the one anticipated by Hannah (1 Sam. 1:6-8) and the one celebrated by Mary (Luke 1:51-53).

We reflect on *the character of that verdict*, which is supported, enhanced, and fleshed out by the various formulae. What is the nature of the verdict? I suggest four possible characterizations of the verdict:

1. It is a *historical decision* reflecting the fact that the center of vitality and authority for Judaism did indeed shift away from Jerusalem to the Babylonian community.[27] As a historical claim, this can hardly be disputed. The reasons for that shift are complex. It is impossible to identify any single explanation. Such a shift belongs to the "cunning of history."[28] One may, of course, observe that the class of Jews deported (cf. 24:1) made possible new initiatives that would come from there, but that seems too flat a reason.[29]

In retrospect this is what happened: It was indeed members of the Jewish community in Babylon that provided the theological and political leadership that gave shape and viability to Judaism, as in the poetry of the second Isaiah, the pastoral concern of Haggai and Zechariah, and the decisive work of Ezra and Nehemiah. But to identify the verdict of Jeremiah 24 as historical in this sense is to place the visionary announcement in a reportive role, which only describes what happened. The historical judgment could not have been made until later and, in any case, the vision-oracle of the chapter does not present what was obvious to everyone. That is, there could have been some who observed the historical emergence of the leadership of Babylonian Jews and still not have drawn a theological conclusion that YHWH had made a fresh covenant commitment. The shift from a historical reality to a theological verdict is by no means clear and obvious. Rather what we have in Jeremiah is a shocking "rereading." While the historical factor is true, it is not an adequate way to understand the theological verdict, which is not determined by such a historical assessment.

2. The verdict is a *pastoral assertion that means to give comfort to the exilic community*.[30] No doubt there was need for such an assurance, for the community in exile was surely filled with doubt, fear, and uncertainty. There was need for an assurance that the deportation did not nullify the identity of that community as the people of YHWH.

No doubt the vision-oracle functioned in this way as an enormous assurance. But such a pastoral concern also is not a sufficient explanation of the surprising verdict for two reasons. First, while the positive affirmation of vv. 5-7 does express such pastoral assurance, it is not obvious why or how the harshness of vv. 8-10 is necessary on that reading. It would be possible to make the affirmation about exiles (as in the salvation oracles of 2 Isaiah) without the derogatory, adversarial comment concerning the other communities. There is nothing polemical in such assurances. It is clear that our text is a very different kind of statement that means to do more than offer assurance. Second, a pastoral assurance has no credibility if it is simply said to reassure, in the sense of telling the exiles what they want to hear. In that case, the assurance is made up and is not to be taken seriously, unless it is established on other grounds. So the pastoral gain may be its effect, but it cannot be its source or its primary intention.

3. The verdict is a *political statement that is self-serving propaganda*. No doubt the claim of this text served the vested interests of this community in exile. If one asks who would make such a claim, it seems probable that no leader or member of the Jerusalem community or the Egyptian community of Jews would make such a judgment. Indeed it is difficult to imagine that the text comes from anywhere except from the Babylonian community or its strong allies and political advocates. This means the verdict is a self-serving claim that is partisan, polemical propaganda. In part, the Babylonian community was able to emerge in prominence (see point 1 above on historical reality) precisely because it was able to express its political and

cultural ambition in the language of religious legitimacy. Because the vision oracle does not hang in the air but belongs to historical concreteness, the verdict sounds like ideology that masks political goals in religious language. It is the Babylonian community of Jews that claims and asserts God's special commitment to the Babylonian community. This explanation merits serious consideration.

4. This historical, pastoral, political verdict, however, is here presented as a *theological verdict*. That is, its casting as a vision from God and an oracle with a messenger formula effectively claims that it is the very voice of God announcing a decision that YHWH has made, which is accepted not only as a truth about Judah but also as a truth about God. As the text now stands as a part of scripture, this is the enduring judgment the community has received.

This decision made about Judah and the future of Judaism is that the future belongs to the exilic community that refuses both *assimilation* into Babylonian definitions of reality and *despair* about the prospect of return. This verdict of YHWH thus is a ground for Jewish hope in a historical circumstance that would otherwise lead to despair or assimilation.

The disclosure about YHWH is of overriding importance. It is the assertion that YHWH has taken sides and that YHWH has taken the side of the exiles against the landed (a judgment sustained in the tradition of Nehemiah).[31] This decision by YHWH is of crucial importance for theology, both for Jews and Christians. The interpretive move I propose in what follows is that this choice of *exiled* over *landed* may be extended to a choice of the *marginal* over the *established*. In retrospect, it may be argued that members of the group exiled were not all that marginal, given their trades and status in society. But in that moment of displacement, they were indeed symbolically the marginal, subject to the punishment of exile and politically powerless in the face of the empire. Politically they were marginal for they had to start life over in a context that reduced them to weeping (Ps. 137:1).[32] This decisive moment of YHWH's verdict fixed irreversibly YHWH's commitment in this direction and declared YHWH to be the one who attends to the homeless.[33] The textual decision may be concrete but the theological claim is necessarily generalized.

This long-term verdict, of course, is not a contextless theological statement. It is at the same time and without apology a historical, pastoral, political act that no doubt has an ideological dimension to it. For all its theological importance, it cannot be doubted that it is self-serving on the part of the Babylonian community, or if not self-serving, it at least serves that community. The oddity is that this decisive *theological judgment* is made by and for and in the interest of a particular political opinion. One might conclude that such a theological decision is contaminated and suspect by such a political factor. But that is the character of biblical disclosure and that is the nature of biblical faith, not only mediated through but decisively shaped by political, historical, human factors. It comes no other way. Thus, of the four possible understandings we have identified, all are in some way correct and none can stand without the others.

The verdict on the basis of historical, pastoral, political grounds has immediacy and specificity. The verdict is about this community in this situation. But the undeniably theological factor transfers this immediacy and specificity into a paradigmatic statement concerning who YHWH characteristically is and where the power and faithfulness of YHWH characteristically turn up in the historical process. The *literary activity of the Deuteronomists*, in moving to the "second stage" of the tradition of Jeremiah, and the process of *canon-building* are ways in which immediacy and specificity are transferred into something paradigmatic.[34] That transformative factor gives this text a theological future for Jews and for Christians. It is a disclosure that God is partisan in the historical process in ways that have crucial political implications. The reason finally is concealed in the purposes of YHWH. That astonishing verdict, given without reason, opens this text to a theological future.

The methodological point here is an important one. We are facing the issue of holding together *critical and canonical* judgments. The critical judgment to which we assent (as do critical scholars generally) is that the verdict of Jeremiah 24:1-10 is the work of the Babylonian community in its own interest. That judgment seems beyond dispute, but we will press the implications of that critical insight further. In times past, that critical judgment would have precluded making a theological judgment because the fact that this is partisan, if not ideological, denies its theological legitimacy and because theology must be above such partisan claims. But the truth of the matter is that this piece of Babylonian literature, which is admittedly partisan and polemical, became and is canon and we take it as scripture. Therefore, the substantive judgment of the chapter is not dismissed as self-serving but is taken as a rule and norm for life and faith. The judgment made by this community is thus taken to be a faithful and correct judgment, rightly discerning not only its own historical vocation but also rightly confessing who God is and what God does. The move from critical to canonical thus is important. It does not deny the critical insight to nullify the canonical theological claim.

We have thus far tried to explicate the nature and problematic of the critical claim. Now we turn to see about the canonical spin-off. The critical investigation has tried to trace how this text arrived in this form. We have seen it is a *collage of formulae in the interest of a partisan historical judgment.* When we turn to the canonical question we are not studying the process of which this text is the end result. Rather we are concerned with how this text stands at the beginning of a textual-theological process that moved the textual community into a different future with a different perspective. The continuing community of the text takes the disclosure as faithful, true, and binding, articulated by the originary community in a moment of conflict and insight.[35]

VI

Out of this verdict of immediacy and specificity, which becomes paradigmatic, we ask how this text continues to speak in the ongoing theological tradition. At the outset, we may concede that the text is not used explicitly, so we do not have such an easy time identifying its function for the future. But we may suggest that this text, with this decisive verdict for Judaism and its decisive disclosure about YHWH, continues to stand at the center of the theological tradition. Its claim is that *YHWH acts in partisan ways, characteristically in solidarity with the marginal*, in ways that decisively shape and impinge upon the process of public history.

1. This partisan reshaping of the public process of history is characteristic of Israel's "rereading" of reality. Thus this text does not stand alone but is congenial to a characteristic Israelite propensity. Quintessentially this decision—which *chooses and rejects* (Ps. 78:67-68), which *creates and destroys* (Isa. 45:7), which *scatters and gathers* (Jer. 29:14), which *raises up and brings low* (Luke 1:52)—is experienced and articulated in the Exodus tradition in which YHWH sides with the slaves (peasants) against the empire (Exod. 11:7). The same freedom for solidarity is the key hope of Hannah (1 Sam. 2:1-10). In the tenth century B.C.E., a decisive turn was wrought in the history of this people by their choosing David and rejecting Saul (1 Sam. 16:1-3). These decisions, like the one in Jeremiah 24, are simultaneously

political, ideological, and theological. The theological claim is not nullified by conceding its partisan, political characteristic.

2. This sense of YHWH, so specifically articulated in our text, stands at the center of the gospel presentation in the story of Jesus. The formula tha best expresses and reflects the verdict of Jeremiah 24 is that "the first will be last and the last will be first" (Mark 10:31, Luke 13:30). This formula is a free-floating saying that is variously attached to teaching and actions. The saying may appear at different points in the tradition, but it contains the main claims of Jesus' ministry and the main claims of Israel's tradition. The saying asserts that the assignments of power, worth, and value made by worldly standards are false and will not endure. The tradition bears witness to the inversion wrought by God that happens concretely in the historical process. Thus Jeremiah 24 is for the Christian tradition an anticipation of the history of Jesus.

3. The central verb of Jeremiah 24:5 is *'akir*, "regard." We have seen that there may be some ambiguity in the term, whether it means *to see* what is there (i.e., good) or *to assert* with authority a new reality. Insofar as the latter is correct (the opinion we have taken following Reventlow), the verb reflects the free sovereignty of YHWH that goes under the name of grace. It occurs to me that this verse is a more powerful assertion of grace than is Genesis 15:6, because it is not only a positive regard (as in Gen. 15:6) but also a radical inversion of the excluded and devalued so that the exile is the one to whom the future is given.

Insofar as *'akir* is a free act of God, this free decision continues in the Pauline program of graciousness and in the Reformation teaching of "grace alone," rooted only in God's free sovereignty. It is important that the "regard" of Jeremiah 24:5 is utterly without explanation. It is this absence of explanation, because YHWH appeals to no norm outside his own resolve, which permits the historical inversion. Thus I suggest that the Pauline-Augustinian-Reformation trajectory of God's free sovereign act explicates in Christian modes and categories this shaping verdict of Judaism. What is discerned and affirmed here is that future Judaism is a community wrought only by the free sovereign assertion of YHWH. To the extent that Judaism revolves around the question of land,[36] it is free and given without qualification to a people that does not qualify.

4. The verdict of 24:5, however (unlike the "religion of grace" in the tradition of Augustine just mentioned), is not simply a matter of religious

justification. Unlike that tradition, it has *concrete, material implications*. The verdict concerns precisely who will have land and who will not. The promise to bring the exiles back is *to give land to those who have none*. The curse formula of vv. 8-10 asserts that those with land will be denied land. The two parts bespeak land redistribution.[37] The text therefore asserts *free sovereign graciousness in the arena of historical materiality*.

I can think of no theological assertion of grace in historical experience that is as dramatic and unmistakable as the formulation of Medellín, Colombia, in 1968, which acknowledged and celebrated the "preferential option for the poor."[38] This programmatic statement stands at the center of current efforts of liberation theology. There is no doubt that this formulation by the bishops is a deliberate pastoral, political statement. It is *pastoral* in the sense that it means to give meaning and assurance to the marginal. It is *political* in the sense that it is a quite partisan and polemical statement. It remains to be seen if it is a *historical* statement in the sense that the poor do in fact again reenter the historical process. But there is no doubt that it is a *theological* statement. The bishops take the formulation as an affirmation about the resolve God works in the historical process. The pronouncement of Medellín has been perceived as dangerously radical in a destabilizing sense. And so it is. But it is no more so than the vision of Jeremiah in its own context. That is why it is a "rereading" against the first reading of the historical process, which is so obvious and conventional, and which assumed that the ones in the land were the blessed. The first reading in Latin America would be to affirm that there is preferential option for the rich, but this "second reading" contradicts and intends to refute the first reading.

Theological exegesis is a rereading that has paradigmatic power in the future of the text. The danger of the text is characteristically reduced in two ways. The first is to hold the text to its originary historical situation so that is has no authoritative future. This temptation is served by some forms of historical-critical study. The second way is to *spiritualize* the text into a religion of grace so that God may reach a new verdict—a religious verdict, even though the text is vigorously material concerning *land, land displacement*, and *land repossession*. As the text has paradigmatic power, it concerns a decision YHWH has reached about land. In its original statement and in its contemporary claim, the ones without land are in YHWH's "regard" for good, for land, for covenant. The bad figs who may now have land cannot, so Jeremiah 24:1-10 asserts, withstand this verdict of God.

CHAPTER NINE

A Shattered Transcendence

Exile and Restoration

The Exile—as event, experience, memory, and paradigm—looms large over the literature and faith of the Old Testament. Together with the restoration, the Exile emerged as the decisive shaping reference point for the self-understanding of Judaism.[1] Moreover the power of exile and restoration as an imaginative construct exercised enormous impact on subsequent Christian understandings of faith and life as they were recast in terms of crucifixion and resurrection.

I

We may take as foundational for our theological reflection three propositions that are beyond dispute:

1. The Exile was indeed *a real historical experience* that can be located and understood in terms of public history.[2] It is clear that a considerable number of persons were deported by the Babylonians, though different accounts yield different results. In any case, much of the leadership of the community was deported. It is conventional to conclude that the sociopolitical situation of the exiles was not terribly difficult, though Daniel Smith has made a strong case for the notion that, in fact, the deported Jews in exile faced enormous hardship.[3]

2. While the actual number of persons exiled must have been relatively modest, the Exile as a theological datum became a governing paradigm for all successive Jewish faith.[4] That is, the experience, articulation, and memory of the Exile came to exercise influence upon the faith, imagination, and self-perception of Judaism quite disproportionate to its factual actuality. As a result, the Exile became definitional for all Jews, many of

whom were never deported. Part of the reason that a modest historical fact became a dominant paradigm for self-understanding can, no doubt, be understood in terms of the exercise of social imagination and social power by the Jews who were in exile, who insisted upon and imposed their experience on Judaism as normative for all Jewishness. The community of the deported established ideological, interpretive hegemony in Judaism, insisting that its experience counted the most. Such a sociopolitical explanation, however, does not fully account for this interpretive turn in Judaism.

In addition to the interpretive authority of the exilic community in the political process, the intrinsic power and significance of the Exile must be acknowledged. Since the Mosaic articulation of covenantal faith, built as it is around stipulation and blessing and curse—an articulation appropriated in the prophetic tradition—Israel has been subject to the moral seriousness of its own covenantal-ethical enterprise. Thus, power politics notwithstanding, the Exile required construal in Israel in terms of those covenantal categories. As a result, the Exile is an event not only of historical displacement but also of profound moral, theological fracture.

That moral, theological fracture generated two primary responses. On the one hand, the paradigm of exile/restoration is concerned with the *moral failure* of Israel, so that exile is punishment and judgment from God. This is a dominant stream of "exile [*golah*] theology," voiced especially in the tradition of Deuteronomy. On the other hand, however, it is clear that the crisis of exile cannot be contained in the categories of covenantal sanctions. Thus there was also the posing of urgent questions concerning the *fidelity of God* that are more profound than a simple moral calculus of blessing and curse. These questions are voiced, for example, in the prophets, in the priestly tradition, and perhaps in Job. The immediate questions of *moral symmetry* and the more subtle question of theological fidelity, therefore, created a large arena for Israel's venturesome theological reflection.[5]

3. The experience and paradigmatic power of the Exile evoked in Israel a surge of theological reflection and a *remarkable production of fresh theological literature*.[6] The Exile decisively shattered the old, settled categories of Israel's faith. It did not, however, lead either to abandonment or despair.[7] Israel was driven to reflect on the moral, theological significance of exile. The characteristic tension between acknowledgment of shattering on the one hand and the refusal of despair and abandonment on the other hand, required, permitted, and authorized in Israel daring theological energy that began to probe faith in wholly new categories that are daring and

venturesome. Indeed it is not an overstatement to say that exile became the matrix in which the canonical shape of Old Testament faith is formed and evoked.[8] In that context, the old traditions are radically revamped and recharacterized,[9] and the theological process strikes out in quite fresh and inventive ways.

These three factors, historical experience, paradigmatic power, and inventive literary imagination, are crucial for recognizing the context of the Exile as decisive for shaping Old Testament faith. These three factors, however, in and of themselves, do not constitute a theological probe. They are the context for such a probe. Our intention here is to push beyond historical-literary issues to theology proper.

II

The literary-historical-cultural aspects of the Exile have posed the general overarching question of *continuity and discontinuity*. This rubric permits us to consider a number of subpoints in relation to the general problematic. The dominant Wellhausen paradigm for Old Testament history and interpretation revolves around this question of continuity and discontinuity.[10] Julius Wellhausen's powerful model insisted upon a significant discontinuity between the earlier faith of Israel and the later development of Judaism. It is not clear to what extent Wellhausen's model was designed to critique and even depreciate later Judaism, which he found inferior to earlier prophetic faith, nor is it clear to what extent that depreciation was either motivated by or served (unwittingly) a kind of anti-Semitism. In any case, very much critical Christian scholarship has regarded the emergent faith of the Jewish postexilic community as inferior, so that a clear line has been drawn from the earlier prophetic faith to the New Testament.[11]

Distinct from Wellhausen's powerful paradigm, none has thought more carefully and perceptively about the continuity and discontinuity than has Peter Ackroyd. In a series of four articles, Ackroyd has carefully and judiciously reflected on the crises of history and culture and the powerful drive for continuity in the midst of the cultural, historical break.[12] Ackroyd has considered the ways in which cult objects (temple, vessels), theological constructs, and reutilization of textual formulations have served the concern for continuity.[13] It does not surprise us that in the end Ackroyd concludes that continuity is the overriding reality for Judaism: "The restoration and the destruction are all of a piece, discontinuity is resolved in the discovery of a continuity within it."[14]

There are two very different reasons why Ackroyd comes down on the side of continuity. First, there was in and through the Exile a surviving continuity of vibrant Judaism as a community. As a historical fact, the Jews did indeed have continuity, and they claimed that continuity for themselves. Second, Ackroyd poses questions of social history; he is concerned with the community over time and through time. Moreover Ackroyd is interested in institutional sociology and therefore is attentive to the gestures, textual and otherwise, that sustain continuity. A historical critic could hardly entertain the notion of deep discontinuity, so that there is an inevitable bias toward continuity in our common work of criticism.

I do not at all suggest that Ackroyd has misconstrued the data, for his historical methods serve well to understand the community that lives in and through an ongoing tradition. I suggest, however, that Ackroyd's analysis has not, in fact, penetrated beyond cultural, institutional, community-generated continuities to the more difficult theological question, namely, what happened to God in the process of the Exile? Or to put the question more critically, what does the text say happened to God?

In putting the question in this way, a methodological acknowledgment is required. To do biblical theology, I suggest, requires us to leave off the kind of critical observation that stands outside the text and to enter into the dynamic that operates inside the text and its claims. In other words, biblical theology, unlike historical criticism, requires us to approach the text more "realistically," as though this were indeed a word about God and about God's life, very often a word from God about God's life.[15] Such an approach may appear critically to be naive, but it is the only way we have to penetrate the difficulty of God's own life in the Exile.[16]

When we ask a theological question of the text, as distinct from a literary, historical, or sociological question, the issue of continuity and discontinuity takes on a different configuration. Whereas concerning literary, historical, and sociological questions one can point to evident continuities that override discontinuities (as Ackroyd has done so well), a theological focus on the rendering of God's own person as a character in Israel's large drama of faith is not so ambiguously on the side of continuity. The text attests that the Exile constituted a significant crisis in God's own life. As a character rendered in Israel's "covenantal discourse," as a character central to the plot of Israel's self-preservation, God is deeply impinged upon by the crisis of the Exile.[17] The theme of continuity asks whether the character of YHWH continues to be the same character in, through, and beyond the Exile. The theme of discontinuity asks whether (and to what extent) the character of God is decisively changed by the crisis of exile, for example, if God ceases to be in some crucial way who this God was heretofore.

The evidence is not clear and consistent. The articulation of the text, nonetheless, makes clear that the displacement and suffering of exile breaks something of God's own self, both permitting and requiring YHWH to be presented in a different way. It is clear that such a substantive theological argument depends upon (a) the texts being taken as "realistic" speech about God and (b) the metaphor of personhood as the governing image, so that a rendering of the person of God in this drama is what is available to Israel (and derivatively, available to us). Clearly, there are in the Exile literary continuities through reused speech formulae, historical continuities through genealogy, and sociological continuities through cultic acts and gestures. These continuities, however, all appear to be organized to cope with the peculiar reality of discontinuity with which God struggles.

In putting the theological question in this way, I note two implications that more directly relate to J. Christiaan Beker's own work and writing. First, the continuity/discontinuity of Israel's God in exile is a theological counterpart to the christological problematic in the New Testament concerning the relation of the "Jesus of history" to "the risen Christ."[18] The New Testament Church struggles to assert continuity in the person of Jesus through the events of Good Friday and Easter, but also must assert that in those events there is a decisive, transformative discontinuity in the person of Jesus. So it is as well concerning the God of Israel in the Exile.

Second, Beker's own poignant and remarkable discussion of suffering and hope is a reflection on the power of hope in the midst of suffering.[19] Beker's mode of expression asserts that hope confronts and overrides suffering. An alternative model might be that hope arises precisely in and through suffering. In either case, the life of the God of Israel in the midst of exile, a life of suffering in solidarity, and of powerful resolve against displacement, is a life that struggles for continuity in the brokenness. I mention this connection to Beker's work in order to suggest that the question I pose is an intensely practical issue, for Israel sees through this crisis of God how real suffering is, how seriously suffering is taken, and how suffering impinges even upon the life of God, both to shatter something old in God's own life, and to evoke something utterly new in God's life.[20]

I have selected three texts from different exilic sources that explore different dimensions of the way in which God is voiced.[21] To be sure, one can understand the different voices in these texts critically, in such a way to explain their different theological claims by referring to the literary historical sources. But if one is theologically "realistic," the diverse voicings evidence the struggle in God's life over the way God will be God in the face of such a crisis.

III

The critical problems concerning the history and unity of the first text, Deuteronomy 4:23-31, are considerable.[22] They are made more complex by the dominant judgment of two redactions by the Deuteronomic tradition.[23] Specifically, vv. 29-31 are widely judged to be a secondary redaction.[24] Thus the text may be composite. In any case, the entire passage as it stands reflects a concern about the Exile. Verse 26 speaks of "utterly perishing from the land," and v. 27 of "scattering." The phrase *from there* (v. 29) no doubt refers to exile, so that the text as we have it advances from a warning about exile (vv. 29-31) to a situation in exile and an anticipation after exile. And if vv. 29-31 are indeed an intrusion, as critical study has concluded, then they are an intrusion reflective of God's new exilic situation.

In this sustained and extended speech, Moses traces a remarkable move in the character of YHWH. Put concisely, Moses voices YHWH *before* exile and *after* exile around the geographical/temporal reference to "from there" (v. 29). Prior to "from there," Israel is not yet "there," not yet in exile, nor is YHWH yet addressed "from there." Prior to exile, Mosaic Israel is defined by the demands, sanctions, and warnings of Sinai. The burden of the speech of Moses is that attentiveness to the Torah is the condition for remaining in the land (vv. 25-26). The theological dimension of this preexilic warning is that YHWH is "a devouring fire, a jealous God" (v. 24), a God who will brook no rival and tolerate no disobedience. The entire warning and urgency of Moses grows out of the character of YHWH, a God who is uncompromising about demand. Thus the ominous warning of Moses is appropriate to preexilic Israel and grows from the jealousy of YHWH.

Were the character of YHWH sustained into exile in continuity, we would expect Israel, in exile and beyond exile, to continue to deal with a jealous, uncompromising God. The God who is available "from there," however, is not the devouring God from preexile. In the middle of the text, in the middle of Israel's experience, and, we may believe, in the middle of God's life with Israel, there is a new "there"—exile. When Moses continues his testimony about the God with whom Israel has to deal, everything is changed. Of course one may say that this change reflects layers in the redactional process and therefore different theological perspectives. Or the change may only reflect the pastoral emergency of the Exile when the producers of the theological literature said something different to meet new needs. If, however, we are to do theology, what emerges in the text is a real break in God's way with Israel, such as a real break in God's way of being God. Now there is no more talk of devouring fire and jealous God. Now Moses speaks of a "merciful God" (v. 31). The *'el qanna'* (v. 24) has become the *'el raḥum* (v. 31); the one who scattered in anger is the one who will not forget covenant.

There is, of course, continuity in this God to whom Moses bears witness. If one follows the rhetorical pattern of the text, however, there is also a discernible discontinuity in the move from *'el qanna'* to *'el raḥum*. This God who keeps the same name has ceased to be, so far as the text is concerned, a jealous, devouring God and has now become a God of compassion. Of course one may conclude simply that the God of Israel has all along been *'el qanna'* and *'el raḥum*. That however is not the way the text works. I submit, rather, that in this one text, the voice of Moses expresses a profound break in the character of God, and that break makes visible the emergence of a God of compassion whom YHWH has not been before in this text, an emergence evoked by the Exile.

Thus we may provisionally suggest that as hope arises in the midst of suffering, hope that did not heretofore exist, so the mercy of God is evoked, formed, and articulated just here. The formal reality of discontinuity permits a substantive assertion of compassion. And if one follows Phyllis Trible's notion of compassion as "womb-like mother love,"[25] then the Exile becomes the place where the character of God turns in a quite fresh direction.

IV

Perhaps the most remarkable text for our theme is Isaiah 54:7-10. Having just utilized the metaphor of a wife (Israel) deserted by her husband (YHWH; vv. 4-6), the poem asserts the restoration of the relationship when the husband takes a fresh initiative to restore the relation. Within this metaphor, the husband makes two quite distinct assertions, each reiterated in a parallelism. First, "I forsook you" (*'azabtîk*), "I hid my face" (*histartî*).[26] Second, "I will gather you" (*'aqabbeṣēk*), "I will have compassion" (*riḥamtîk*).[27] The contrast of the husband's two moves are abandon/gather and hide/have compassion.

Three interpretive questions may be posed about these assertions: (1) Was the abandonment a real abandonment? (2) Was the absence a real absence? (3) Did God in truth abandon covenant partner Israel? The wording of the poem is candid and unambiguous. The abandonment is real and complete, without qualification.

Such an assertion is difficult when there is a felt need to claim that God's resolve is unbreakable, for example, when continuity is stressed in every circumstance.[28] Thus John Calvin seeks to find a way around the clear statement of the text in the interest of continuity:

> When he says that he *forsook* his people, it is a sort of admission of the fact. . . . What the prophet says in this passage must therefore refer to our feelings and to outward appearance, because we seem to be rejected by God when we do not perceive his presence and protection. And it is necessary that we should thus feel God's wrath, even as a wife divorced by her husband deplores her condition, that we may know that we are justly chastised. But we must also perceive his mercy; and because it is infinite and eternal, we shall find that all afflictions in comparison are light and momentary.[29]

Such a reading, however, clearly goes against the wording of the text itself. Serious theology is placed in jeopardy when texts are, in this way, explained away. Calvin's comment is an example of the way in which a concern for theological continuity (transcendence) wants to outflank and override the text.

In the face of postwar tragedy in Europe, Kornelis Miskotte voices a much more sober reading of the text, directed against an interpretive posture like that of Calvin:

> The very first thing that is said here makes it clear that this situation actually cannot be understood on the two-dimensional level of experience and its interpretation [so Calvin]. It is a real abandonment. And those who did not recognize and understand it as an actual abandonment by God are now compelled to hear it proclaimed as God's own

word. It was an actual abandonment by God. Without this proclamation of the (partially recognized and partially unrecognized) abandonment by God, the prophetic word is not in the full sense the word of
God. He scattered the people, he hid his face from them. The fact is
that we have actually lived under the condition of this act; but it is only
the Word that reveals to us that it is an act of God.[30]

Miskotte's reading poses much more difficult theological questions than
does the reading of Calvin, but it surely is more faithful to the text. The
poem asserts a profound discontinuity without qualifications, as Israel's
condition vis-à-vis God. All transcendental guarantees about God are
shattered; God's goodness in Israel is decisively broken. It is instructive
that it is Miskotte's European experience of discontinuity that both permitted and required a radical rereading of the text.

The break in abandonment and anger is "for a brief moment" (rega'; vv.
7-8) We may ask, as Israel must have asked, How long is rega'? The word
suggests that while the abandonment by God was total and without qualification, it was only for an instant. Or we may reverse the proposition; the
abandonment was only for an instant, but long enough for it to be massive,
total, and decisive. The other uses of rega' do not illuminate us very much
because they are not the same appeal to brevity, but to decisiveness.[31] That
is, "a moment" is long enough for a total inversion or transformation. I
suggest that in this word, as it is used here, we are at the crux of the issue of
discontinuity and continuity for Israel in exile. The time span of the break
interests us because we wonder if it was so brief that the carryover of God's
commitment still prevails.

In considering "for a moment," perhaps an analogy will aid us. The
moment of God's abandonment is like the effect the breaking of an electri-
cal circuit has on a digital clock. The breaking of the circuit may be only
for an instant. To my unscientific observation, it appears that sometimes
the circuit breaks briefly when the power goes off, but not so long as to
disrupt the time reporting of the clock. The clock continues to function
through the brief break in power. At other times, or with other clocks,
the seemingly same disruption of current does break the functioning of
the clock, and it must be reset. In both cases the break is "for a moment,"
but in one case continuity persists, and in the other it does not. Thus the
"instant" of circuit breaking is a delicate one, and one does not know when
a clock (or one clock rather than another) will be disconnected and cease
to function accurately.

In like manner, this poem, I suggest, intends us to focus our theological attention on the instant of the breaking of God's loyal love. We are left by the poem to ponder whether the "breaking of the circuit" of God's faithfulness precludes the continued function of the covenantal commitment of God. It is for Israel a close call; whether or not the current leaps the break for YHWH determines continuity or discontinuity for Israel. This poem deliberately lodges the entire issue of continuity or discontinuity on the freight of one word, a word so delicate we cannot decide precisely. Thus the hard verb *abandon* is set next to the adverb *for a moment*, and there the matter rests. The verb in the end is more decisive than the adverb. The husband did indeed abandon the wife in wrath; but it was only for an instant, "a twinkling of an eye."[32] It was enough of a circuit break to cut the connection, briefly, but decisively.

This double statement of the acknowledgement of real abandonment by God is followed with a counter theme introduced by an adversative conjunction:

> . . . but with great compassion I will gather you. . . .
> . . . but with everlasting love I will have compassion on you,
>   says the LORD, your Redeemer. (vv. 7-8)

Miskotte comments on the "reverse" of the rejection:

> This at the same time reveals that this word is a saving word—by reason of the fact that the event [for example, the Exile] is now past and is no longer the ultimate truth about our condition. . . . Therefore the church must be all the more aware of the reverse side of this truth, namely, that grace, which is the annulment of judgment, confirms and corroborates the judgment as God's judgment. In the multidimensional realm of his freedom, God does not arbitrarily pass from one to the other, from yes to no, from rejection to acceptance. He resists the resistance. He breaks the rebellion by breaking his own heart.[33]

Abandonment, *wrath*, and *hiddenness* are countered by *steadfast love*, *compassion*, and *redeemer*.

Because of the adverb *'ōlām*, we may inquire about the relation of the negative and affirmative triads. When *'ōlām* is rendered "everlasting," we might conclude that God's *ḥesed* was at all times operative, for example, before, during, and after the abandonment. On that reading, the abandonment by the husband does not cut deeply, and an underlying continuity is affirmed in spite of the hiddenness of God's face (so Calvin). An alternative reading, however, does not regard the qualifying *ʿōlām* as mercy before and during but only after the abandonment. The relation of rejection and embrace is, therefore, not an ongoing parallelism whereby *ḥesed* denies ultimate serious-ness to abandonment, but the two are sequential. *Ḥesed* arises out of, after, and in response to the rejections, so that *ḥesed* stands on the other side of the discontinuity and not in powerful opposition to the discontinuity. Thus the "everlastingness" of *ʿōlām* is into the future but not through the past of Israel's exile.

We may answer our three interpretive questions: (1) The abandon-ment is real and not only "seems" so. (2) The abandonment is *for an instant* but long enough to matter decisively. (3) The promised *ḥesed* is *after and in response to* the abandonment and not in its midst as an antidote. The upshot of this reading is that there is discontinuity in God's own resolve for Israel, a discontinuity that evokes, permits, and requires a new response by the compassionate God who is redeemer.

This reading of discontinuity is sustained by the following lines in vv. 9-10. "This [the Exile] is like the days of Noah" (RSV).[34] God swears "from wrath" (*miqṣop*) and from "rebuking" (*migʿār*), as YHWH "swore that waters would not again pass over the earth" (cf. Gen. 8:21-22; 9:11). In the analogue of the Flood, it is clear that the promise in Genesis is a promise that it will not happen "again"; it is a promise *after* the Flood that pre-cludes its replication.[35] There was a real flood, a real release of chaos, a real abandonment of the earth that left creation bereft of God's protective care. Thus, in the flood story, the promise and assurance do not persist through the Flood but come in sequence after the discontinuity of the Flood.[36] The analogue supports our reading vv. 7-8 as a statement of deep discontinuity, with the same "again" implied; that is, the exile of abandonment will not happen again, as it manifestly has happened this time.

The sequencing of abandonment and compassion in v. 10 is not a denial of recently experienced discontinuity but an assurance against future dis-continuity. Mountains and hills are juxtaposed to God's *ḥesed* and *berît šālôm*.[37] Now in light of the promise, God's compassionate resolve is more reliable than the ordering of creation. That assurance is given and received post-Flood, post-Exile, post-abandonment. Out of the massive disconti-nuity of chaos (flood, exile), God arrives at a new overriding resolve for fidelity and compassion that wells up out of the discontinuity. The husband who has abandoned now embraces. The God who has been wrathful acts in compassion. The relation that has been breached is now solidified. Out of discontinuity comes a profound decree of continuity, after the discontinuity. The text exhibits no interest in and makes no comments on how it is that the newness arises out of, from, and in the midst of the break. The movement of this sequence is not unlike the sequence we have found in Deuteronomy 4:23-31; in Isaiah 54:7-10, it is from wrath to compassion; in Deuteronomy 4:23-31, it is from jealousy to compassion. The situation of exile features a profound recharacterization of God.

V

The cosmic reference of Isaiah 54:10 that contrasts "mountains and hills" with "steadfast love and covenant of peace" leads us to our third text, Jeremiah 31:35-37. These verses immediately follow the new covenant passage (vv. 31-34). The announcement of "new covenant" appears to accent the discontinuity between the new covenant and the old covenant that it is not like (v. 32). Indeed the dominant tendency of the Jeremiah tradition is to accent the discontinuity of exile. Oddly, vv. 35-37, immediately following, are a stunning statement of continuity. These verses counter the main tendency of Jeremiah and make a high claim of continuity. Whereas Isaiah 54:10 acknowledges that the structures of creation may indeed "depart" (*môs*) and "be removed" (*môt*) in this text it is assumed that the "fixed order" of creation will not "depart" (*môs*).[38] In Isaiah 54:10, God's *ḥesed* to Israel is more reliable than creation; in this text, God's guarantee of Israel "all the days" is as assured as the fixed order of creation, which is utterly assured. The argument on the same subject, to make the same claim, is stated very differently. Whereas Isaiah 54:10 moves beyond the experience of discontinuity to make its claim,[39] our verses appeal to the experience of continuity to make a similarly large claim.

This assertion of utter continuity is not one we expect in Jeremiah. It is as though the tradition cannot finally settle the matter of continuity and discontinuity. Each time it makes an assertion, it must follow with a counter assertion. As a result, even in the Jeremiah tradition, preoccupied as it is with discontinuity, there is added this counter voice that insists that God's guarantee of Israel is not and cannot be disrupted.[40] The ostensive protasis-apodosis structure of the passage, twice voiced, appears to be governed by a conditional "if"; the rhetoric, in fact, denies any conditionality (against the grain of Jeremiah), and assumes an unconditional relation between God and Israel. In this text, even the Exile allows no disruption in Israel's life with God because of God's steadfast love and fidelity. Unlike Isaiah 54:7-8, Israel's partner does not abandon and does not act in wrath.

VI

We may take these three texts, Deuteronomy 4:21-23, Isaiah 54:7-10, and Jeremiah 31:35-37, as representative of the theological reflection evoked by the Exile. These three disclosures together suggest that the issue of continuity and discontinuity was for Israel an urgent issue, one that admitted of no simple or settled solution. Four observations arise from this analysis:

1. While the historical, sociopolitical dimension of the Exile is hardly in doubt, the Exile cannot be treated simply as a historical problem concerning the continuity of the community. The Exile is a *deep problem for the character of YHWH*, as well as the community of Israel. Exile constitutes a profound theological problem and must be treated theologically as a crisis for God. The texts we have considered are all decrees in the mouth of God, for example, disclosures of a moment in God's own life that cannot be explained simply as a historical or sociological issue.

2. The theological crisis that these texts enunciate and with which they struggle is that the *transcendence of God is placed in deep jeopardy* by the Exile. From this it follows that even God's abiding commitment to Israel is at risk, impinged upon by the reality of the Exile. It is our common theological propensity, as indicated by Calvin, to exempt God from such jeopardy, to imagine that at bottom, Israel's God is not subject to the terms of the historical process. Such transcendentalism, of course, offers assurance but must necessarily refuse to take either the text or Israel's experience of exile with real seriousness. These texts entertain the thought that God is radically vulnerable to the realities of Israel's life.

In making this affirmation, Israel breaks with magisterial "common theology" that reduces God to a part of a fixed, predictable retribution system.[41] Such a "common theology" cannot countenance Exile as a crisis for God and cannot entertain the stunning affirmation concerning God's own life that emerges in the midst of such jeopardized transcendence.

3. The texts assert the jeopardy of transcendence but cannot finally adjudicate the extent or depth of that jeopardy. That is, the texts refuse to come down cleanly either for continuity or discontinuity. In each case, the text

tends to counter the tradition in which it is embedded. Deuteronomy 4, which ends in compassion "from there," counters the familiar "theology of command" featured in Deuteronomy. Isaiah 54 is embedded in the vibrant affirmation of exilic Israel but pauses over God's radical abandonment in the Exile (cf. 40:2). The affirmation of continuity in Jeremiah 31:35-37 lives in tension with the Jeremianic inclination to discontinuity. In this way, the texts keep the question of the jeopardy of God's life with Israel delicately open. Every tilted statement is promptly corrected by a counterstatement, thus permitting no statement to be a final one. Israel's way of doing theology, or more fundamentally, God's act of self-disclosure, bespeaks a profound and ambiguous lack of closure that resists every systematic closure.

4. The texts *move toward God's compassion*. This is true more directly of Deuteronomy 4 and Isaiah 54 than Jeremiah 31, but see Jeremiah 30:18, 31:20, 33:26. Indeed God's compassion seems to be the primary and powerful theological emergent of the Exile. The exile evokes new measures and fresh depths of compassion in the character of God. Taken pastorally, the articulation of God's compassion is a humanly needed assurance. Taken theologically, the Exile evokes in God a new resolve for fidelity, a resolve that was not operative prior to the hurt and dread of the Exile.[42] That resolve on God's part is, to be sure, seeded in old texts (cf. Exod. 34:6-7); the Exile, however, provides a rich array of texts voicing this newly central and newly appreciated theological datum. The Exile permits God to become toward Israel who God was not.[43] The fresh characterization of God seems to arise, inexplicably but freely in, through, and out of exile. The tone of God's speech toward Israel is dramatically transformed through this terrible jeopardy, a jeopardy that God shares with Israel.

VII

The Exile is the moment in the history of Israel and in the life of God when an irreversibly new theological datum is introduced in the horizon of faith. In conclusion, I suggest three dimensions of our interpretive work that are impinged upon by this theological reality emerging in exile:

1. The paradigm of "exile and restoration," which has as its theological counterpart God's abandonment and God's new compassion, provides crucial and decisive categories for understanding the crucifixion and resurrection of Jesus and the New Testament "*dialectic of reconciliation*."[44] While

Trinitarian theology has opened a variety of ways of getting from Friday to Sunday,[45] the typology of exile suggests two things:

a. The abandonment of God is real and decisive, albeit brief.

b. The God who is evidenced in Easter is decisively different from the God who abandons and is abandoned on Friday.

The theological reality of the Exile warns against any protective transcendentalism in the midst of the failure of God's life with Israel and Israel's life with God.[46] Thus New Testament theology might take more seriously this paradigm that comes to govern the imagination of Judaism, as a way of reflecting upon the abandonment of Jesus and the rule of the risen Christ.

2. The new theological datum of exile impinges upon the crisis of modernity and postmodernity in theology. There is in the Exile a decisive disclosure of God that should warn us against certain theological temptations. Three aspects of our crisis occur to me in this connection.

a. Much theological work has been a search for universals, an attempt to articulate "truth" that lies outside the concrete experience and testimony of the confessing community.[47] Against every such universal, the claims of the biblical God come down to particular moments of embrace and abandonment, to particular verses of texts, and to particular moments (*rega'*) of crisis. More than anywhere else in the Old Testament, in the Exile, Israel faces "the scandal of particularity" in all its pathos. Such an exilic voicing of God stands powerfully against any would-be universals.

b. Much of theology, particularly as voiced in conventional confessional traditions, has sought to voice God in transcendental categories that leave God freed from and untouched by the vagaries of historical discontinuity. The disclosure of God in these exilic texts refuses such a posture and allows no certitudes about God beyond the jeopardy of discontinuity.

c. The moral propensity of modernity is ragingly enacted in the brutality expressed in technological categories, most dramatically (but not exclusively) in the Holocaust. It may indeed be that the Exile is no adequate paradigm for the technological brutality quintessentially expressed in the Holocaust;[48] nonetheless we are the generation that has witnessed massive hurt generally through technological strategies that bespeak the power of death and the absence of God. The technological production of massive pain makes all our conventional theology open to questions and drives us to the more elemental categories of God's presence and absence and God's abandonment and reemergence.[49] In the exilic texts, human failure evokes

God's absence and abandonment; *mutatis mutandis,* our shameless linkage of brutality and technology may evoke a moral calculus that requires God's absence. It may, however, be that same shameless linkage of brutality and absence that evokes God's reemergence in a fresh posture. In, with, and under the brutality and pain, God emerges anew as the generator of human possibility.[50] The new theological data of exile has much to teach us about our current theological situation, much that we should already have learned but did not.

3. The importance of the new theological data of the Exile not only offers decisive material for the shaping of New Testament theology and crucial illumination of a substantive kind for our current theological task. Its major offer to us is the suggestion of new ways of doing theology in poetic, narrative forms that eschew conventional modes of discourse, that offer God as a speaker in the poetry, a character in the narrative plot, a God who moves in and through terrible disjunctions to newness. Thus the rhetoric of these texts shapes God's own life with Israel:

a. "from there" (Deut. 4:29),
b. "but . . . but," (Isa. 54:7-8), and
c. "if . . . then, if . . . then" (Jer. 31:35-37).

Such a way of theology is concrete, particular, and inherently subversive of every settlement, spilling over from daring rhetoric into public reality, where exiles must live and trust.

CHAPTER TEN

Haunting Book—
Haunted People

W e are, all of us, children of the biblical text. We have been conceived and birthed, generated and summoned, given life by this text and none other. This text keeps having its say among us, by translation and interpretation, by commentary and proclamation, by study and enactment. We must always again, always afresh in every circumstance, come to terms with it. We spend our lives struggling with this text, sometimes struggling for the text, sometimes struggling against the text. The text always has its say among us; it will not go away. Its voice is a haunting one, sounding promises, uttering commands, voicing stories, proclaiming oracles, ejaculating pain, authoring hope. The voice of the text haunts us because we know very well it is a human text filled with endless critical problems—and yet we hear in it the very voice of God: majestic sovereignty, awesome holiness, passionate grace, weakness made strong. Because of this text, which will not go away or finally keep silent, we live haunted lives, filled with yearnings for what is not in hand, promises not yet filled, commands not yet obeyed, desires not yet granted, neighbors not yet loved. The old text becomes new text; old story becomes new song. For all those reasons, in gratitude and awe and fresh resolve, we celebrate the publication of the NRSV, made freshly aware by it that we are indeed haunted children of this haunting text. And because the text will not go away or be silent, we are destined to be endlessly haunted, uneasy, restless, and on the way.

I. There Was a Time: The Emergence of a Text

There was a time before which we were not children of this biblical text. There was time when our Jewish fathers and mothers had no text. It seems most likely that our Jewish parents became children of this authorized, authorizing text only somewhere in the seventh or sixth centuries B.C.E., a happening linked to the reform of Deuteronomy, to the disaster of 587, and to the danger of exile. It is in times of reform, disaster, and exile (times not unlike our own), that this community first was seized by the text, and in such times is always again seized by the text, for such times are primal times for retextualization.

I have chosen for this occasion a very early textual moment, perhaps the earliest. Jeremiah 36 is indeed the only clear account in the Old Testament of how the text came to be. Earlier there were powerful oral traditions, and later there was canon. But in this text we are at the pivotal moment between oral tradition and settled canon. There is an awesome moment of redefinition. In this awesome moment of text-making, we have the intrusion of heavenly holiness into a region that would so much like to be immune to the haunting. This pivotal invasion happened in the career of the subversive Jeremiah. I shall trace the emergence of this dangerous text in six moments, perhaps the same six moves always enacted when we rehear the text and accept its haunting.

1. *The text is initiated by God;* it intends always to *evoke a drastic change* (Jer. 36:1–3). It is God who initiates the notion of a scroll, which Jeremiah perhaps would not have thought of or have risked. It is the speech of God and the passion of God and the purpose of God that are the driving forces of this event. It is as though Jeremiah is a passive receiver who can exercise no choice in the matter. The Lord says to Jeremiah:

> Take a scroll and write on it all the words that I have spoken to you against Israel and Judah and all the nations from the day I spoke to you, from the days of Josiah until today. (v. 2)

The scroll initiated by God constitutes a threat, for it is three times "against"—against Israel, against Judah, against the nations. The speech-scroll of God casts God's terrible rule against the orders of the day.

The purpose of that dangerous, holy scroll from heaven is to evoke in the listeners massive, drastic change:

> It may be that when the house of Judah hears of all the disasters that I intend to do to them, all of them may turn from their evil ways, so that I may forgive their iniquity and their sin. (v. 3)

"It may be . . ." Perhaps. The scroll is God's risk. It may be that the listeners will hear and turn from their deathliness. It may be that the conditions for God's forgiveness will be established. It may be that the scroll will set in motion the required gestures, permitting reconciliation and new life. It may be. The scroll is a chance God will take. And whenever heard, the scroll invites to such life-giving change.

2. *The scroll is wrought in and through human fidelity.* The fidelity and risk of Jeremiah is enormous in fashioning this scroll, and the fidelity and risk of Baruch is even greater. The biblical text, human in its articulation, is not an easy or obvious enterprise, but a dangerous political act, committed in utter obedience and at high risk. That is how this text is always formed. This community that holds the text in its hands, holds the outcome of a long history of risk-taking obedience:

> Then Jeremiah called Baruch son of Neriah, and Baruch wrote on a scroll at Jeremiah's dictation all the words of the Lord that he had spoken to him. And Jeremiah ordered Baruch, saying, "I am prevented from entering the house of the Lord; so you go yourself, and on a fast day in the hearing of the people in the Lord's house you shall read the words of the Lord from the scroll that you have written at my dictation." (vv. 4-6a)

Jeremiah is no coward. He knows, however, that his reading will get no hearing. Jeremiah knows that the scroll stands in deep otherness and deep over-againstness. The text is a danger and would evoke resistance. It requires careful human strategy in order to gain a hearing.

The passion for the scroll in this narrative is undiminished. That passion is as deep with Jeremiah as with God, as freighted on earth as in heaven. Everything rides now on the text. The scroll stands outside the human enterprise with the great "perhaps" of God now sounded again. Jeremiah says to Baruch:

> It may be that their plea will come before the Lord . . . for great is the anger and wrath that the Lord has pronounced against this people. (v. 7)

The scroll, which is threat, is in fact an act of grace. The scroll lives in the terrible anger and fury of God, and seeks a way of survival and well-being in the face of God's majesty. The scroll struggles with the definitional fact that this people is en route to death in the face of the reality of God. It is as though this scroll, now rooted in these two daring men of faith, is not a carrier of God's anger but a modest provision for escape. It authorizes and permits a return to God and an embrace of life. Around the text, human persons do offer the chance of life to each other.

3. *The scroll is a public question*, taking place in the public square. There is here no private religion, no pious oasis, no sectarian retreat. The public square is not naked. The rhetoric of faith will have its say and create its own listeners. Baruch, at the behest of Jeremiah, runs the risk, all the way to the temple. The temple is the place of public hearing; it is also, however, the royal chapel, the king's media center, the central shrine of civil religion, the engine of dominant ideology. The temple may be hospital of the safe prophets of *šalôm*, but this terrible scroll of ominous possibility pushes its way into the arena of settled, safe religion:

> Baruch the son Neriah did all that the prophet Jeremiah ordered him about reading from the scroll the words of the LORD in the LORD's house. . . . Then, in the hearing of all the people, Baruch read the words of Jeremiah from the scroll in the house of the LORD, in the chamber of Gemariah son of Shaphan the secretary. . . . (vv. 8, 10)

Right there in downtown political Jerusalem, we hear the scroll of "perhaps"; the scroll makes no accommodation to settled civic reality, no adjustment to dominant ideology. The scroll contains "all the words," the words of plucking up and tearing down, of destroying and overthrowing (cf. 1:10). Truth is indeed uttered in the face of power! And power must willy-nilly heed.

4. *The dangerous scroll receives a positive hearing* from some folk in high places. In all our accent on "over-againstness" and the inherent resistance to the summons of the scroll, this point should not be missed. After the first reading in the public square, Micaiah, the grandson of Shaphan, reports the reading to the cabinet of the government (vv. 11-14). Micaiah immediately recognizes that this scroll is not only dangerous but also warrants a hearing. He knows at first hearing that this scroll, which will become scripture, is as big a deal as the Pentagon Papers. This civil authority recognizes the validity and urgency of the scroll and is sympathetic to it. The cabinet of scribes and royal officers want to hear the scroll. There is a

second reading of the scroll (v. 15). Now the action has moved from temple to cabinet room. The text, with its dangerous say, moves toward the center of power and ideology where the haunting voice of God speaks its rule in the face of all other rulers:

> They said to him, "Sit down and read it to us." So Baruch read it to them. (v. 15)

Remarkably, or perhaps predictably, the text evokes a response. The "perhaps" of God is promptly answered:

> When they heard all the words, they turned to one another in alarm, and said to Baruch, "We certainly must report all these words to the king." (v. 16)

The response is of two kinds. First, they are afraid! The scroll attests on its own terms to its heavenly authority. Without being form critics or doing carbon-14 dating, the cabinet members know as they listen that this is true stuff and therefore dangerous stuff. The long history of this text, all the way up until this revision of the RSV, is that the biblical text has its say. The rulers of this age (including us) have not been able to nullify or restrain its dangerous voicing of another reality.

Their second response is, "We will surely tell the king." That response may be filled with such fear they want to hand the "hot potato" of the text over to somebody else, get it out of their presence and off their desks. More likely, the listeners in the cabinet room are sympathetic to the scroll. Some of them had long believed that current royal policy was suicidal, but they lacked leverage to resist the king. Now they have a voice other than their own over against dominant policy. These leaders know that Jerusalem must host a deep sovereignty in its otherness, a sovereignty that speaks their only chance for life. They have this dangerous scroll in their hands. Like any careful official, they receive secret documents from odd sources only gingerly; they investigate this one's provenance: "From where did you get this scroll?" (v. 17). Baruch answers: "He dictated all these words to me, and I wrote them with ink on the scroll" (v. 18).

The response is immediate and clear: "Go hide, you and Jeremiah" (v. 19). Go hide, because you are in big trouble. Go hide, because the scroll is so subversive and its authors are so vulnerable against the terrible ruthless power of an unprincipled state. Go hide and do not tell us where you hide. This is on a "need-to-know" basis. The scroll has located its faithful constituency even in a high place. The scroll is not in the end welcome, but in every dangerous context it is matched by a responsive remnant that acknowledges its terrible authority. So the scroll is at last on its way to meet the local Pharaoh, the one who tolerates no scroll, no voice other than his own.

5. *Royal power can indeed eliminate the text.* Whenever established power is threatened, it eliminates the text:

> As Jehudi read three or four columns, the king would cut them off with a penknife and throw them into the fire in the brazier, until the entire scroll was consumed in the fire that was in the brazier. (v. 23)

The king cannot tolerate the threat of the text. The king wants an unhaunted life and so must banish the haunting text. He can and he does. This is a very early example of shredding documents. The powerful of the world, and we with them, often prefer a textless existence. We may use somewhat less violent strategies to banish the text, like scholastic theology, or liberal ideology, or "higher criticism," or pious neoconservatism. There are endless ways to silence the text. In the end, all the ways aim at one outcome, a life untroubled and uninterrupted by this dangerous scroll.

The king was indeed not interrupted by the text:

> Yet neither the king, nor any of his servants who heard all these words was alarmed, nor did they tear their garments. Even when Elnathan and Delaiah and Gemariah urged the king not to burn the scroll, he would not listen. (vv. 24-25)

He was not alarmed. He did not tear his garments. He did not hear the urgent summons. He continued, as he had power to do, to manage his regime on its deathly path.

But of course such a continuation of an untroubled regime, personal or public, in the face of this text, evokes a terrible uneasiness. It requires endless vigilance, alertness to conspiracy, and defensiveness that culminates in isolation and violence. The last action of Jehoiakim in this text, not surprisingly, is this:

> The king commanded Jerahmeel the king's son and Seraiah son of
> Azriel and Shelemiah son of Abdeel to arrest the secretary Baruch and
> the prophet Jeremiah. (v. 26)

All the energy of the king was devoted to stopping and silencing the dangerous text. The intransigent status quo, public or personal, private or corpo-
rate, liberal or conservative, seeks finally to end this haunting scroll, because
a haunted life is too demanding, too restless, too costly. Dreams must be
killed, promises stifled, commands explained away. In the end, the scroll is
savaged, the authors made fugitives, and the king remains in charge.

6. *There is, however, an odd addendum* to this royal episode, an addendum
the king little anticipated but that is the key point of the entire narrative.
The authors are kept safely: "But the Lord hid them" (v. 26). And then
the text continues:

> Now, after the king had burned the scroll with the words that Baruch
> wrote at Jeremiah's dictation, the word of the Lord came to Jeremiah:
> Take another scroll and write on it all the former words that were in
> the first scroll which King Jehoiakim of Judah has burned. . . . Then
> Jeremiah took another scroll and gave it to the secretary Baruch son
> of Neriah, who wrote on it at Jeremiah's dictation all the words of the
> scroll that King Jehoiakim of Judah had burned in the fire, and many
> similar words were added to them. (vv. 27-28, 32)

The scroll is not defeated. The scroll will prevail. The scroll is not finished or closed. It contains new and added words in its power and resil-
ience. The scroll makes its continuing claim.

But there is also a counter theme that concerns the royal resister to the
scroll:

> Concerning King Jehoiakim of Judah you shall say: thus says the
> Lord, You have dared to burn this scroll. . . . Therefore . . . He shall
> have no one to sit upon the throne of David. . . . They would not listen.
> (vv. 29-31)

In the end, self-serving power evaporates before the truth of this uttered
disclosure of holiness, an utterance undiminished, unbanished, relentless,
resilient, fashioning another existence in the world, the only viable one.

II. Haunted by This Text: Life with the Holy One

We are, all of us, children of the text, awed and not self-congratulatory. These are not words said to comfort. I do not suggest that we are positioned as friends of the text against all others who are wrong. Rather I suggest that this text in its dangerous offer of life stands over against us all—liberal and conservative, dove and hawk, pro-choice and pro-life—with its radical invitation, its severe warning, and its uncommon possibility. We are not the pets of this text, but we are the community that accepts the burden of struggling with this text on behalf of all humanity, sometimes struggling on behalf of the text, sometimes against it.

So what did the scroll of Jeremiah voice that the king could not tolerate? Not just right policy, crucial as it is. Not just right morality, urgent as it is. Not just right doctrine, decisive as it is. In and around and behind right policy and right morality and right doctrine, the text fashions a life with the Holy One, a life of terrible freedom, a life of savage commitment and rigorous demand, a life of magisterial hope that refuses present despair. In this scroll, Jeremiah sketches out a character and a drama much too large for the king's timid royal horizon. Indeed that large drama that stands over against the king has a haunting, cunning dimension that is endlessly unnerving and destabilizing. This haunted God, carried by the haunting of the text, is like a beloved husband in the wilderness (Jer. 2:2); like a well of living water (2:13); like a weatherman who withholds showers (3:3); like a shepherd who scatters and gathers (23:1-4); like a leopard ready to spring (5:6); like a suffering, adoring mother (31:20); like a terrible seducer (20:7)—keeping the drama open, keeping the king off balance, keeping the future well beyond the reach of royal control.

If we move beyond Jeremiah's scroll to the larger biblical text, the same God who stalked the slave camp at night for freedom (Exod. 11:4-7) is the God who sent lying spirits to destroy King Ahab (1 Kgs. 22:19-23). The same God who raised Jesus from the dead (Acts 2:24) is the God who told Samuel to lie en route to Bethlehem (1 Sam. 16:2). The same God who birthed the baby to the old lady (Gen. 21:1-7) is the one who scandalized the virgin with a pregnancy (Matt. 1:18-25). The same God whose summons us to leave everything and follow (Mark 10:17-22) is the one who sent bread to the hungry (Exod. 16:15; Mark 6:30-44). Israel and the church have on their hands a haunting text, filled with dark shadows and an inscrutable presence, not predictable, not held in our ideology, not confined to our familiar worlds. This haunting text, which always surprises us at the edge of reality, is inhabited by the Holy One who makes a restless home in the text. The text is a haunted place like the old houses we used to fear to visit as a child. And like those old houses, we mostly go by quickly at a distance, not wanting to come into serious contact, because whenever we do, our prefab world is put at risk.

It matters that this haunted text is not reduced by any of our passions or ideologies to flat, predictable, manageable, usable proportion. Because this text is finally not reduced, we remain a haunted people, haunted with severe duty and ecstatic delight, haunted with heavy truth and free compassion, haunted with freedom and courage, energy and hope. This haunting text haunts us. As a result we are never so sure as to have a single settled story, even the one we like, because here are many stories told toward us. When haunted, we are not so trivial in our morality as to voice one tired, relentless proposal. Instead we confess utterances like "Go to a new land," "He is risen," "We are forgiven," "It is finished," "Comfort my people."

The text is characteristically somewhat remote, not obvious and available. It is more a night creature, never quite in our grasp or fully focused in our vision. We hear the haunting sounds of God's "otherness"; we find our principal delight in our uneasiness. If perchance you think this is a terrible overstatement, think where we would be without this text. We might then only be good liberal do-gooders or the self-assured guardians of order we cherish too much. Or we would be frightened and in control like Jehoiakim, contemptuously burning the scroll and sending out search parties, fearful, frozen, failed and dying.

But we have this text; better, the text has us, and we are being endlessly haunted beyond ourselves. So we pause in our weary ideologies when this text speaks. We remember that the world is more open and more at risk than we usually imagine. We are grateful that in our trembling, God has authorized a text, and a text, and another text, to which "more words were added."

In beginning his ministry, Jesus came to the synagogue, that is, the place of the text (Luke 4:16). He unrolled a scroll (v. 17). He read it (vv. 18-19) and commented on it (vv. 21, 24-27). He showed how dangerous and contemporary the text is. The scroll in its danger almost got him lynched (vv. 28-29). He took a scroll and jarred all settled reality. What else could he have taken? What indeed would you have taken in such a crisis, except a scroll?

III.

Carrying Forward
the Prophetic Task

Prophetic Ministry

A Sustainable Alternative Community

The formation of a religious *community*, the practice of a disciplined *spirituality*, and the embrace of *prophetic faith* are dimensions of Christian obedience that converge and cannot be separated from each other. While my theme concerns the formation of religious community, that is, an ecclesiological matter, I make my beginning with prophetic faith, for that is the most likely entry point in the conversation for my discipline of Old Testament study.

Prophetic faith is a voice for life in a world that is bent on death. Prophetic faith is a risky practice of sanity in a world trapped in madness. I stake out such a radical, one-sided posture because I imagine the call of the gospel today to be urgent, subversive, and therefore dangerous in the face of a society in pursuit of its own destruction. In my consideration of prophetic faith, I will focus on the person, tradition, and book of Jeremiah as an exemplar.[1]

I settle on Jeremiah in the recognition that Jeremiah faced and entered into a situation not unlike our own. In his situation, the requirements and possibilities of faith seemed to him clear and unambiguous. Yet his contemporaries in culture, state, and "church" resisted, ignored, and denied his witness and made their relentless way to death.[2] Jeremiah stands isolated in his historical, cultural context, a voice of sanity in a world of madness, discerning so much, summoned to care, driven to anguish.[3] I suggest that a faithful, witnessing community of faith is now situated in a like destiny, in the same way discerning, summoned, and driven.[4]

I

As a model and embodiment of prophetic faith, Jeremiah is rooted in *four realities* that shape and authorize his terrible and awesome ministry.

1. Jeremiah is rooted in and infused by Israel's normative covenantal faith, which is focused at Mount Sinai and linked to the memory, person, and office of Moses.[5] In Deuteronomy 18:15-18, Moses is remembered to have said that there would be a prophet "like me." It is plausible in the Old Testament to assume that Jeremiah is indeed the one "like Moses," who is to do for his generation what Moses did for his, to form and shape a whole new community of obedience as an alternative to the dominant community of disobedience, obdurateness, and oppression.[6]

Jeremiah is embedded in the old recital of God's saving deeds, which is centered in the acts of Moses. He knows that the continued recital, embrace, and practice of the old saving deeds is essential to effective faith, and indeed survival in the presence.[7] In chapter 2, Jeremiah traces the old destruction course of Israel's life in covenant. That long story is a move from devotion, trust, and loyalty to a broken relation of indifference and recalcitrance. The old memory is reiterated as a model of effective devotion:

> I remember the devotion (*ḥsd*) of your youth,
> > your love (*'hb*) as a bride,
> how you followed me in the wilderness,
> > in a land not sown. (2:2)

That treasured memory, however, is only a foil for Israel's present indifference. Israel no longer names the name or tells the story.[8] Israel is cut off from its shaping memory. The story of rootage, which gives perspective and proportion to Israel, has been neglected and jettisoned; Israel can no longer remember who it is. The reason for alienation is that,

> They did not say, "Where is the LORD
> > who brought us up from the land of Egypt,
> who led us in the wilderness,
> > in a land of deserts and pits,
> in a land of drought and deep darkness,

in a land that none passes through
where no one lives?" (2:6)

As the people have forgotten, so also the leaders have been neglectful:

The priests did not say, "Where is the Lord?"
Those who handle the law did not know me;
the rulers transgressed against me;
the prophets prophesied by Baal,
and went after things that do not profit. (2:8)

Notice two things about this rooted memory that Israel has abandoned. First, the shaping memory is not a set of certitudes, propositions, or truths, but it is a concrete narrative that lives behind and underneath packaged intellectual formulations. Second, the content of Israel's story concerns land, land that must be had for life, land that is an utter gift.[9] The people have forgotten the gift of the land and the priests have forgotten the Torah traditions about the care of the land. In the end, the priests "do not know me," that is, no longer live in close and intimate loyalty to YHWH.[10]

Thus Jeremiah has to practice his ministry and his faith in a community alienated from and cut off from its founding, authorizing memory. It is a main insistence of Jeremiah that Israel's whole life must be resignified and redescribed through that primal memory. When that memory is forfeited, the land is misperceived as an achievement, a possession, or an accident. Such a false perception of land encourages self-sufficiency and autonomy, and this predictably ends in destruction (cf. Deut. 8:17-26). Everything depends on the normative memory. Jeremiah articulates that memory in the face of self-serving, self-legitimating, and in the end self-destroying ideology. For the Jerusalem establishment, royal ideology has crowded out the memory of covenantal transformation. Faith has become a defensive holding action without vitality or power to transform. The question posed in the time of Jeremiah is whether the old memory of transformation still has power and compelling authority in a community that prefers a more convenient discernment of reality.

A second Mosaic aspect of Jeremiah's rootage is that Jeremiah functions as an intercessor to God on behalf of troubled, needful Israel. Before Jeremiah, Moses was a daring voice of prayer who pressed God and reminded God who to be.[11] Moses turned out on occasion to love Israel more than God loved Israel. There is nothing polite or bland about such an intercessory function in the manner of Moses, for the prayers of Moses are contentious assaults against God.

Jeremiah could function in the same role as did Moses, in the same abrasive voice. That possibility of prayer, however, is foreclosed by YHWH:

> As for you, do not pray for this people, do not raise a cry or prayer on their behalf, and do not intercede with me, for I will not hear you. (7:16)

In 15:1, intercessory prayer is even more directly linked to Moses, again with an interdict against intercession:

> Though Moses and Samuel stood before me, yet my heart would not turn toward this people. Send them out of my sight, and let them go!

The greatest intercessors in Israel, Moses and Samuel, are reduced to muteness; how much more is Jeremiah silenced![12]

Jeremiah's faith must be practiced in a theological situation of enormous danger, when engagement with YHWH is so strained as to be nullified. Jeremiah knows about and accepts his Mosaic function. In doing so, he is enormously frustrated because he is precluded by God from enacting the ministry he accepts as his own. The personal wound of such a magisterial foreclosure by God is a hint of the deep public crisis in Israel. The political-religious establishment has become so obdurate as to be rejected by God. Jeremiah's silencing by God reflects the larger antipathy God has toward Israel. The memory of Moses is a poignant tradition that makes Jeremiah's faith and ministry so costly and burdensome. The Mosaic traditioning process is decisive rootage for Jeremiah's disputatious faith.

2. A second, very different, rootage, expressed in very different categories, is the *mythic, metaphorical claim of authority*. A dominant image of God's rule is that there is in heaven a functioning government, organized like a cabinet meeting in which YHWH presides over an assemblage of angels, lesser gods, and heavenly functionaries.[13] This assemblage legislates and forms policies governing the world. It dispatches messengers to earth, often to reigning kings, to announce the decrees that will shape the world. Among the messengers who are dispatched are the prophets, human agents sent from the heavenly council to articulate policy on earth.

This image of a heavenly government serves several important functions. On the one hand, it asserts that real and important decisions about the shape of the earth are made beyond human reach and access. The "rulers of this age" are not autonomous agents but must reckon with another governance that is serious, and over which they have no control. On the other hand, the notion of "divine council" is a device whereby prophets claim legitimacy and authority beyond the reach of the established agent of society. Thus the prophet, in using this metaphor, insists that his message carries with it a transcendent authority that even established royal authority cannot nullify. That is what is meant when the prophet said, "Thus says the LORD."[14] The message to be announced is not "my" word, but the word of the government of God that dispatches "me." The power that shapes the world has not been put at the disposal of human arrangements and preferences.

This is indeed transcendent authorization whereby the prophet is emboldened to perceive and articulate reality well beyond the categories and perceptions of the ruling elite. This is an alternative authorization that subverts conventional authority. The metaphor of divine council is a political metaphor that concerns policy and power and is not simply a "soft" religious, psychological experience. It is the sovereign will of YHWH for the public process that is at issue in this foundational metaphor. Jeremiah claims to have been authorized by God in this way. That is the substance of 1:4-10.[15]

Jeremiah's prophetic assertions collide with other voices, other prophets, with different messages. These other voices make the same claim as Jeremiah: to have been sent by the divine council. It turns out, so the text asserts, that the opponents of Jeremiah are simply echoes of establishment ideology.[16] It is exceedingly difficult, however, to discredit the claim of legitimacy made by the opponents of Jeremiah, for they also claim to have been where authority is given beyond official scrutiny.

Jeremiah stands against them by arguing that the message of his opponents, which he regards as false, is a self-invented message, a piece of propaganda that is not from the council of the gods and is therefore not to be taken seriously:

> For who has stood in the council of the LORD
> > so as to see and to hear his word?
> > Who has given heed to his word so as to proclaim it?
> > . . . I did not send the prophets,
> > > yet they ran;
> > I did not speak to them,
> > > yet they prophesied.

But if they had stood in my council,
> then they would have proclaimed my words to my people,
> and they would have turned them from their evil way,
> and from the evil of their doings. (23:18, 21-22)

In this metaphor, the issue of authorization is pushed one step back behind Moses. The question of prophetic authority is posed in this way: Who brings a true word from the government of God, and who is inventing his own fanciful message without proper authorization?

The substantive conflict concerns the future of Judah and Jerusalem. Jeremiah wants to assert that there is a deep conflict between the government of God and the royal-temple establishment in Jerusalem. Because there is such deep conflict, the present sociopolitical, economic arrangement of Jerusalem is in deep jeopardy. Jeremiah's opponents stand much closer to organized, legitimated earthly power and believe that God's government is congruent with the present order. Thus the image of "divine council" is employed in the book of Jeremiah to explicate the abrasion between the Mosaic covenantal faith and present human forms of power and authority. Jeremiah, with his odd, unprovable claim of authority, speaks in Jerusalem as an unwelcome voice. The issue of faith and spirituality is how abrasively the intent of God stands vis-à-vis our conventional modes of faith and power. The issue, I imagine, turns on the question of whether there is standing ground for courage, nerve, and authority outside social convention and accepted legitimation. Jeremiah claims to be rooted elsewhere, in a source uncompromised by establishment authority, unaccommodated to the status quo.

3. These first two rootages, Mosaic tradition and divine council, are very different. Both, however, are remote from the actual situation of Jeremiah's own time. Mosaic memory is voiced in the face of self-serving social *amnesia*, for a society that remembers nothing is free to do anything. The scenario of divine council is offered as an alternative to social *autonomy*, for those who live completely outside divine authorization can do what they please and can count on ideologues to give legitimacy for what they do. The combined testimony of *narrative memory* (from the Mosaic tradition) and *divine authorization* (from the divine council), I submit, is measured by a third rootage. Jeremiah's faith is sanctioned by his participation in the *concrete pain, anguish, and pathos of his actual situation.* Jeremiah takes the hurt of injustice in his society to be a pathology that reaches clear to the heart of God. It is this notice and embrace of pain among

his contemporaries that legitimates the terrible words of the prophet. We should not miss the explosive power in the move of the prophet from social injustice to hurt in God's heart. This daring poetic move is an interpretive clue to Jeremiah's power, his passion, and his threat.[17]

Jeremiah's pain, matched by his bold, discerning speech, notices and voices what his contemporaries perceive about their situation. His contemporaries were committed to the self-deceptive slogan, "It doesn't get any better than this." Jeremiah, however, noticed more and saw the suffering rooted in cynical greed:

> For scoundrels are found among my people;
> > they take over the goods of others.
> Like fowlers they set a trap;
> > they catch human beings.
> Like a cage full of birds,
> > their houses are full of treachery;
> therefore they have become great and rich,
> > they have grown fat and sleek.
> They know no limits in deeds of wickedness;
> > they do not judge with justice
> the cause of the orphan, to make it prosper,
> > and they do not defend the rights of the needy. (5:26-28)

The prophet saw that the marginal are put at risk by the powerful. He saw that such social contradictions are not only socially dangerous but also unbearable for God. So he has God ask defiantly and indignantly:

> Shall I now punish them for these things?
> > says the LORD,
> and shall I not bring retribution
> on a nation such as this? (5:29)

God has seen what the prophet sees and will not let the affront go unanswered. Jeremiah pondered long the resolve of God to punish God's own people. He dared to suggest that the expansionism of the Babylonian Empire was in fact God's way of dealing with the injustice of Israel's social life. Jeremiah, however, does not ignore politics and geopolitics.

Like every good poet, Jeremiah incorporated great world events in a poignant, concrete, personal scenario. He does not speak about Babylonian imperial policy or about Judah's foreign policy, but about the coming of one soldier into his bedroom to terrorize him. He imagines how terrified he will be when the judgment of YHWH comes, embodied in a specific imperial soldier who disrupts his sleep:

> My anguish, my anguish! I writhe in pain!
> Oh, the walls of my heart!
> My heart is beating wildly;
> I cannot keep silent;
> for I hear the sound of the trumpet,
> the alarm of war.
> Disaster overtakes disaster,
> the whole land is laid waste.
> Suddenly my tents are destroyed,
> my curtain in a moment.
> How long must I see the standard,
> and hear the sound of the trumpet? (4:19-21)

In fact there have been no soldiers yet, no invasion. Jeremiah discerned "beforehand" the pain, grief, loss, and terror that injustice will bring. He speaks the coming pain well before it is enacted. On the lips of this daring poet, the destruction is voiced, even if not yet visible.

The suffering the community has provoked upon itself, however, is more than Jeremiah's personal agitation. The nightmare the poet envisions is given larger public scope in his rhetoric. The poet dares to imagine that death has struck all parts of society—by sword, famine, pestilence—and no one can resist. Death will come because Israel has abandoned its identity. Those who die are not nameless numbers. Each one is the child of some hurting mother.

In order to articulate the anguish Jerusalem has brought on itself, the poet gathers all the mothers who grieve and calls them all "Rachel," the "Ur-mother" in Israel, who will not be comforted:

> A voice is heard in Ramah,
> lamentation and bitter weeping.
> Rachel is weeping for her children;
> she refuses to be comforted for her children,
> because they are no more. (31:15)[18]

In the vision of this poet, Jerusalem becomes a city of deep, unmitigated grief. The city with its temple and palace cannot withstand the exhaustion of YHWH's steadfastness. When YHWH quits, the city dies.

In his eloquence and daring, Jeremiah wants his contemporaries to notice the pain they have chosen for themselves. The prophet escalates his subversive rhetoric one step more, so that the hurt reaches clear to God's own heart:

> My joy is gone, grief is upon me,
> my heart is sick. . . .
> For the hurt of my poor people I am hurt,
> I mourn, and dismay has taken hold of me. . . .
> O that my head were a spring of water,
> and my eyes a fountain of tears,
> so that I might weep day and night
> for the slain of my poor people!
> O that I had in the desert
> a traveler's lodging place,
> that I might leave my people
> and go away from them! . . .
> for they proceed from evil to evil,
> and they do not know me, says the Lord. (8:18—9:3)

The speaker in this poem is God. There is grief that impinges upon God's heart. God asks about a balm in Gilead, but the asking is only a basis for accusation. God wishes for larger tear ducts in order to cry more and wishes for a place in order to escape. This is not a cry of rage but of deep grief at having committed and risked such love. And now God is utterly disregarded and forgotten: "They forgot me."

Notice how the poet has changed the subject by his inventive rhetoric. The grief the poet has experienced about the present hurt and the coming death of Israel is transformed from the life of the poet to the life of God. It is now God's own self that is consumed in grief, yearning for a balm, knowing there is none, and breaking into inconsolable tears. The poet is not an exhibitionist, nor is he manipulating his audience. He does not ask his audience to do anything, nor does he scold for what has happened. In this pain, there is no anger or reprimand, but only terrible, bottomless grief. The poet only wants his listeners to see and know what in fact is happening, and perhaps to understand. That is all.

It is the poet's discerning grief, however, that finally counts. It is that acute grief that causes him to notice so much. The grief overrides even the memory in its radicalness. The poet's horizon is utterly present tense, present to the grief of reality, to the hurt of God, and to the dulled life of his listeners, who miss nearly everything. Dorothee Soelle has seen that sound feminist theology begins in pain.[19] The same large dose of anguish is crucial for every prophetic theology, which requires poetry as the only adequate mode of articulation. The rootage in current rawness requires raw language not reasoned discourse. The language of the poet expresses a cosmic ache that causes the very person of God to tremble in the pain.[20]

4. The grief and cry of God will carry us as far as our ears can tolerate. The grief in which the prophet is rooted is, however, not limitless. The grief is finally curbed by another reality that does not yield to the tears. The prophet is rooted in a *powerful vision of an alternative future.*[21] Precisely in the midst of the grief, the poet can become lyrical about a common social possibility that is rooted in the heart and resolve of God. We may first characterize that vision and then consider its rationality. In chapters 29–33, that vision of an alternative future is multifaceted. I will mention four aspects of that alternative vision:

a. There will be *restored land* (29:14). The very people who were sent away homeless into exile will reclaim and reenter their patrimony. The land is guaranteed in the face of present circumstance. The land is an inalienable right and gift, rooted in God's very promise that is not yet voided.

b. The *city will be rebuilt* (30:18-21). This is an astonishing poetic certitude, uttered while the city is still smoldering ashes. Moreover there was no social organization or political muscle to initiate any rebuilding. God's promise, however, is not rooted in discernible progress but in the dogged fidelity of YHWH who wills, dreams, and intends a restored city, an adequate place for presence, an assured centering for a destabilized people without home or focus. This will indeed become a Jerusalem rejoicing. There will no more be heard in it grief, tears, or hurt.

c. Best known to us, in a very different idiom, is the promise of *new covenant*, a relation no longer rooted in violated commandments, but a relation that begins afresh, a change of heart, a renovated will, a quickened resolve for following, a glad embrace of what is required, a convergence of desire and obligation (31:31-34).[22] In the new covenant, restored Israel desires to do exactly what it must do. The promise of new covenant is against all data, bespeaking both reorganized institutions and reordered communion. At last Israel becomes the yearned-for Israel of God.

d. The possibility articulated by the poet is social, concrete, visible, and public. The vision is nonetheless a theological vision, offered and assured only by God's resolve. The poet speaks a hope that lives only in the speech of God and in God's generous intention. It is for that reason that the newness is rooted in *an affirmation of forgiveness*. The future of Judah is an utterly forgiven future, forgiven by the One who has no reason to forgive, but who can and does. It is this God who has said "fear not" (30:10-11), and who has assured that God's own self is watching over Israel's promised destiny to bring it to well-being (31:27-28). Finally, the poet imagines a world fully at home in God's presence.

The central theological issue in the tradition of Jeremiah is the deep and raw shift from pain to possibility, from judgment to promise. Both aspects of God's way with Israel, judgment and promise, are necessary. The connection between them, however, or we might better say the discontinuity between them, is as hidden and inscrutable as the move from Good Friday to Easter Sunday, from death to life. It is this radical and unpredictable shift that so startles Israel and powers the gospel.

Jeremiah does not simply respond to circumstance. He is not presented as a social commentator. He dares rather to probe God's own heart and disclose to us what it is that happens there. It is odd but crucial that the turn in Jerusalem's prospect is matched by a stunning turn in God's own heart. It is the very God who announces in 30:12 that Israel's sickness is beyond cure who dares to say, five verses later, "I will cure."[23] God does not simply mirror what happens in Israel's historical experience. God's hurting, hopeful heart leads reality. In the loss and dismay of exile, God discovers for a first time how deep is God's love for Israel. The disaster does not nullify God's yearning but powers and intensifies it. It is the turn in God that evokes the turn in Israel's history. It is God's resolve to heal that permits Israel's hope. The exile is not only the displacement of Israel. The exile is also the moment in which God discovers the depth of God's own love for Israel. In that unmeasured, unutterable love is Israel's lean chance for a new life in the world.

Rootage for prophetic ministry, I submit, is situated *in the divine council*. The poet reaches back to the *sanctions of Sinai*. The poet reaches forward to the *imagined, assured newness promised.* In this remembering and hoping, the poet *embraces present pain* as the place wherein God will come with newness. These several factors in the tradition of Jeremiah are all identifiable and discreet.

In the end, however, all we see of these factors are lean, crafted words. The work of prophecy is a poem, a poem that bespeaks the world subversively, resignifying, redescribing, and reimagining. It is the practice of such artistic speech, so tentative and so daring, that permits Israel one last chance in the world. The poet is one who can dare to probe underneath official reality to the place where pain does not deceive but must be honored. The poetic voice has no concrete proposal or program for the future. The poet has only words that are a burning fire (20:9) and must be uttered. When uttered, something new is thereby permitted and insisted upon. The old, denied hurt is now visible. The old, repressed hope is now released. There appears in the world, on the awed lips of the poet, a new people in the world, a people endlessly problematic, but also relentlessly under promise. This relentless insistence for the future makes sense only to those who depart the conventional world and are willing to enter the new world voiced by the poet. This new world that has substance only as abrasive, angular words bring to existence things that do not exist.

II

Prophetic faith is aimed, in the first instance, at *reconstruction of social reality.*[24] It believes that the world of social transaction is redeemable and subject to change. It affirms, moreover, that human agents can make a difference in the shape of that world. Out of this four-fold rootage I have explicated, the prophets are in the first instant *reformist.*

The reformist tendency of prophetic faith is boldly and affirmatively "this-worldly." This tendency is embedded in a thoroughly Israelite tradition that stretches from Moses to Ezra, the two great administrators of public possibility in Israel. I suggest that the prophets can only be understood if they are seen as falling between, bracketed by, and defined in terms of these two great reformers who had such confidence in historical possibility.

On the one hand, in the daring of the Exodus and in the constitutive events of Sinaitic covenantalism, Moses was precisely concerned with the refashioning of public institutions.[25] Not only the Decalogue, but also the initial legal traditions of Exodus 21–23 evidence both a powerful realism and a daring critique of realism.[26] This legal collection dares to urge and summon Israel to "a more excellent way" in the world, a way of compassionate justice.

On the other hand, Ezra (in concert with Nehemiah) refounded Israel (Judaism) after the shattering displacement of exile. Ezra taught, translated, and interpreted the Torah as the normative summons of Judaism, insisting that every aspect of Israel's life, domestic and public, economic and liturgical, must adhere to the will and purpose of YHWH.[27]

This reformist tendency is also expressed in a prophetic summons to repent.[28] The repentance urged by the prophets is both theological-covenantal, urging Israel to return to YHWH, and socioeconomic-political, urging Israel to enact the radical public claims of Yahwism. The convergence of covenantal theology and public policy is at the heart of prophetic faith.[29]

Jeremiah is peculiarly important for the reformist tradition of the prophets. Jeremiah, however, is also very complex about this theme because the tradition of Jeremiah has been much influenced, shaped, and transformed by Deuteronomic redaction.[30] It is the Deuteronomists who are the principal carriers of reformist faith in the Old Testament. The relation between Jeremiah and Deuteronomy is notoriously difficult. For our purposes, it is sufficient to observe that in the traditioning process, the voice of Jeremiah has been thought (by the Deuteronomists) to be a convincing vehicle for reformist thought, even if this requires a considerable recasting of the voice of Jeremiah.[31] Jeremiah, as now given to us in the redactional process and in its canonical outcome, is a reformist voice insisting on covenantalism as a mode of public practice.

I cite two texts in this regard. First, Jeremiah 11:1-13 is a text that urges covenantalism and that has often been regarded as an intentional link between the prophet and the reform of Josiah. Jeremiah is commissioned by YHWH to proclaim the covenant:

> Hear the words of this covenant, and speak to the people of Judah and the inhabitants of Jerusalem. You shall say to them, "Thus says the LORD, the God of Israel: Cursed be anyone who does not *heed* the words of this covenant which I commanded your ancestors when I brought them out of the land of Egypt, from the iron-smelter, saying, *Listen* to my voice, and do all that I command you. So shall you be my people, and I will be your God. . . . *Hear* the words of this covenant and do them." (vv. 2-4, 6, emphasis added)

The key word is *shemaʿ*. The voice of Jeremiah given here believes that willingness to heed covenant requirements will transpose the public life of Israel and preclude the coming judgment.

The reformist tendency of this prophet, however, is soon exhausted. Immediately after the summons to "listen" in v. 7, v. 8 continues:

> Yet they did not obey or incline their ear, but every one walked in the stubbornness of an evil will.

And because they did not listen, the judgments of covenant are given:

> So I brought upon them all the words of this covenant, which I commanded them to do, but they did not.

Israel must listen. Israel did not listen. Therefore Israel stands under covenant curse. In the reformist tradition, this harsh logic is irresistible.

After v. 8 the voice of Jeremiah draws the conclusions that soon nullify Judah's only change for reform. A weighty and sober lawsuit is voiced, given by YHWH against God's people, governed again by the term *shemaʿ*.[32] First there is the *indictment*: "They refuse to hear my words." This is followed by the *sentence*: "I will not listen to them." They did not listen. I will not listen.[33] The possibility of reform is forfeited and abandoned, because reform requires what Israel will not give, namely, responsive, attentive listening. YHWH is prepared to abandon failed Israel to the gods who are unable to save:

> Then the cities of Judah and the inhabitants of Jerusalem will go and cry to the gods to whom they make offerings, but they will never save them in the time of their trouble. For your gods have become as many as your towns, O Judah; and as many as the streets of Jerusalem are the altars to shame you have set up, altars to make offerings to Baal. (vv. 12-13)

The other gods cannot save. And YHWH will not save. Judah is hopeless.

There is one final development of the *shemaʿ* theme. After the lawsuit about a mutual "not listening," Jeremiah is now directed by YHWH to cease his intercession on behalf of Israel, for now YHWH will not listen, not even to Jeremiah:

> As for you, do not pray for this people, or lift up a cry or prayer on their
> behalf, for I will not listen when they call to me in the time of their
> trouble. (v. 14)[34]

This prohibition for YHWH surely ends the reformist possibility for the
prophet. Any hope Jeremiah may have had for such a turn in Israel is now
nullified. The hope-filled, society-affirming prophet is exhausted through
"not listening." Israel's obdurateness is matched by YHWH's decisive
rejection of God's covenant partner. YHWH also refuses to listen, but the
fault clearly belongs to Israel.

The second reformist text I cite is in chapter 34, with its foil and contrast in chapter 35. The narrative reports of an attempt at reform, instituted
by King Zedekiah. Jerusalem is under assault from the armies of Babylon.
In a desperate act of Torah obedience, in an attempt to avert the impend-
ing disaster, the people covenant with the king to release all their slaves
(34:8-9). This act is a faint-hearted recognition that the Babylonian threat
results from a failure of covenant obedience, for the people of Jerusalem
hope to avert the pending invasion by covenant obedience. They propose a
drastic economic reform, for the slaves are debt slaves, poor people in hock
for credit they cannot pay.[35] The people promise to cancel debts and liberate slaves, in obedience to the law of Deuteronomy (cf. 15:1-11). They make
that promise, solemn as it is desperate.

They renege, however (v. 11). They force the poor back into bondage,
so that the initial act of obedience was in the end only an act of bad faith.
Jeremiah is not in this case a poet of reform. He is not present in vv. 8-10
where the reform is under discussion. Only in v. 12 with Judah's failure to
act in obedience does Jeremiah appear in the narrative, after the reform
is aborted. Only now does the prophet speak. His speech is no longer
reformist, as in chapter 11. Remote from hope of reform, the prophet speaks
with a terrible, dread soberness (vv. 13-22). He offers a review of the entire
history of Judah, under the rubric of covenant requirements (vv. 13-14).
He redescribes the present crisis with Babylon with reference to the old
memory of Exodus and Sinai; he speaks of the profanation of life enacted
in rebonding the debt slaves. Finally the prophet arrives at the massive,
ominous "therefore" that is central to a prophetic perspective:

> Therefore, thus says the Lord: You have not obeyed me by granting a
> release to your neighbors and friends; I am going to grant a release to

you, says the LORD—a release to the sword, to pestilence, and to famine. I will make you a horror to all the kingdoms of the earth. (v. 17)

Jeremiah reverts to the language of *shema*: "You did not listen!" You
did not grant a release; you did not proclaim liberty. So now I, YHWH,
proclaim liberty. But what a liberty! It is liberty granted to the covenant
curses, sword, pestilence, and famine. The power of death is released, to
work destruction and shame. Death is given "the freedom of the city," as
the debt slaves were not. The prophet articulates and certifies a terrible
ending to the people of Jerusalem. There is no longer any hint of reform,
no summons to repentance, only a despairing conclusion that Israel has
passed the point of no return. That long, unworkable season of life with
YHWH has come to its terrible, unutterable end.[36]

III

Because the prophet has rejected reformism, he is now led by his vocation
underneath thinkable public possibility. The social ideologues imagine they
are prophetic by urging their particular sets of reforms. "Do-gooders" always
imagine there is something to be done that will salvage present arrangements. Prophetic faith and prophetic spirituality, however, are always
pressed back behind public possibility to something more hidden and more
subversive. Prophetic faith and prophetic spirituality probe how to speak,
think, discern, trust, and dare when public possibilities seem to be fully
exhausted. Jeremiah is an awesome embodiment of faith and speech when
no public possibilities are on the horizon.

In such time, when reform is unutterable, the prophet is driven back to
words for which there are no visible public realities, words that serve either
to voice *the depth of trouble*, and by speaking, keep one sane; or conversely,
the prophet speaks words that go so deep they touch *the madness of caring
and knowing*, which has no discernible public possibility. Oddly, Jeremiah
does not withdraw into muteness or private community but is mandated
to speak the reality that lies beyond available rationality. He speaks to keep
the conversation of faith under way, a conversation that affirms a reality everywhere else rejected. The hostility evoked by Jeremiah among the
leadership types indicates that Jeremiah spoke in a rationality so subversive
that it would not be tolerated in official Jerusalem (26:7-11).[37]

In this terrible, awesome, urgent, futile practice of prophetic faith in a society that is profoundly inhospitable, we may identify the following elements of prophetic practice:

1. The prophet does *imaginative rereading, resignifying, and redescribing of social reality.* He does so by bold, daring, and offensive metaphor, in an attempt to disclose and reveal what otherwise would not be seen or noticed.[38] In Jeremiah, two metaphors may be identified as thematic, though many other metaphors are offered almost in passing.[39]

First, the metaphor of marriage, honeymoon, adultery, and possible remarriage is offered as a rereading of Israel's life and faith. Jeremiah articulates with gentleness the initial devotion of the two partners. Jeremiah's rereading is a reiteration of the old Mosaic discernment of passionate covenantal commitment:

> I remember the devotion of your youth,
>> your love as a bride,
> how you followed me in the wilderness,
>> in a land not sown. (2:2)

Then the poet can wedge into Israel's ears the awesome word *'azab* (abandon, forsake, leave, divorce):

> they have *forsaken* me,
> the fountain of living waters. . . .
> Have you not brought this upon yourself
>> by *forsaking* the Lord your God,
>> while he led you in the way? . . .
> Know and see that it is evil and bitter
>> for you to *forsake* the Lord your God.
> (vv. 13, 17, 19, emphasis added)

The poet sounds the pained voice of God the lover, who wants the adulterous partner to come home, to come home regardless, to come home transformed for truth, justice, and mercy (4:1-2). Affronted YHWH still hopes for another, better way of relating:

> If you return, O Israel,
>> says the Lord,
> if you return to me,

if you remove your abominations from my presence,
    and do not waver,
and if you swear, "As the LORD lives!"
    in truth, in justice, and in uprightness,
then the nations shall be blessed by him,
    and by him they shall boast. (4:1-2)

The second metaphor is that of sickness and healing. Jeremiah employs radical language that is necessary for the reality of pain he senses. Israel has an incurable disease, a terminal illness. A distorted heart has ended in heart disease. As a result, YHWH also has heart disease, through empathy with diseased Israel. In 8:18, 21, the prophet articulates his profound heart sickness over Jerusalem:

My joy is gone, grief is upon me,
    my heart is sick. . . .
For the hurt of my poor people I am hurt,
    I mourn, and dismay has taken hold of me.

It is the wound of Israel that wounds the speaker. The speaker is ostensibly the poet. At the end of the unit, however, we have the decisive signature, "says the LORD" (9:3). It is YHWH who speaks. It is YHWH who grieves. It is YHWH who has a sick heart.[40]

The same metaphor is sounded in 30:12-15, to describe a situation of abandonment and hopelessness:

For thus says the LORD:
Your hurt is incurable,
    and your wound is grievous.
There is none to uphold your cause,
    no medicine for your wound,
    no healing for you. . . .
Why do you cry out over your hurt?
    Your pain is incurable.

Astonishingly, in the same poem, v. 17 reverses the metaphor and answers with healing:

> For I will restore health to you,
>   and your wounds I will heal,
>   says the LORD ...

For our purposes, both the sickness and the healing, the "divorce" and "reconciliation" are crucial. Together they show the prophet skillfully rereading historical reality. Without the pain (of "sickness" and "divorce"), one might imagine Judah's historical jeopardy occurs because of poor foreign policy, weak military preparation, foolish government, or aggressive imperialism. One might even imagine the trouble pertains to "morality." These metaphors of divorce and illness, of broken marriage and broken heart, however, cut underneath such notions to a more fundamental reality, enunciating the scandal of infidelity and the aching power of fidelity. The work of imagination is to cut through conventional perceptions and underneath commonsense explanations, underneath both morality and policy, to the real issues that are covenantal and theological.

In parallel fashion, the metaphors of restoration ("healing" and "reconciliation") are crucial. They affirm that the deathliness of termination has not nullified Israel's future with God. The reason the negative metaphors do not lead to historical nullification is that Israel's hope for the future is rooted in God's will for a relation. Thus it is God's yearning that leads to reconciliation; it is God's passion that leads to healing. In anticipating such a future, the prophet is not extrapolating from Israel's present nor making "predictions" about what comes next in the historical-political process. Rather he is penetrating into God's resilient intention, which can only be voiced in imaginative poetry and powerful metaphor.

The prophet redescribes Israel's future reality. In so doing, there is very little of moral urging, no didacticism, no advice or coercion, but only a passionate articulation of the realities that transpire between YHWH and Israel, realities utterly preoccupying YHWH and only late noticed by Israel. The world of reality is recharacterized to show that the main presuppositions of the dominant culture are unreal. Society specializes in "non-issues," completely missing the realities that finally count with YHWH. Society notices neither that fidelity to YHWH will destroy, nor that YHWH's overriding fidelity will recreate.

2. The purpose of prophetic imagination is to engage in *prophetic interpretation*, to assert that Israel's public experience needs to be seen from a wholly different perspective. The metaphors to which I have referred, and many others used by the prophet, seek to mediate current experiences

through the prism of the old memories of Exodus and covenant. In its naked sense of self-sufficiency, Israel had scuttled the old memory as a working premise. Israel paid lip service to that memory, but the community no longer understood what that memory was in fact about (cf. Isa. 29:13).

The voiding of the memory leads to a misreading of present reality. That misleading in turn leads to mis-action and mis-policy. Without the redefining voice of the old memory, the present historical process deteriorates into an enterprise of brute power and intimidation, a juggling of interests, an ideological manipulation of symbols. Everything becomes, in one of Jeremiah's favorite words, "false."[41] Everything is perceived wrongly when the memory is scuttled:

> What wrong did your ancestors find in me
>> that they went far from me,
> and went after worthless things and became worthless themselves?
> They did not say, "Where is the LORD
>> who brought us up from the land of Egypt,
> who led us in the wilderness,
>> in a land of deserts and pits
> in a land of drought and deep darkness,
>> in a land that no one passes through,
> where no one lives?" (2:5-6)

When the true story is abandoned, the result is false trust and false practice:

> The priests did not say, "Where is the LORD?"
>> Those who handle the law did not know me;
> the rulers transgressed against me;
>> the prophets prophesied by Baal,
>> and went after things that do not profit. (2:8)

The leadership misunderstands reality and leads the people to death.

The prophetic response to this misreading is to reread the present in light of the memory that has been scuttled and is thought to be irrelevant. When world history and Israel's modest place in it are reread in terms of the normative Mosaic memory, three matters become freshly central.

First, the old memory asserts that Judah's entire life is founded in *God's liberating purpose*, which persists as God's sovereign resolve. The old deeds of God are a protest against every illusion of self-sufficiency (cf. 10:1-16).

Second, the old memory asserts that *God's primal commandments* are still in effect and are still the norm of Israel's destiny (cf. 7:9). The mandate of obedience, the summons to justice, the insistence on righteousness and equity, are not abrogated by Israel's heady assertion, "I will not serve" (2:20). The commandments contain the clue to Israel's survival and well-being. Any hope for *shalom* apart from obedience (*shema'*) is a distortion (cf. 6:13-15; 8:10-12). The commandments are not optional.

Third, *the old covenant sanctions* of blessing and curse are still operative and inescapable. There is a moral coherence to reality that takes human response seriously. Said another way, Israel's life in the land is profoundly "iffy":

> For if you truly amend your ways and your doings, if you truly act justly one with another, if you do not oppress the alien, the orphan, and the widow, or shed innocent blood in this place, and if you do not go after other gods to your own hurt, then I will dwell with you in this place, in the land that I gave of old to your ancestors forever and ever. (7:5-7)

Where the "if" of obedience is not enacted, Israel's sure future holds only the dread curses long ago pronounced:

> Those destined for pestilence, to pestilence,
>   and those destined for the sword, to the sword;
> those destined for famine, to famine,
>   and those destined for captivity, to captivity.
> And I will appoint over them four kinds of destroyers, says the LORD:
> the sword to kill, the dogs to drag away, and the birds of the air and the wild animals of the earth to devour and destroy. (15:2-3)

In Jeremiah's time, Judah had imagined that the old covenant threats were obsolete and irrelevant (cf. Jer. 5:12; Zeph. 1:12). A prophetic rereading counters such emancipated "modernity" by a powerful reiteration of those old sanctions.

This covenantal rereading of present reality is polemical. It polemicizes against (a) the notion of *self-sufficiency* by its statement of God's liberating purpose, (b) the seduction of moral *autonomy* by a reiteration of primal commandments, and (c) the assumption that the future can be had *without paying* for the present, by a reassertion of covenant curses.

This rereading, based on the normative Mosaic theological tradition, must have seemed irrelevant and outrageous to this community of self-deception. That community long ago had imagined it had outgrown and superseded such covenantal insistence. The prophetic rereading is more insistent than it is clever or innovative. It refuses to accommodate the categories of "modernity," autonomy, and self-sufficiency.[42]

In a succinct statement, Jeremiah juxtaposes the two perceptions of reality competing in Jerusalem, one rooted in the old, uncompromising Mosaic covenantalism, and the other expressive of self-serving self-sufficiency:

> Thus says the LORD: Let not the wise boast in their wisdom, do not let the mighty boast in their might, let not the wealthy boast in their wealth; but let those who boast boast in this, that they understand and know me, that I am the LORD; I act with steadfast love, justice, and righteousness in the earth; for in these things I delight, says the LORD. (9:23-24)[43]

Between these two systems of reality there can be no compromise. The prophet thus is engaged in a profound battle for a faithful discernment of the present, insisting that the scuttling of covenantalism will lead to illusion, which he labels "idolatry." Idolatry is not only a theological error, but it is an emptiness that leads to a fundamental failure of energy and power. Idolatry results in a community without the vitality necessary to receive and sustain life. Going after worthlessness ends in worthlessness (2:5). Israel becomes like that which it worships (cf. Hos. 9:10). The prophetic task is one of daring reinterpretation.

3. Prophetic rereading and reinterpretation brings a discernment of present social reality that is ominous. Israel is under sentence and bound for death. The harsh logic of covenantalism leads to a death sentence, uncompromising and nonnegotiable. That is a conclusion on which prophetic discernment might rest.

The Jeremiah tradition, however, pushes beyond this closed fate of curse. It is this push beyond that evidences Jeremiah's liberating imagination and embodies the power and cruciality of prophetic spirituality. There is an inexorable conclusion to Mosaic covenantalism, a conclusion of death. Jeremiah, while holding to the categories of such Mosaic covenantalism, pushes beyond that conclusion.

a. In his "lamentations" the prophet prays at profound risk and puts himself in jeopardy before God. In this regard Jeremiah seems to replicate the risks of Moses. Jeremiah refuses the fatedness of his own situation and he refuses the fatedness of Israel. The critical questions surrounding the prayers of lamentation and complaint are very difficult.[44] It seems fair to conclude that the profound assaults on God are both self-preoccupied petition and concerned intercession. Jeremiah, unlike Moses, does not persuade God, but he does keep the conversation with God going. He is seemingly convinced that as long as there is this conversation, there is a hope that YHWH will begin again with Judah. Thus the poet dares to pray for justice, even against God's injustice:

> You will be in the right, O Lord,
>> when I lay charges against you;
>> but let me put my case to you.
> Why does the way of the guilty prosper?
>> Why do all who are treacherous thrive?
> You plant them, and they take root;
>> they grow and bring forth fruit;
> you are near in their mouths
>> yet far from their hearts. (12:1-2)

The raising of the question of theodicy keeps matters open for a possible future from YHWH.

b. Jeremiah, following Hosea, dares to imagine God's heart is conflicted, with grief, pathos, and regret beyond one-dimensional anger. At enormous risk, the prophet probes the innards of God's heart. He finds there not only anger and rage but also anguish and wistfulness. The poet brings to speech from God's heart the yearning of a rejected father and an aching mother. In these poetic moments of exquisite grief and elegant yearning, the political failures and moral bankruptcy of Israel are shelved. The poet cuts underneath, to dare to speak about a theological reality unencumbered by political urgency or moral implications. The image offered is of a God who moves behind indignation to tears of release and embrace. The most daring and poignant push beyond is this anguished, trembling scene:

> Is Ephraim my dear son?
>> Is he the child I delight in?

As often as I speak against him,
    I still remember him.
Therefore I am deeply moved for him;
I will surely have mercy on him,
        says the LORD. (31:20)[45]

The God of Israel cannot cease to care. Even when God thinks to quit, to nullify Israel, and to banish the memory, God's mind is crowded with precious memories, and so yearns beyond betrayal.

Why does the poet subject himself and his listeners to this excruciating pain? Two reasons may be suggested. First, the pain of God, so he believes, is true. This is what is happening. This is how God is. The poet, any serious poet, has no other vocation than to exhibit reality in all its danger, even the reality of God. Second, the poet speaks in this way because such an articulation of unanticipated reality has strategic importance in his address to Jerusalem. This poet knows, like no one else in Israel, that grief bespeaks possibility.[46] Without this grief, there is no tomorrow. The pathos of God, formed by anger, powered by hurt, marked by yearning, releases the frozen alienation to make a new gesture possible. Ungrieved life blocks all new gestures. Now, for Jeremiah, for YHWH, and for Israel, suffering produces hope. The power of God's grief releases a third push beyond.

c. Out of God's grief comes utter new possibility. It is as though God has come to God's senses. Newness for Israel is not wrought or chosen by Israel but by God. The release of evangelical possibility comes exactly from grief articulated. In this torrent of possibilities, jumbled as it is, we may sort out three themes.

First, there is "building and planting," the actual resuscitation of public life (31:3-6).[47] There is nothing spiritual or ephemeral in this hope. The newness is a reconstituted Judah, a restored Jerusalem, the resumption of public life in Israel on a new basis. Note, however, this envisioning is exactly a vision, not blueprint, or program, or design. The crisis then and now is not lack of concrete plans, but lack of imaginative space among the visible givens that inevitably lead to despair. Jerusalem will be rehabilitated!

Second, not only urban renewal but also the reconstruction of the fabric of human life is anticipated. This is not unrelated to the previous motif, but now there is a quite different accent. The poet speaks not only of public reconstruction but of beginning again in intimate, domestic, primary covenanting, epitomized in family, marriage, and worship:

They shall come and sing aloud on the height of Zion,
    and they shall be radiant over the goodness of the LORD,
over the grain, the wine, and the oil,
    and over the young of the flock and the herd;
their life shall be like a watered garden,
    and they shall never languish again.
Then shall the young women rejoice in the dance,
    and the young men and the old shall be merry.
I will turn their mourning into joy,
    I will comfort them, and give them gladness for sorrow. (31:12-13)

The practice of humaneness has been choked off in preoccupations of greed, fear, idolatry, self-sufficiency, and deception. Now, at the most elemental levels, God will give life back to this people. The poet makes extensive use of the phrase *restore the fortunes*.[48] God will give back to Israel all that was promised, all that is needed, more than is possible. God promises to be restorative and rehabilitative. What is promised is resurrection "to a new and righteous life."

Finally the push beyond is expressed in covenantal categories. In the end,

> They shall be my people and I will be their God, for they shall return to me with their whole heart. (24:7)

The public reconstruction of Jerusalem and the rehabilitation of life for Judah are crucial. Along with that hope comes the restoration of covenantal communion, made possible precisely because of God's passionate love, wrought out of God's deep grief. The God who had quit now resolves to be faithfully the God of Israel. Everything hinges on this fresh resolve of God.

Prophetic spirituality is preoccupied now with the question: Is there a future? Can we hope and if so, on what grounds? This sequence of *risky prayer–grief–new possibility* in all its parts is subversive and countercultural. Jeremiah's words dare to act out a different scenario of human reality. That scenario is subversive because it breaks with immobilizing ideology of *polite prayer–denied pain–domesticated hope*. On all these counts, prophetic spirituality rejects the reductionism of a failed spirit and a crushed hope. It is countercultural because it bears witness to and acts from a God the world has long ago excluded from purview. It insists that life arises from a source other than our own energies. It calls us away from broken cisterns back to living water (2:13).

In the end, this spirituality of exile and homecoming, of crucifixion and resurrection, of grief and hope, is situated in a gap, an abyss where we scarcely dare go, but whence comes newness the world greatly fears and deeply doubts. Jeremiah is tough and uncompromising in facing the abyss and seeing beyond it.

In his toughness, Jeremiah anticipates that other embodiment of grief and hope that we have taken to be normative. Jesus said,

> "Blessed are you who weep now,
>> for you shall laugh. . . .
> Woe to you who are laughing now,
>> for you shall mourn and weep." (Luke 6:21, 25)

There is a time to weep—a time of candor about our true situation. There is a time to laugh—a time of surprised healing. There is a time to mourn, to grieve over utter loss. There is a time to dance—with the Lord of a post-exilic dance. Jeremiah did not believe in timelessness. He believed there are different times, all held in God's hand. He knew, moreover, exactly what time it was. The prophetic community is the one authorized and compelled to know exactly what time it is.

CHAPTER TWELVE

A World Available for Peace

Images of Hope from Jeremiah and Isaiah

A growing breach exists between the dominant values of American
society and the claim of the gospel. It has been held for a long time—
and with some truth—that there was a congruity between America and
the gospel. It did seem that in important ways American values had been
shaped and informed by Christian faith. But no more.

There is now a sickness (or madness, depending on how deep you cut it)
in American society that receives no sanction or legitimacy from biblical
faith. That madness may go by many names, but I shall call it consumerism—the notion that life consists in having and getting and spending and
controlling and using and eating. This value system places stress on accu-
mulation and believes that meaning and security come by "more."

Such consumerism in which we are enmeshed requires militarism to
sustain it. Our consumerism, our excessive standard of living, depends
on our having a disproportionate amount of goods and disproportionate
access to markets, and on our having while others do not have. Indeed, it is
not a great oversimplification to suggest that our militarism exists to support our consumerism, so that we may identify the disease of our society as
consumer militarism, which means an endless effort to gather more of the
world around us for our benefit.

These dominant values have received much support from religions, but
in fact the values of consumerism and militarism cannot, in any way I know,
square with Jesus' embrace of death and Jesus' resurrection into new power
for life. I believe that this growing tension, this collision course between
the two sets of values—consumer militarism and Christian faith—is the
central religious fact of our contemporary situation. Our dominant cultural
values are in deep conflict with Christian faith and will lead us to death.

The central promise of the gospel is peace that is God's good gift (John 14:27). But it is clear upon any reflection that the ways of consumerism do not lead to peace, but only to anxiety. The ways of militarism do not lead to security, but only destruction, violence, and dehumanization. In the midst of this mad scramble toward death are Christians, the church, with this conviction that the crucified risen One matters even here, because this One and only this One is Lord and Savior.

As a way to think about the issue of peace and our commitments to death, I will explore two scripture passages. These are God's living words to us, which may illuminate our situation and the choices we must make.

The first is Jeremiah 6:13-15. The poetry of Jeremiah seems peculiarly appropriate to our setting. Jeremiah lived in a time when destruction was very close at hand. Yet he lived among people who did not seem to notice, did not seem to care, or were unable to act. The poetry goes like this:

> For from the last to the greatest of them,
>> everyone is greedy for unjust gain;
> and from prophet to priest,
>> everyone deals falsely.
> They have treated the wound of my people carelessly,
>> saying, "Peace, peace,"
>> when there is no peace.
> They acted shamefully, they committed abomination;
>> yet they were not ashamed,
>> they did not know how to blush.
> Therefore they shall fall among those who fall;
>> at the time that I punish them,
>> they shall be overthrown,"
>>> says the LORD.

There are four points in this text that we may notice. First, at the center of the text the leaders say, "Peace, peace," when there is no peace. The poet insists that the kings, priests, and leaders in Jerusalem are engaging in an enormous deception.

The Hebrew word for peace, *shalom*, means a harmonious, properly functioning, life-giving order to society. The leadership asserts in its policies and propaganda that society is harmonious, properly functioning, and life-giving. But, says this poet: "It is a lie. It is not so."

The opposite of *shalom* is not war but chaos. The poet wants his community to notice the chaos and to experience the destructive disorder that is everywhere in the life of the community.

Christians are people who must tell the truth. Christians are people who reject the lie, the deception, who refuse the propaganda. This text is a summons to face the chaos among us that destroys, chaos evidenced in hunger, violence, unemployment, and land loss.

Second, at the beginning of this poetic passage is the poet's judgment about why this is happening among his people. It is because everybody has sold out. The prophets in Israel had always been hard on the leadership, not the common folk. It is the leadership who use position for self-advantage, who use office to feather their own nests, who form alliances for personal gain.

The poet makes no exception in his indictment, which includes prophets who say what must be said and priests who pray too easily. And it is, says he, for economic gain.

We are back to consumerism, to the ground of the lie in v. 13. Until this society comes clean about its economic fascinations and pursuits, we will not have peace. The political issue of peace is tied to the economic issue of greed and gain and injustice, to the benefit of some at the cost of others.

The third element, in v. 15, cuts underneath policy to attitude: "They did not know how to blush." What is required, first of all, is not a big disarmament program but the simple capacity to be embarrassed. Blushing and embarrassment depend on moral sensitivity, on being aware that our actions and our policies are in the presence of the Holy One. Shame and blushing refer life back to God and remind us that our public life is accountable to the God of healing and justice known in the Bible.

Jeremiah's prophecy comes to life now in a crucial question that the world of poverty and hurt is asking Americans and U.S. policy: Have you no shame? Can you not blush?

The economic resources of our great nation are used on foolishness in a world of fear—have you no shame? Violence and terror grow because we are so fearful of our markets and our affluence in the world—have you no shame? Our country supports tyranny and torture in the name of democracy—have you no shame? We have enormous well-being, and yet people live in poverty and in hunger and without homes—have you no shame?

We have gotten so used to the barbarianism of word and act that we no longer notice. What might have been an act of shame and a moral affront now becomes standard operating procedure. Jeremiah, of course, was called a traitor (38:4) because he refused to go along with the mindless celebration of his government, which claimed a "moral right" to do anything it wanted. He asked not about guns and arms and policy but about shame and blushing and moral sensitivity.

You see, the real issues about peace are, in fact, religious. And religious voices must not be silenced by the "realism" of policymakers, because now the real issue is what is happening to our humanness and what will happen when we have a new generation of young people who are incapable of blushing over the inhumanity. But Jeremiah's contemporaries called him traitor because they were cut off from noticing and feeling and caring and being transformed.

The passage culminates in v. 15 with a massive, ominous "therefore." The word *therefore* always means that a judgment is coming: therefore a time of fall, of overthrow, of punishment. In downtown Jerusalem, it was thought that Judah would always be safe because it was God's people and God's city. In our society, we imagine we are immune because we are the "leader of the free world."

What Jeremiah asserts is that the real danger is not Babylon or Assyria or the Soviet Union or China. The threat, finally, to our way of life is the sovereign God who will be pushed only so far and then not mocked any further (Isa. 37:23).

Now let me acknowledge that this text is only a poem. It is not theology, and it is not a political program. The poem invites us to see the world differently, not in terms of our ideology or our precious habits, but in terms of a poetic vision that tries to get underneath our usual assumptions.

There is another voice in our life. It is not the voice of ideology or propaganda. It is not the voice of Left or Right, or hawk or dove. It is not an echo of our pet projects. It is rather a holy voice that asks us about life and about blushing, and about selling out for gain. It is a harsh voice, but it is an honest voice. If we are to think seriously about peace, we shall have to listen to this other voice.

As it happened, the poetry of Jeremiah was true. The end did come. In 587 B.C.E., Judah was harshly assaulted. The city ended, the temple burned, the walls crumbled. It did not seem like it could happen, but it did. And when it happened, everything that seemed so secure, so promised by God, so guaranteed, turned to ashes. There was an exile into Babylon, where a group of Jews lived under imperial rule. They were robbed of their freedom and much of their dignity. Their faith ebbed, and God seemed weak and distant.

Then there comes this second poem, sixty years after Jeremiah. It is from second-generation exile in Babylon. In Isaiah 52:7-9, the poet speaks this way:

> How beautiful upon the mountains
>> are the feet of the messenger who announces peace,
> who brings good news,
>> who announces salvation,
>> who says to Zion, "Your God reigns."
> Listen! Your sentinels lift up their voices,
>> together they sing for joy;
> for in plain sight they see
>> the return of the Lord to Zion.
> Break forth together into singing,
>> you ruins of Jerusalem;
> for the Lord has comforted his people,
>> he has redeemed Jerusalem.

The scene is the forlorn, hopeless, abandoned city of Jerusalem. According to the poet, hopeless Jerusalem has been in smoldering shambles for two generations. There seems no way to turn things around.

The Babylonians have their ruthless way about everything. The Babylonian armies are powerful; the Babylonian rules are harsh; the Babylonian gods prevail. All things Jewish are diminished. The city of Jerusalem is gone and its glory departed.

The covenantal tradition is terminated. The God of Israel is driven from the field. It all turned out to be a bad gamble with God. The Jews are indeed the people who walk in darkness.

The gloominess of the scene is one we might feel if we try to think about peace in our world. One can despair if one looks carefully, for one cannot imagine how the foolishness of fear and brutality and arms can ever be overcome. We are all so trapped in it.

Yet if peace is to come, it will come on the tongues of evangelical poets who, out of uncommon faith and nervy speech, dare to say something new; because poets do create new realities.

So this poet speaks, this poet so enmeshed in exile, surrounded by defeated Jews who had lost heart. In such a situation, the poet constructs this imaginative scene. There is the waiting, hopeless city of Jerusalem. It has waited for news for a long time and there has never been any news. Watch after watch, there is nothing—waiting for a runner, waiting for news, waiting for a break, waiting for an announcement that the Babylonian armies have fallen.

But then the sentinels on the wall start to sing and shout and dance. Because as they look over the hills to the north toward Babylon, they see a runner coming, a messenger. They do not have to wait until the messenger gets there. They can tell by the way the messenger runs that there is good news. They had hoped while there was no real hope. And now the messenger has come. How welcome the messenger, and what a sight for sore eyes.

Verse 7 is of interest because it has the words "brings good news." Three times it appears: good news, good news, good news. The messenger arrives breathless all the way from Babylon with a stunning piece of news. The sentinels who have been waiting in long years of despair say, "Yes, yes, spit it out!" The whole message is reduced to three simple phrases, which are words that can change the world. They are the words that matter most, which speak the very center of biblical faith: Your God rules. Your God is king. Your God has just become king.

Your God, the God of Israel, the Lord of the Exodus, the one who fells cities and gives offspring to barren women, the one who seemed to be defeated by the Babylonians in 587—this God has now gone back into the dispute and won. That is the heart of the gospel, that this God, who seemed to be defeated, in fact, is the God who governs.

I make four observations about this remarkable text. The first is that the announcement in v. 7 that God reigns is in substance peace, good, salvation, or liberation. They assert together that this God has reclaimed power and what this God is about to do is restore community, well-being, and life-giving order. That peace is specifically characterized as the rule of God, which entails well-being and liberation. Peace is derived from the affirmation that God governs and will have God's way.

Second, the precise context of this poetry is that the God of justice and freedom and liberation has been in deathly conflict with the gods and imperial power of Babylon. For fifty years it had seemed that Babylonian power was to have its way. Babylonian authority, technology, intelligence, and hardware seemed beyond challenge. People were docile and obedient and passive and hopeless because it seemed that Babylonian modes of reality were absolute and eternal.

According to this poetic scenario, the rule of God's peace turns out to be more powerful and more decisive than anything Babylon can do. It has always been so in the Bible. As early as the Exodus, the power of Egypt seemed stronger, but Moses and Miriam assert the rule of the God of freedom and justice (Exod. 15:1-18, 21).

It is not different in the New Testament, where the power of Roman oppression or the power of harsh law or the power of guilt and death seem always to dictate our life. But then there is the gospel which, in a most subversive way, announces that all of these powers that rob us of our humanness have lost their legitimacy and their clout and their credibility, and we are free to go home. That is why the sentinels danced and sang and the messenger hurried, because God's power permitted Israel to go home.

What I find so stunning about this is that this gospel of poetic alternative ends the fixity of the world. Was it not assumed among us that there would always be a Soviet threat or a Chinese threat? Has it not seemed that there will always be terror in the Near East and racism in South Africa and religious war in Northern Ireland? Does it not seem in this country that there will always be a rapacious Pentagon and an underbelly of poverty? Of course it seems it will always be so.

But we are privy to another cast of characters. We know about the sentinels on the wall who do not cease to expect. We know about the breathless runner who brings the gospel, who says, "Good news: Our God lives and rules and has won." We know about the power of this God. And wherever "Your God rules" is blurted out breathlessly, there the fixities of the Soviet Union and China and the Pentagon and apartheid and terrorism and fear and hatred are dismantled. The world is made available again for peace, and new life is possible.

But new life and peace are not possible unless there are those who watch, unless there are runners who run, unless there is news of victory, unless there are moments when the fixities are shattered. Peace is not a policy of deterrence and repression and control. Peace is an act of God's rule that shatters all the tired ways in which we have organized the world.

My third observation is that this assertion of peace is a liturgic, poetic act of imagination. The scripture of Isaiah 52:7-9 is poetry. That is all. But peace is, first of all, a poetic, imaginative, liturgic enterprise. It depends on having the freedom and imagination to speak the world differently.

We grow so old and so tired and so accustomed to the way we habitually speak the world. We speak the world into armed camps. We speak the world into good guys and bad guys, into winners and losers, into haves and have nots. We speak of the world as though it were an adversarial place, as though there were no one in charge, as though we had to decide and manage it all, as though we could have it our own way, on our own terms, if we claim it that way firmly enough.

But we are baptized, and because we are baptized, we discern the world differently. Because of our baptism, we trust a different poet and we believe a different poem. We speak the world differently. I am not engaging in naiveté or romanticism. I am pointing to the fact that peace comes as we participate in liturgy.

Characteristically, Christians speak differently, which thus shapes the world differently. When we say, "The grace of our Lord Jesus Christ be with you," or "Praise God from whom all blessings flow," this poetic speech asserts that the world is indeed under the rule of this other God.

We must start speaking seriously to each other about the rule of God over the troublesome, peaceless parts of our life, in order to find out if we believe our own poems. To be able to say to each other "Your God reigns" could be the beginning of a new way in the world. It asserts that we do not need to take with excessive seriousness the rulers of this age. We do not need to concede too much, nor trust too much, nor be intimidated too much. Because if one starts with very poetic speech, such as "Your God reigns," then one finds oneself publishing peace and good and liberation.

The foremost peace action of the church is to recover our own language of God's governance to find out if we mean it. To assert the rule of God is not to be stupid in a dangerous world. But it is to begin to turn loose of the fear that immobilizes.

It is a dream and a hope. But it is a subversive peacemaking activity because it announces that the empire is finished. At a liturgical level, we shall have to decide if we believe enough to make such a remarkable claim in the face of enduring imperial power.

My fourth point is that powerful poetry can lead to new action. Or, in other words, worship leads to ethics. New imagination leads to fresh obedience in the world.

The poetry of Isaiah 52 was not just liturgical entertainment. It was a permit, an invitation, a summons to depart the empire and go back home. Peacemaking requires that serious people go back home to the places from which we have been exiled. Going back home means to return to our places of obedience with new liberty and imagination.

We have lived so long in this competitive, adversarial place, defined in terms of empire, that we have come to think it is where we belong. We are so alienated from our true life, so habituated in this other world, that we no longer notice how alien it is. We are children of the language of the Cold War, of the rhetoric of competition and the ideology of individualism, of the practice of fear and hate and greed, so that it feels to us like normalcy.

The poet comes to people like us to say that this is not our home. We have forgotten our home. We don't belong to the military system that tries to find security through armed strength. We don't belong to the consumer ideology that believes more is better. We don't belong to the enduring propaganda of the Cold War that believes the world is divided up into camps.

So, where do we who have been baptized belong? Home is not heaven. It is not life after death. It is not protected church space. Where actions of peacemaking, deeds of love and mercy, decisions of justice and liberation are taken—that is our true home.

To go home, as we can when we hear the poetry, is to become who we are baptized to be. Home is to be engaged, wherever we have access, in the chores and tasks of peacemaking, to become peaceable people who know that the world is ordered and willed by God toward peace.

Imagine the nerve and freedom and power of the Jews who believed the poem. They stood tall in the face of the empire. They mocked the fears and hopes of the empire. They disengaged from all of those administered ways.

Peacemaking depends on believing we have the power to stand tall in the face of the empire. We are now all caught in the war machine. The baptized disciples of Jesus disengage and stand tall and refuse to have our hearts and imagination administered, because we know our place is not in the midst of the war-making energies of our society.

This poetry says to all believers who are exiled in the empire: The war machine is not your place. It's not your place politically and economically, not your place psychologically, not your place liturgically, not your place morally. Let the poets of the church make our true place real and available, because it is a gift to come down where you ought to be.

It is important to look at the relation of these two texts. The first speaks a hard truth that asserts that peace is not present, not available, and that the community is engaged in a big lie. Jeremiah announces to the city that peace is not available and there will be only punishment and devastation. On the other hand, Isaiah, in joyous celebration, announces that God's sovereignty is sure and that peace is now to be announced as the present gift of God. The interesting question is how to move from the negatives of Jeremiah to the affirmations of Isaiah, from no peace to real peace, from the judgment of God to the gift of God. Indeed, I judge that hard move to be the one we are working to embrace in our society.

How do we move from "there is no peace" to announcing "peace" and "good news"? The answer is that peace, which is impossible and not available, becomes possible and available when, and only when, the holy city is dismantled and God is driven back to square one to create a new people and to rebuild a new city. Peace could not be announced to Jerusalem, God would not rule in power, until its idolatrous organization of public life had come to an end. Peace is not possible until there is a dismantling of the holy citadel and an embrace of exile as the place of God's newness.

I do not know how literally or how drastically this must be taken. But what seems very clear is that peace is not possible in our world, anywhere in the world, until modes of domination and control are given up. I sense that the main flow of God's governance is to take these powers of domination from us, and as God takes all of that from us, it is painful and scary. But it is what is required if we are to have peace, to be peacemakers, to be children of God.

In Mark 6:7-13, we are given a glimpse of peacemaking. The disciples preached repentance, cast out demons, anointed the sick and healed them, had authority over unclean spirits.

The gospel puts disciples at the places where humanness is at issue. There were many forces in that society, like ours, that wanted the unclean spirits to have authority, that resisted repentance, that supported the demons, that perpetuated the sickness. But the gospel is about the transformation of all of life toward humanness. The gospel frees us to act in human ways.

So what should we put at the hard place between "no peace" in Jeremiah and "Your God reigns" in Isaiah? I suggest that right between these texts we place the story of Jesus in Luke 19:41-44:

> When he came near and saw the city, he wept over it, saying, "If you, even you, had only recognized on this day the things that make for peace! But now they are hidden from your eyes. Indeed, the days will come upon you, when your enemies will set up ramparts around you and surround you, and hem you in on every side. They will crush you to

the ground, you and your children within you, and they will not leave one stone upon another; because you did not recognize the time of your visitation from God."

The scene presents Jesus approaching the same Jerusalem about which Jeremiah spoke. This is the city where the new age is to come. It is the city whence may come the new king and the place where God's presence is promised. But now it is a place of grief and loss.

I take Jerusalem here as a metaphor for every concentration of political-religious power that is self-serving, including our own. Jesus grieves over such a city because he knows that such a city will be destroyed.

Perhaps Jesus weeps over our country also, even as Jesus weeps over Moscow and Beijing and Havana and Johannesburg and Belfast and Beirut and Baghdad (and Washington) and all those concentrations of power and money and security and hate and fear that prevent and deny peace. I do not know if it is too late. It is always a debate to know if it is too late, or if there is yet time.

But I do know it is very, very late. It is very late for a society that does not know how to blush. Jeremiah and Jesus weep over a city that does not know the things that make for peace.

Against the dominant value system that does not blush and that keeps on lying, it is the task of the peacemaking church in America to grieve, to speak the truth, to dismantle, to turn loose, to face the exile, all for the sake of peace. The only way from here to there, from despair to hope, from death to new life, is by way of weeping, of grief, of exile.

Life comes differently when read through the gospel, when heard as being crucified and raised to new life, of dying with Christ to be born again. The primary peacemaking work of the church is to consider the story of crucifixion and resurrection again, to see in what ways it really is our story, to see what must be given up to death in order to be surprised by God's new life.

Thus I believe the first, dangerous, difficult, and urgent issue is to reshape our imagination. It is the central vocation of the church to reshape our public imagination around different images. The real issue is that we must learn to discern all of life, personal and public, around the truth-telling of Jeremiah and the surprise of Isaiah, around the strange cost of letting go of the city and the equally strange gift of receiving a future from God.

The church tradition knows something unshakably true about peace-making. It goes like this: "For those who want to save their life will lose it; and those who lose their life for my sake, and the sake of the gospel, will save it" (Mark 8:35). That is as true with public policy as with prayer. It is the strange central insight of the gospel.

In our baptism, we know of no alternative to this truth. Peace begins in communities of bleeding that will give their life. That bleeding may indeed lead to repentance, then to healing, and finally to homecoming, and with it, peace.

"Is There No Balm in Gilead?"

The Hope and Despair of Jeremiah

The word that came to Jeremiah from the LORD in the tenth year of King Zedekiah of Judah, which was the eighteenth year of Nebuchadrezzar. At that time the army of the king of Babylon was besieging Jerusalem, and the prophet Jeremiah was confined in the court of the guard that was in the palace of the king of Judah, where King Zedekiah of Judah had confined him. Zedekiah had said, "Why do you prophesy and say, Thus says the LORD: I am giving this city into the hand of the king of Babylon, and he shall take it; King Zedekiah shall not escape out of the hands of the Chaldeans, but shall surely be given into the hands of the king of Babylon, and shall speak with him face to face and see him eye to eye; and he shall take Zedekiah to Babylon, and there he shall remain until I attend to him, says the LORD; though you fight against the Chaldeans, you shall not succeed?"

Jeremiah said, "The word of the LORD came to me: Hanamel son of your uncle Shallum is going to come to you and say, "Buy my field that is at Anathoth, for the right of redemption by purchase is yours." Then my cousin Hanamel came to me in the court of the guard, in accordance with the word of the LORD, and said to me, "Buy my field that is at Anathoth in the land of Benjamin, for the right of possession and redemption is yours; buy it for yourself." Then I knew that this was the word of the LORD.

And I bought the field at Anathoth from my cousin Hanamel, and weighed out the money to him, seventeen shekels of silver. I signed the deed, sealed it, got witnesses, and weighed the money on scales. Then I took the sealed deed of purchase, containing the terms and conditions, and the open copy; and I gave the deed of purchase to Baruch son of Neriah son of Mahseiah, in the presence of my cousin Hanamel, in the presence of the witnesses who signed the deed of purchase, and in the presence of all the Judeans who were sitting in the court of the guard. In their presence I charged Baruch, saying, Thus says the LORD of hosts, the God of Israel: Take these deeds, both this sealed deed of purchase and this open deed, and put them in an earthenware vessel, in order that they may last for a long time. For thus says the LORD of hosts, the God of Israel: Houses and fields and vineyards shall again be bought in this land. (Jer. 32:1-15)

My joy is gone, grief is upon me,
    my heart is sick.
Hark, the cry of my poor people
    from far and wide in the land:
"Is the LORD not in Zion?
    Is her King not in her?" . . .
For the hurt of my poor people I am hurt,
    I mourn, and dismay has taken hold of me.

Is there no balm in Gilead?
    Is there no physician there?
Why then has the health of my poor people
    not been restored?
O that my head were a spring of water,
    and my eyes a fountain of tears,
so that I might weep day and night
    for the slain of my poor people!
O that I had in the desert
    a traveler's lodging place,
that I might leave my people
    and go away from them! . . .
for they proceed from evil to evil,
    and they do not know me, says the LORD. (8:18—9:3)

Holding to a vision of how it will be is the business of prophetic faith. It is a key mark of ancient Israel's prophets that they held to a vision of an alternative world in season and out of season. And they could hold to such a deep and abiding hope precisely because they understood that the new alternative to come was not to be derived from the present circumstance.

Their hope was not grounded in their sense that things are going to get better, nor in the notion that things were evolving in a desired direction.

And therefore they were not utterly undone when things got worse, for that also was not finally relevant to their vision. Their hope had an independence from the present, because the new world would be a gift from God, who would act in unqualified freedom.

It is that uncompromised rootage of vision to which the prophets cling. It is the memory of the Exodus that seems to be the root for that vision. As the prophets and all of Israel reflected on the Exodus, they understood that the newness of Israel was in no way derived from its context, but it was a new gift wrought by God. If God could do that, then prophets could still hope God might do that sort of newness again.

The maintenance of the prophetic vision thus depended on distinguishing between the gifts God would give and the possibility of the present situation. Certainly the prophets were not uninterested in the present situation. They were acutely aware of it and observed it most discerningly. Indeed their emotional life was very much in response to the ache they saw in the world around them. But they never confused present possibility with divine impossibility. And that, I suggest, is a terribly important distinction for radicals, both those who are tired and those who are not. There is a tendency to care so much and invest so deeply in the present struggle that it appears to be God's last, best hope. Then the historical process turns thin in its promise. It is tempting to become hopeless.

For that reason, the fundamental distinction between social prospect and divine promise is crucial. We need to be saying to each other that our energies are rooted in and aimed toward God's promises and not social prospects.

There is no prophet who had to face this problem of prospect and promise more acutely than did the prophet Jeremiah. His career stretched over the period of Judah's last gasp, its deepest obduracy, and its eventual demise. Jeremiah surely understood, above all, that Judah would not change and indeed was incapable of change. He did not flinch from announcing judgment, harsh and inescapable. It was he who understood that Judah must fall into the terrible hands of Babylon, and he discerned that this was God's awful will for his very own people. For all this, he was reckoned a traitor against king and people. All of that we might have expected from such an acute and candid social critic.

But Jeremiah is more than social critic. He is holder to a vision rooted in nothing other than God's promise. In the very midst of the hopelessness of defeat and inescapable judgment, he continues to articulate an alternative vision for the future.

The critical judgments about the "Book of Consolation" (Jeremiah 30–33) are difficult and disputed. One cannot know for sure if these poetic ventures are from the poet. In any case, as it now stands, Jeremiah is remembered and presented as having spoken these remarkable promises. Of all the promises that are found in this section, Jeremiah 32:1-15 has the ring of authenticity. It is a narrative that does not sound theologically tendentious. It is carefully rooted in the exactness of history. The action is enacted with legal precision. This could hardly be a fiction, for the grounds of the narration argue and are intended to argue against that. Thus there seems no reason for doubting the authenticity of the report.

As the report stands, it is an awesome moment in which to act. It is 588 B.C.E., just one miserable year before the final collapse of Judah. The inept Zedekiah is on the throne. The Babylonian armies are at the gates of the city. The prophet is imprisoned as a subversive agent. This is no time for a wager on the future. The word of YHWH with a promise acts in contradiction to every social possibility. It is a free word of hope, utterly underived from or linked to the current circumstances. It is on this word that Jeremiah stakes his life and future.

Jeremiah anticipates a divine command; it is as though he already knows that God's hope would not cave in to this hopelessness. The command comes from his cousin, and Jeremiah knows he must act, since he does not, even now, doubt the future. So he buys a plot of land just at the moment of disaster—surely a foolish investment. He is willing to bet against all historical circumstances.

As every hope dwindles, he purchases a piece of land for the future. He puts himself on the record as a hoper against circumstance. The basis for his action is an unprovable, unmeasured word that there will be a future underived from the present. This is incredible buoyancy, in which everything depends on the free word of God that is not supported by any visible prop. It takes enormous chutzpah to act in a concrete way toward the future when it is clear that the known present is about to end.

The basis for this boldness is articulated in vv. 16-25. Whether this comes from Jeremiah is debatable. But at the very least, it is an early reflection on the prophet's buoyant, defiant act. The only ground for such an act is the conviction that YHWH can do the "impossible"—create a future out of a hopeless present.

The reality of judgment is not denied. But the gamble is based on the rhetorical turn of v. 25: "Yet You." *Yet*—against the data. The reason for acting against the data is *You*. It is free, named, trusted, unrestricted You who makes buoyant hope possible. This You is the only warrant for action against all circumstance. Radicals who would not grow cynical must stay very close to this You, for whom nothing is too hard. Only then is there the prospect of a newness in this context of deep hopelessness.

But how do we stay close to this hope-giving You? That is the tricky question. Staying close under arrest, under siege, cannot be easy. One way might be to stay so close to such a triumphant God that one simply denies the trouble and looks to "alabaster cities . . . undimmed by human tears." But Jeremiah does not have such nerve, and YHWH is not that triumphant. And anyway, he is not dealing with alabaster cities, but only with troubled, fickle Jerusalem.

Rather Jeremiah stays close to YHWH in his articulation of pained, anguished, overwhelming despair. With good reason Jeremiah is known as the most troubled of the prophets. He aches and grieves, protests and rages. My point is simply that these "questionable" acts are Jeremiah's faithful way of staying close to YHWH. Indeed it is these actions that make the hope found in 32:1-15 possible and credible.

Here we can consider only one such articulation of despair. The poem of lament in chapters 8 and 9 provides a heavy, hurting glimpse at the prophet who does not flinch from all the darkness of reality. This sounds not just like a tired liberal, but a radical grown cynical with fatigue. It is hard to know if the speaker is Jeremiah or YHWH, for in v. 3 we have the divine verification. In any case, even if the words are those of the prophet, they reflect a deepness beyond the political convention. But it does not matter greatly who the speaker is, for Jeremiah has fully committed himself to the grief of God. The poem serves to express the grief of both the prophet and the God of the prophet.

The poem begins with a cry of hopeless hurt, sick of body and sick of spirit. The people had grown testy, wanting God to be a ready answer to every need. It is God's business to save—and God has not. The prophet (or God) is immobilized with grief. He sees deeply into the irreversibleness of things. He understands that conventional resources for rehabilitation have all been tried. And all have been found wanting. He slowly speaks his way to the horrendous conclusion: The sickness is terminal.

The prophet then violates every nicety, no longer giving to any the benefit of any doubt. He calls it as he sees it. Rottenness, falseness, treachery— an unending process of evil. He has hoped longest and best for his people.

He has such deep faith that he believed in Judah long after everyone else abandoned hope. But he cannot persuade even himself any longer.

So, he has two wishes, both utterly anguished. We do not know if they are serious wishes or only for rhetorical effect. But that does not matter. Either way, we are confronted by a man who is betrayed for having hoped too long, too passionately, too unreasonably. He wants first to have adequate crying equipment, to be up to the task of grief that is now thrust upon him. His tear ducts and eyes are inadequate for his grief. This is undisciplined, unstructured, unlimited grief. Second, he wants to escape it all, for the whole plight of Judah is not really his problem.

The last line of v. 3 gives pause. Psychologically this should be the voice of Jeremiah. But the Hebrew texts make it the speech of YHWH.

Jeremiah brings YHWH's thought to speech. Despair is not only pervasive on earth, it has reached heaven. God can think of no way out. God has no thoughts about a newness, but only a dissolving of all reality into tears. If this be the speech of God, then God also is ready to pack up, for Judah is by now no longer his concern or problem either. Because Judah is so unresponsive, this people is not only prophet-forsaken, it is now also God-forsaken.

Jeremiah is competent beyond reason in bringing grief to speech. God stands with and for and among all those prophetic types who have bet too much, hoped too long, risked too greatly. And now they have had to face reality. No wonder the professional mourners must now be summoned (9:17-19). The grief work now to be done requires the best experts available.

Now we can consider the strange juxtaposition these two texts offer us. The grief of the poem (8:18—9:3) is unqualified. It reaches the person of the poet. But it also touches the person of YHWH. It is, taken by itself, surely an act of unqualified despair. It is the voice of a radical who is now broken. The hope found in chapter 32 is also unqualified. It compels the person of the prophet. But it clearly comes from the speech of YHWH. It is, taken as it stands, an act of bold hope.

The lament of the poem provides a glimpse of the broken heart of God. The promise in chapter 32 opens the buoyant, expectant heart of God. In both, Jeremiah has been very near to God, near in despair and near in buoyancy.

The deep hope of the promise, perhaps, is how we would like to be. But as our society drifts toward its death, we find ourselves smitten with the cancer, helpless and astonished that our people do not know. We might like to speak the hope of Jeremiah. But we find ourselves more drawn to the honesty of his despair.

In these two pieces we meet the buoyancy and despair of the prophet, this one who believes so powerfully and yet who sees so clearly. How could these belong together? Is this juxtaposition of texts at all a responsible one? More is at stake than a critical, literary question. More is at stake than the matter of psychological possibility. What is at issue is how a griever can be a hoper.

I submit that holding these two texts together may be our most important agenda in our societal context. The vision of the promise cannot be abandoned because we are charged with a vision and cannot renege. But the poet of grief cannot be silent, for the word burns to be spoken. Our problem is how to hope so convincedly and yet to discern so deeply at the same time.

Of course there are several safe ways of handling this juxtaposition by disposing of it. One is to say the second text, the promise, is not from Jeremiah. I suggest, however, that the texts do indeed reflect the same person. The narrative of 32:1-15 has about it sure marks of being the person of Jeremiah.

Another way is to observe the chronological distance between the two texts. That is, even if they come from the same person, they are separated by as much as a decade. This is altogether possible. I suggest that the articulations of despair and buoyancy are not to be dated in isolation from each other, as though in one decade Jeremiah despairs and in the next decade he is buoyant. More plausibly, these two statements reflect abiding tendencies in Jeremiah, who is persistently a man of despair and buoyancy.

A third way is to observe that our two texts are related as private despair and public hope. There is something in that. The poetry of Jeremiah 8:18—9:3 may or may not be public. It may well be a personal reflection shared only intimately. The texture of this poetry is nevertheless contrasted with the quite public presentation of 32:1-15. In any case, we can readily see that despair is indeed a more intimate matter.

So perhaps we have a poet who had grave doubt and misgiving, and who lived with these constantly, but who managed to keep a composed public face on things. Though smitten with despair, he kept his public articulations focused on buoyancy. If that is true, we still may wonder about the resources that permitted and generated such a buoyant, public articulation of hope. There must be some genuine basis for it.

Thus none of these three possibilities finally removes the strangeness of this juxtaposition. And for bewildered or disheartened radicals, that juxtaposition is well worth noting. The same speaker knows about an awesome despair and a confirmed buoyancy. The one does not negate the other. In the very midst of a realistic despair that sees life in its rawness, there is nevertheless a word of hope. Despair does not override or drive out buoyancy but succeeds it and lives with it.

But I suggest an even more helpful dimension of this juxtaposition. Our question is how hope in 32:1-15 is possible in such a context of siege and imprisonment. The answer given provisionally is this: Such hope was possible because Jeremiah stayed close to the hope-giving You of 32:25. And in what way did he stay close?

The answer I submit is this: Jeremiah was able to continue to hope buoyantly in this You because he stayed close to the You in his articulation of despair. It is the embrace of and engagement with the hurt and forsakeness of 8:18—9:3 that permits Jeremiah to move on past despair to buoyancy. Indeed it is in the specific, concrete expression of despair that there come the seeds and possibilities of hope.

I conclude that tamed cynics and chastened radicals, if they are to continue their vision of an alternative world, must find concrete ways of giving voice to their despair that is likely also the despair of God. It is the utterance of the hopeless poem of 8:18—9:3 that creates the rhetorical, psychological, theological possibility of hope in 32:1-15.

Consider the alternative. If Jeremiah had not spoken the despair of 8:18—9:3, it would not have been verbalized anguish but would have become immobilizing, unexpressed rage. It would have stricken him and blocked any possibility of hope. Thus the despair of 8:18—9:3 is not the antithesis or denial of hope. It is an essential "door to hope" (see Hos. 2:15).

The poem speaks honestly to God. It speaks honestly for God. It speaks honestly about the human prospect. But human speech has this strange power: It liberates, brings to expression, releases, and permits movement beyond. After this speech of despair, neither YHWH nor Jeremiah is as fully despairing. They can move on to other things, free from the hopelessness of the human prospect and freed for the "new thing" from God.

Out of this I submit a liberating juxtaposition for radicals who can move in and through and beyond despair to a new buoyancy. On the one hand, there is need for concrete, public acts of hope, public risks for newness, and public assault on conventional hopelessness. That is the meaning of the land-buying in 32:1-15, which is based only on God's surprising, unadministered word. This word is neither besieged by Babylon nor imprisoned by Zedekiah.

On the other hand, and prerequisite to the concrete public act of hope, is the pathos-filled expression of despair. Both Jeremiah and God engaged in that despair. Would-be radicals, who are sobered by the human prospect, must fully grieve and lament the emptiness of the human prospect. Only then is the new word of hope given or received.

So I argue it is the grief of Jeremiah that is the ground of hope. It is the pained word that precedes the anticipatory word. It is liturgy that grounds public action.

If radicals, tired or otherwise, cling to human prospects or are unable to release despair into speech, then there are no new hopes and the promise is dead. Jeremiah (and Jeremiah's God) understood the strange dynamic of fully speaking as the way of full surrender and liberation. Speechless radicals are bound to be hopeless radicals, left only with their wishes, stridency, and coercion. Grief-filled speech permits hope-filled action.

Prophets and Historymakers

History—and how it's made—is a question I got into some time ago when I went to a PTA meeting for my son who was in fifth grade at the time. I knew it was going to be a big night because, when I walked in, the teacher was wearing a white suit and walking around with a baton. In time the reason became evident: the fifth graders were doing a choral reading.

The choral reading turned out to be a review of American history. One fifth grader got up and said, "George Washington was the father of our country." Another said, "Thomas Jefferson wrote the Declaration of Independence." Another said, "Abraham Lincoln freed the slaves." After each of these statements, the baton got waved, and all the fifth graders said, "And America goes on forever; and America goes on forever."

I got to thinking what my tax dollars were going for—and what my son was learning about American history. He was learning two things. First, he was learning that history is made by officeholders who have public positions of power and who were then and mostly still are now white males. History is made by white men who hold public office. And the other thing he was learning is that American history is absolute history. It is ultimate history, for it goes unto perpetuity.

Through many people, perhaps most visibly Alex Haley, we are learning that there's an alternate mode of history. It's history made by people who have suffered, who have never held office, who have never been saluted in any PTA recital. It has to do with nameless blacks, nameless women, and nameless people of all kinds whose main contribution is that they suffered with hope.

The nicest thing about this notion of history is that I have at last been able to remove Millard Fillmore, James Buchanan, and some more recent occupants of the White House from my list of historymakers.

Though these nameless histories never got into the textbooks, they survived. And not only did they survive in spite of being censored for so long, but they are even now surfacing in ways that assault and critique and undermine the dominant ideological notion of history. That's remarkable.

I

I've been thinking lately about what I teach seminarians about history, meaning the history of ancient Israel, which is more or less my specialty. (Now *that's* history.)

The first thing I teach them is the time line: "You must know the time line." Teaching Israelite history is wonderful for a time line because all the kings ruled one at a time in a straight row. It's like studying English history: All the monarchs ruled one after another, not like German history, where all those princes were ruling at the same time.

The time line goes like this: Josiah was a great king, but he died too quickly. Jehoiakim was his son, and he lasted three months (he reminds me of Millard Fillmore or Gerald Ford). This son of Josiah, Jehoiakim, lasted eleven years and was a very bad king, though he died a good death. Upon the death of Jehoiakim, his son Jehoiachin, who lasted three months before having the misfortune of living thirty-seven years in exile. Then came Jehoiachin's uncle Zedekiah, who spent eleven years on the throne. The last thing Zedekiah saw was his sons being killed before his eyes, then they poked his eyes out.

Those are the historymakers. It's a pretty impressive list. If you read the book of Kings uncritically, you would think that it was *about* the kings. But I believe the book of Kings ought to be named Kings not because it is interested in the kings but because it knows that kings are definitionally *not* historymakers.

I can imagine that somewhere in the middle of this time line, down at the PTA in Jerusalem, there were fifth graders saying, "And Jerusalem goes on forever; and Jerusalem goes on forever." The terrible thing about time lines is that the last monarchs on them never know they're the last. There will be a last American president, a last pope, a last seminary, a last magazine, a last everything. When you get too absorbed in the time line, you lose all perspective.

Another thing I teach seminarians is that you must learn the headlines. You must learn the stuff that was printed in the paper in Nineveh and in Jerusalem. Take Jeremiah, a person I've been particularly looking at lately. He lived at a time of *incredible* headlines. Not many people get to watch it like Jeremiah did—and like we do. In one generation, in fifty years, the Assyrian Empire was at its peak—and disappeared. Within ten years, the Babylonian Empire, which came from nowhere, controlled the whole Fertile Crescent.

History really does have to do with the rise and fall of kingdoms and empires and nations and nation-states—and large concentrations of power. But those of us who gather around the Bible learn, if we pay any attention, not to pay too much attention to those headlines and time lines.

My thesis is this: According to the Bible, history is primarily made by voices of marginality who have tongues to bring hurt and hope to speech. A city or a nation does not consist in a collage of officeholders. It consists of all those unnoticed conversations that are imaginative conversations— about people who are in touch with their pain and through their pain arrive at human possibility. What we have to learn to do in the church, after the manner of Jesus of Nazareth, is to *participate* in those conversations of marginality.

Back in the time of Jeremiah, the true historymakers were not Josiah or Jehoiakim or Zedekiah, or even Nebuchadrezzar or Sennacherib or Ashurbanipal. The true historymaker, the Bible would have us believe, was Jeremiah, the voice of marginality who creates new historical possibilities.

Here we have to get free of all liberal notions of prophetic ministry as going out and whacking people with criticisms. Real prophetic ministry has to do with having tongue enough to make the hurt and the hope of the human community available.

Historymakers, I submit, are first of all people who have imaginative and poetic playfulness, who can talk about the incongruity and pathos that is present in the human community. Second, historymakers are not overly impressed with official forms of power. They believe the real stuff of history is breaking out underneath that—in ways the dominant ideology does not even notice.

Whenever historymakers like Jeremiah do their work, they come face to face with history stoppers. These are the folks who want to silence the poetry and keep the pain from being noticed and close everything down. So it is the work of the historymakers to dis-close, un-close, reveal, and make available.

II

Having said that, I would like to explore with you now five theses that I have either read out of or into Jeremiah—the reader may be the judge of that—about Jeremiah as a historymaker.

First, Jeremiah and all real historymakers have a profound sense of anguish, pathos, and incongruity that touches the historymaker quite personally. Now I know all about the futility of the historical quest for Jeremiah, the impossibility of recovering the full chronology of his life, and all those other critical things we like to debate in seminaries. But what really strikes me when I read the book of Jeremiah is the poetry of a man who is in grief. "Woe is me, my mother, that you bore me," he says in chapter 15. "I have not lent; I have not borrowed. Yet they all pick on me all the time." And in chapter 12 we find this incredible statement of anguish, "Why does the way of the wicked prosper?" Once that question has been spoken, it cannot be unspoken. "Why do we live in a world that doesn't work out equitably?" He lives this reality. He lives it in his body.

Even more poignant is the poem in chapter 4 where our bourgeois translations begin, "My anguish, my anguish. . . ." Commentators tell us that more authentically it reads, "My bowels, they twist in pain! The walls of my heart—my heart is beating wildly. I cannot keep silent. Listen, do you hear the sound of the trumpets? The armies are moving—and you don't notice! I'm the only one who hears the trumpets. Disaster follows hard on disaster; the whole land is laid waste. Tents are destroyed, my curtain in a moment. How long must I watch and see that enemy army? My people are foolish; they are stupid; they do not understand anything!"

Jeremiah has this shameless capacity to bring to speech his trembling body. He gives voice to the terror he feels about his city being burned up even when nobody else seems to notice.

Second, Jeremiah, like every serious historymaker, believes in the moral coherence of the world. The world, these historymakers believe, is not a technical operation in which might makes right. The world is governed by nonnegotiable realities of justice and righteousness, truth and order, and it will not be mocked.

It's absurd, of course. All the data argue against it. Because we live in a society that believes might and technique and knowledge and intimidation and self-interest and brutality and pragmatism and ideality have their way, it gets harder and harder to stand up in public to say that. But you'll never be a historymaker unless you believe what Jeremiah believed. You will only be led to cynicism and resignation.

Jeremiah dares to hold to his belief against all the data. So he has God say in chapter 4, "If you will return, if you will remove your abominations and swear in truth and justice and righteousness, then the nations will be blessed." And in chapter 7, which sounds like it was written yesterday, "If you truly exercise justice, if you do not oppress the alien"—isn't *that* interesting—"or the widow or shed innocent blood or go after other gods, then I'm going to let you keep your land." And the implication is that if you don't, I won't.

What do you think? Do you think we're in process of losing the land?

In chapter 5, Jeremiah quotes God as saying, "How can I pardon you? Do you think I'm going to forgive you? I fed my people to the full; yet they committed adultery. They were well-fed stallions, each neighing for his neighbor's wife. Should I not punish them for this? Everyone is greedy for unjust gain; everyone deals falsely. They heal the wounds of my people lightly, shouting, 'Peace, peace,' when there is no peace." And then Jeremiah adds this incredible statement: "Were they ashamed when they committed abomination? No, they were not at all ashamed; they did not know how to blush."

I've been thinking that church education ought to be teaching people how to blush. To blush over Grenada, to blush over Libya, to blush over Iraq, to blush over unemployment, to blush over the rip-off that goes in the name of opportunity. We who would be historymakers have to ask what has happened to our sense of the moral coherence of the world when we no longer can be ashamed about anything. We who would be historymakers must have the wisdom—and faith—to see that righteousness will win out.

Does anyone imagine that there are enough U.S. bombs to crush local traditions in Iraq? Does anyone entertain the thought that there is enough U.S. hunger for oil to silence the moral power of the disinherited in Venezuela? "Oh, my people are foolish! They do not know me; they are stupid; they have no understanding."

Third, Jeremiah, like every serious historymaker—see if this is an overstatement—asserts the raw rule of God's sovereignty. Now I want to tell anyone who is all hyped on meeting the needs of the poor and oppressed, you must be a critical theologian. We're not talking about a social work movement. We're talking about the move of a sovereign God in the social process. Until we gain a deep and personal awareness of that, we haven't a chance in the world of being historymakers.

Canvass the globe for every movement of freedom and justice, if you will, and you'll find everyone fed, in one way or another, by the church—and by the peasants who gather around the gospel. Maybe in China, maybe in Russia, maybe in officially secularized societies it isn't so, but I doubt it.

It does seem to me, out of the strange poems in the book of Jeremiah, that the freedom of God is something we will have to recover on our bourgeois lips. The theological issue must be joined against privatism, against personalism, against immanentism, against spiritualism. Jeremiah really could do that. He knew, as we need to know, that historymakers cannot appeal to an anemic God who is a good buddy or a warm fuzzy. This God is not a God to be "experienced."

In chapter 4, he tells us, "A lion has gone off to destroy the nations, a lion has gone forth from its place to make your land a waste. Gird yourself with sackcloth, for the fierce anger of God has not turned back." And then Jeremiah, this hallucinating poet, takes his listeners into a zoo. "Therefore," he says in chapter 5, "a lion shall slay them, a wolf shall destroy them, a leopard is watching, and all who go out of the city shall be torn to pieces because of their transgressions." A lion, a wolf, a leopard—and all of them are nobody but God.

You can hardly do that in the American church. The only warrant for talking that way in the American church is that it's in the Bible. We really ought to stay close to the Bible—and to these poets who have the courage to talk about the raw sovereignty of God. When God is sovereign in such a raw way, history can be made, for only then are all other sociopolitical claims called into question.

Fourth, historymakers are not simply passionate poets, moral energizers, and dangerous theologians. Historymakers are people who are capable of engaging in serious, discerning social analysis. By and large, Americans and American history are incredibly naive about social analysis. How else does a given administration get away with what it gets away with? It's because people don't understand what's going on.

I think the reason we know nothing about social criticism is that as soon as you try to do social criticism somebody hollers, "Terrorism!" So I want to say to any who are in seminary, who are pastors, or who are lay leaders in your churches, you must insist on some classes and seminars that introduce and facilitate the categories of social analysis. Start them yourself if you have to, because we aren't going to be very good at historymaking until we learn how to read social policy and social ideology.

The coming of social analysis to scripture study is an extraordinary turn in theological education. The marvelous book *A Home for the Homeless*, by

John Elliot on 1 Peter, is an extraordinary case in point because 1 Peter talks about being aliens and sojourners and wanderers in the world.[1] And Elliot simply says, "Those are not metaphors: that's how it really was!" See, you let the folks into your house because they haven't got any place to stay. . . .

We are having to learn to reread the Bible, and when we learn to reread the Bible, we learn to reread the historical process around us. Maybe that's part of what makes Jeremiah such an uncommon social critic. He has made a decision about where the historical process is moving, and he is uncompromising in his conviction that the historical process is moving toward Babylon. So get out of the way, he says. If you resist, you're going to die.

Jeremiah even has YHWH say—can you imagine God saying this?— "Blessed be Nebuchadrezzar, my servant." Jeremiah figured out that the great threat from the other side of the Fertile Crescent was the move of God's will. That wasn't idle speculation. It was sound social analysis, rooted in passionate theological reflection. The great theological question we now need to be probing is, where is history moving? Clearly U.S. policymakers believe that history is moving us all toward the Persian Gulf in pursuit of oil. But like those ancient policymakers, such notions may misread what in fact is going on in the historical process.

But like Jeremiah, when we ask our theological questions about where history is moving, we need to probe for what matters. Chapter 22, in which Jeremiah tauntingly addresses the king, presumably Jehoiakim, is one of the most remarkable texts in the Bible. Jeremiah asks, "Do you think you're a king because you have cedar?" Or, to put the question in translation, Do you think you're a president because you've got a paneled office? Do you think you are learned because you've got a briefcase? Do you think you are important because you've got a limousine?

However you translate it, Jeremiah is raising the question, "What constitutes power?" And this voice from below knows that paneled offices and limousines and press conferences and briefcases and laptop computers are not it.

"Consider your father," he says. "He took care of the poor and the needy, and then it was well with him. That's what makes one a king." Jeremiah wants to add, "If you don't take care of poor people, you're not a king." Jesus knew that. In Luke 7, John the Baptist sends and asks, "Are you truly God and truly Man according to the Council of Chalcedon?" And Jesus says, "I am not going to engage in that kind of Hellenistic fantasy. Go tell

John, the blind see, the lame walk, the lepers are cleansed, the dead are raised, and the poor have their debts canceled. Go tell John I'm taking care of these people—so what do you think?"

Jeremiah and Jesus, like every historymaker before and since—they knew the meaning of social analysis.

Fifth, I do not understand it, but historymakers are relentlessly filled with hope. They know that the coming of the kingdom of justice and righteousness may tarry, but they know it will not be defeated. You cannot reduce faith to sociology or psychology and come out with hope. That's why we need to be having conversations in our homes and churches and schools and everywhere else about whether this stuff is true—about these promises that hover in the midst of history.

Maybe that's why Jeremiah, in that great chapter 29, writes a letter to the exiles. "Just settle down and start living there," he says. "There isn't going to be any return to normalcy—and don't believe all these royal fantasies." But then he has God say, "I know the plans that I have for you, plans for *shalom*"—now it's very interesting that before it became a dirty word, the Revised Standard Version translated *shalom* here as "welfare"—"plans for welfare and not for evil, to give you a future and a hope. You will call upon me and come and pray, and I will hear you. You will seek me, and you will find me. I will be found by you, and I will restore you. I will bring you back to your place, from which I exiled you."

The book of Jeremiah moves in these chapters to the unarguable affirmation and conviction that God will do a new thing and that God will finally keep God's promise. That kind of faith lives simply by the preaching and the singing of the church, nothing else.

Similarly in chapter 24 there is this strange business about good figs and bad figs—and God doesn't give a fig for any of them. But what the chapter finally affirms is that these marginal, disinherited, disenfranchised exiles are the wave of God's future. God's eye is on these folks. And God will one day make them the restored community of faith.

III

Here, I would suggest, is enough for any church's curriculum, any seminary's course of study. Here is a theology to keep us from losing our faith and growing cynical, given the mission to which we are called: One, the capacity for anguish, pathos, and incongruity, which we take into our very own persons. Two, a confidence in the moral coherence of the world that is not negotiable. Three, assertion of the raw sovereignty of a God who will not fit into our schemes. Four, the capacity for discerning social analysis and criticism. And, five, the bold conviction of hope that God will not quit until God has done God's thing.

You will notice that all five of these affirmations are easily transferable to Jesus. And you will notice that all five are subversive and unacceptable to the rulers of this age. Yet we have this strange invitation, all over scripture, that we should be historymakers—and that we should notice the history-makers, that we should celebrate and uphold historymakers, even when we ourselves do not have the courage to be historymakers.

I invite you to compile a list of your own historymakers, people you can think of from whom we draw energy and courage—and the capacity to exegete. I think of people like Rosa Parks, whose feet were tired but whose soul was not. So she didn't move to the back—and thereby set in motion a new epic of history. It is not difficult to identify some of the recent makers of history, among them Lech Walesa, Nelson Mandela, and Václav Havel; in each case the force of the empire was against them, but each time they prevailed, because the historical process is not finally controlled by violent power.

I think of Betty Williams and Mildred Corrigan in Belfast who simply said, "It's enough. We mothers can bridge the quarrels and stop the killing." I think of Anwar Sadat, who opened a new era of history in the Mideast and lost his life because of it.

The historymakers are not the great public figures who get on the *Tonight Show*. They are hidden people, often unnoticed people, operating with an incredible dimension of freedom. I will tell you about one, one I have discovered. I leave it to you to name others.

I remember a practicing psychiatrist in Atlanta who, at the age of eighty-six, became concerned that the state of Georgia was, in effect, dumping people out of its mental hospitals onto the streets of Atlanta. So she took her concern to the session of her suburban Presbyterian church. She said to the session, "Don't you think we ought to do something?" And they solemnly voted, "You can if you want to." So she did, and soon she was feeding a hundred and fifty people a week. In taking on that kind of task, in making that kind of life statement, she mobilized other people in her congregation around the problem.

IV

I don't care whether you're a pastor, a student, a lay leader, or just an ordinary Christian. All of this has do to with how you shape your ministry, how you articulate your theology. It also has to do with how you attend PTA meetings and it has to do with how you read your Bible. We must all begin reading our Bibles as historymakers, *noticing* the historymakers.

The tragedy of the church is that it has so many people who read their Bibles as history *stoppers*. I understand history to be an honest conversation about redistribution of power. And I find, whether it's with my family, my colleagues, or my students, that that's really the only conversation that matters. It sometimes *seems* to be about curriculum, premarital sex, or family budget. But it always turns out to be about the redistribution of power, the Dick Cheneys of this world—and they can be found in every faculty, church, and family—don't want the conversation to go on because they've already got the power distributed just about the way they would like it.

The voice of the gospel, of Jesus, of scripture, is the affirmation that the conversation must be continued until the kingdom comes. If the conversation is not continued and kept open, we're going to die.

A friend of mine went to EPCOT Center, the great "World of Tomorrow" fantasy center in Florida. There he saw the marvels of technology that are to be ours in the next generation. "There isn't anything here about the Politics of Tomorrow," he commented to one of the managers. "Of course not," he manager replied, innocently. "That's too messy. We don't want anything messy in the World of Tomorrow."

Making history is messy business. Historymakers walk outside, out beyond our nightmares of repression and hate and revenge. Historymakers walk as though it were light, pursuing new human possibilities. Jeremiah anticipates where we will be walking when he says, "The day is coming when there will be a new covenant. Everybody from the greatest to the least will know the Torah. Everybody will want to obey." And then God says, "I will remember your sin no more."

We live in the promises that injustice and unrighteousness will finally be nullified; all God's children will live in praise and joy.

Blessed, I say, are the historymakers.

CHAPTER FIFTEEN

Why Prophets Won't Leave Well Enough Alone

An Interview with Walter Brueggemann

I. *What does it mean to be a prophet?*

Initially, a prophet is simply a poetic figure who stands outside the mainstream of public power and exposes what's going on. The prophets are people who feel pain and are enormously sensitive to what the public processes are doing to others, and they seem to have amazing rhetorical imagination to get their message said in compelling ways.

In the Old Testament, the prophets in one way or another are propelled by the vision of Moses—of Exodus and Mount Sinai—and insist that the liberation of Exodus and the Commandments of Mount Sinai are a way to organize public policy. Now, that's a big argument because one can easily make the case that the Exodus and the Commandments are idealistic and romantic that and people can't really organize anything seriously that way. So in the Old Testament a prophet is always the counterpart of a king. Kings want to organize public power without reference to the human dimension. The prophets keep insisting that if the king organizes public power without reference to the human dimension, he is going to bring death on himself and a lot of other people. Thus for the prophets, talk of God always carries with it socioeconomic-political talk. You can't separate them.

II. *How does the prophet Jeremiah, for example,*
fit into this description?

Jeremiah is the most extreme case. Jeremiah is situated around the crisis of 587 B.C.E., which is the time when Jerusalem was destroyed, the temple was burned, the king was exiled, and everything came to a crashing end.

Jeremiah is the poet who both anticipates that crisis and after the crisis tries to help people see how to get along without the establishment. So he is a poet of critique and hope.

The assumption in Jeremiah's time was that the kings in David's line were guaranteed a blank check by God: They could do anything they wanted to do and everything would be wonderful. Against this assumption, Jeremiah speaks out of the tradition of Moses, which says that if you don't do the right thing, you're going to die.

The amazing thing about Jeremiah is that, with some few exceptions, he doesn't have any advice to give anybody. He doesn't discuss particular policy questions. What he does instead is use a rich variety of images and metaphors, many alluding to marriage and divorce and illness, to try to cut underneath policy questions to help people see that the practices of the monarchy in Jerusalem will bring death. He keeps his poetry a little bit at a distance from the issues and assumes that his listeners can make the connections.

There was an exchange like that between the great Protestant minister William Sloane Coffin and Henry Kissinger during the Vietnam War. Coffin was attacking U.S. government policy about the war and Kissinger said to him something along these lines: "If you're so smart, why don't you tell us what to do in Vietnam." And Coffin in his usual high-handed way said, "Mr. Secretary, my job is to say to you, 'Let justice roll down like mighty waters.' Your job is to get the plumbing in place."

So the prophet doesn't worry about the specifics of policy. What the prophet wants to do is to have the people in power imagine reality differently on the bet that if they imagine the reality differently, they'll be able to think of policies to work it out.

III. *What was Jeremiah's role in society? Did he have the king's ear?*

That's in dispute. He certainly is not like Isaiah. Isaiah had a key to the Pentagon, so to speak; he was in the councils of power. Jeremiah's situation is much more ambiguous than that. In Jeremiah 7, it says that he preached at the temple door. What we don't know is whether that was a place where official speakers spoke or whether he just walked up and started talking.

What's clear is that because he did this he was arrested, had a trial, and the leaders wanted to execute him. He seems to have been saved by a very powerful family. After Jeremiah was saved, he had to go into hiding and ended up in a cistern where he was punished. So his life as it is reported ends in a miserable failure. The life of the prophet is always problematic because he or she is attempting to speak truth to power.

IV. *Is there any sense that Jeremiah is vindicated?*

One can see in retrospect that Jeremiah's way of talking was vindicated because what he said metaphorically did work itself out in terms of the Babylonian captivity. And it does seem that there was a group of people who paid attention to him and who, after the whole crisis, remembered him and preserved his words because they believed he was telling the truth and that his words were transferable to other situations. That's probably how Jeremiah got into the Bible. But I don't think there were many people while he was living who thought Jeremiah was a great man. I think they thought he was a nut.

V. *What were some of the abuses Jeremiah and the other prophets spoke out against?*

There are two ways in which the abuses are talked about. One is in terms of religious rhetoric: "The people went whoring after other gods." In other words, the problem was idolatry. The other way to look at it is from the perspective that all talk about God is in part socioeconomic-political talk. So "whoring after other gods" is seen to mean having bad socioeconomic-political policies. In other words, the problem was the practice of injustice within the central urban government in Jerusalem. The king just didn't give a damn anymore about what was happening to the peasants.

Some scholars believe that particularly Micah and Jeremiah are really spokespersons for the peasant interest and what they are attacking is agri-business, where the big banks in Jerusalem are buying up all the land, displacing people, and creating a poverty class. It all sounds very familiar, doesn't it? Of course, the Mosaic tradition of the Ten Commandments says that you can't treat people that way. Prophetic speech is always in a lawsuit form and consists of an indictment and a sentence. The indictment says to the accused, "You broke the Torah by your practice of injustice"; and the sentence is something like, "The Babylonians are going to invade and destroy you."

Now the Babylonian King Nebuchadrezzar and the Babylonian army didn't know of or care about the Torah. What they cared about was getting another colony and getting access to the Mediterranean. So their invasion seemingly had nothing to do with policies in Jerusalem. The prophet makes connections that nobody else would make. Saying that the cause is internal and related to justice and that the result is an external invasion would be like saying that the cause is the abuse of blacks in our inner cities and the result is the terrible defeat in Vietnam. Now who would think that racist policies in the United States would produce a defeat in Southeast Asia? To say that world history revolves around the question of justice is an extraordinary argument. And Jeremiah learned that from Moses.

VI. *Does this go back to what you said about talk about God always being socioeconomic-political talk?*

Yes, and it comes from Karl Marx, who says in his "Paris Manuscripts" that the criticism—and by criticism he means careful thought—of heaven becomes the criticism of earth. The criticism of religion becomes the criticism of law. The criticism of theology becomes the criticism of politics. What he's saying is that talk about God, if you pay any attention to it, is talk about public policy.

For example, the Old Testament prophets are regularly attacking Baal, the god of the Canaanites. Canaanite, by the way, is not an ethnic term; the word *Canaanite* means "people who practice sharp, exploitive economics and politics." Baal, their god, then, is the guy who legitimates exploitive economic practice. YHWH, the God of the Exodus, is the God who cares about freedom and justice. The religious conflict is between Baal and YHWH, but that really means there's a policy conflict between the things that these two gods care about. Baal cares more about advantage for the privileged, and YHWH cares about egalitarian economics.

Now, unlike Marx, I do not think that all talk about God is mere socioeconomic-political talk. I'm a believer, so I also believe that talk about YHWH really is talk about YHWH. But YHWH is not just a generic God. YHWH has disclosed YHWH's self as a God who cares about justice. So that when you hear the word *YHWH*, you have to hear justice, righteousness, and faithfulness. We must understand the connection religion has with public policies. People would like to have YHWH as their God and Baal's economic program. It doesn't work that way.

There's a very nice passage in Jeremiah 22 that has God, through Jeremiah, comparing two kings, father and son, Josiah and Jehoiakim. Jehoiakim was a bad king who ripped off poor people. He's accused of spending his time building cedar houses—cedar being a metaphor for enormous luxury—trying to prove his rank among kings. His father, Josiah, on the other hand, was a really good guy. King Josiah did what was "right and just." And God says, "Because he dispensed justice to the weak and the poor, it went well with him." Then God asks, "Is this not true knowledge of me?" That's an extraordinary comment: knowing God means caring for the poor and the needy. The passage doesn't say if you know God, you will care for the poor. It doesn't say if you care for the needy, you will get to know God. It says that caring for the poor and needy *is* the act of knowing God.

VII. *Did the prophets think that God was dreaming up bad things to happen to kings who were unjust?*

What they were trying to say is that the whole process of public history is of a piece, and that God is working through all of it, including those parts where the players have never even heard of YHWH. So in the book of Jeremiah, two times King Nebuchadrezzar, who is the big Babylonian emperor, is called by YHWH, "Nebuchadrezzar my servant." The argument is that everybody, including all the kings of the whole world, are really servants of YHWH's larger purposes.

The prophets argue that one can change God's purpose or change God's way of implementing the future if one acts differently. That is to say that human conduct matters to how God is going to issue the future.

So in Jeremiah 18, YHWH says, "If that nation which I have threatened turns from its evil, I also repent of the evil which I threatened to do"—which means that God is not immutable, that we do not live in a closed, fixed, unchangeable cosmos, and that the historical process is a process of endless transactions between human persons, who are capable of change, and God, who is capable of change at the behest of human change. Prophetic faith insists that human choice and human policymaking is of decisive importance.

VIII. *What was the purpose of prophets when there were no more kings and the Israelites were living in exile?*

After the Babylonian captivity began in 587 B.C.E., the function of the prophet was no longer to criticize the arrogance of the king; now the function of the prophet is to address the despair of the community and to speak hope. In Isaiah 55, which is a well-known text, the poet has God saying, "My ways are not your ways, and your thoughts are not my thoughts." That is to say, "I've got an entirely different notion about this whole thing than you do." The people's notion as near as we can tell was: "We are fated to live in Babylon forever." It must have been the kind of feeling that the Lithuanians had: "We're going to live in the Soviet Union forever."

In Isaiah, when God says, "My ways are not your ways," scholars think that he was talking about the Persian king Cyrus, who overthrew Nebuchadrezzar and had a very different policy from Nebuchadrezzar. Cyrus let all the deported people go home and simply had them pay taxes because he felt that it was too costly to keep people under surveillance. That was simply Persian foreign policy. But in Isaiah 45, like the passage in Jeremiah, the poet has God calling Cyrus, "my anointed," and the word for anointed is *messiah*. So the prophets in exile are saying to the community, "Relax. There's a lot going on to save you even through the characters themselves who do not understand that they're playing out YHWH's purposes."

IX. *So are people manipulated by God?*

No, I wouldn't say manipulated; but on this point the Bible mumbles. It's the age-old talk of the riddle of predestination and free will. It's hard to work it out logically, but one way to say it is that Cyrus decided to do these things for reasons of realpolitik, in accordance with his free will. Then YHWH said, after the fact, "Oh, I think I can use that for my purposes."

You have to remember that this is not logical thought, this is poetry. And the thing about poetry is that it can put things together that you would never put together in a syllogism. So it is an oxymoron to say, "Cyrus, my anointed." But just listen to the poetry—the poetry precludes all of those kinds of questions we would like to ask to get things sorted out. In my own judgment, the reason churches are in such bad shape these days is that they do not understand that their main claims can only be expressed in poetic language. As soon as you try to become explanatory, it's absurd.

X. *So when Isaiah spoke of Israel's coming freedom,*
the people were saying, "What are you talking about, Isaiah?
We're stuck here in the middle of Babylon.
What's your plan to get us free?"

That's exactly right. There's a wonderful passage in Isaiah 45:9-10, in which the poet is responding to a comment not in the text that must have been something like, "I don't want to be delivered by a gentile, and if I've got to be delivered by a gentile, I'm going to stay in exile." The poet says, "Dare the clay to say to its modeler, 'What are you doing?' or 'What you are making has no hands'?" No, the clay just keeps turning and taking shape. That metaphor is God saying, "I'm the potter. Don't you question me about what I'm doing to save you, just get moving." In some hidden, indiscernible way God is indeed working good for his exiled people. But they must understand that they don't have God under control.

XI. *So prophets tell us to imagine a just society.*
Is that more than simply daydreaming?

It is daydreaming. But that doesn't make it false. Since John Locke we really have assumed that speech is mere description of reality, and reality sits there no matter how you say it. That's not true, in my opinion, nor do prophets or poets think it's true. What I believe is true is that social reality is generated, shaped, and driven by speech. So obviously if you've got dull, conventional, routinized speech, reality is going to shrivel to the status quo. The only alternative to the status quo is the kind of adrenalin-laden speech that can imagine and push beyond the status quo.

If you ask who is capable of that kind of speech, I'd say on the whole, if you look around the world, the people who engage in that kind of speech are people who are suffering. So in South Africa and Latin America, the liberation movements have been generated and driven by speech. Mainline Christian churches today, however, have so much to defend in terms of social position and privilege that their speech is largely domesticated. For example, I'll speak from my tradition. If you look at a Protestant sermon, which is really an art form, the domestication plays itself out in long sermon introductions. What long sermon introductions do is present a clever illustration of something that doesn't illustrate anything. The rhetorical purpose of it is to assure the congregation that nothing is going to be said that will upset them. The first sentence of a sermon ought to jar the congregation and put the congregation on notice that "I am not going to talk about anything that fits anything you thought before you came." That usually doesn't happen.

XII. *Are preachers supposed to be prophets?*

Well, I think that evangelical preaching, meaning preaching of the gospel, at least has the potential of being prophetic. There is more to it than that, no doubt; and there are other roles to play and voices to sound. But it always is potentially open for the good news of criticism and hope.

I would like to say that although I'm not romantic about black preaching, good black preaching is much more capable of that poetic stuff. The genre of black preaching permits that. But I assume that most good black preachers have much more access to suffering and hope, and therefore the word is not so domesticated.

XIII. *What about Jesus? Was he a prophet?*

It seems to me that it is right to say that the prophet's mission is to insist that there is another purpose surging through the historical process, and occasionally you can see that purpose if you pay attention—and that is exactly what Jesus' parables do. Like all good poets, Jesus knows you cannot talk about the message and mission directly. If you talk about it directly, you will ruin it. Prophets leave a lot to the imagination. So very often when Jesus told his parables, his disciples said, "What do you think he was talking about?" Jesus says, "Why don't you just think about it for a while." And of course we continue to unpack those parables even to this day.

XIV. *But do you see Jesus in the classic prophetic role of critiquing?*

Oh, yes. I don't have any doubt about that. His most direct criticism is in Matthew 23:23. When he says, "Woe to you, you hypocrites," that's religious talk he's engaging in. He says to the scribes and Pharisees, "You pay tithes of mint and dill and cumin, and have neglected the weightier things of the law; judgment and mercy and fidelity." Now that sounds exactly like Jeremiah. He says people are paying attention to the wrong things. In Luke 15:2, for example, the Pharisees say, "This man welcomes sinners and eats with them," which means he is consorting with not nice people. What Jesus is doing is legitimating these outcast people. He's saying, "These are genuine people in the social process, and you can't pretend that they don't exist."

Jesus is engaged in a sharp practice of social criticism, on the one hand, and social hope (for the losers in society), on the other. He wants to restore people to full participation in the public process. But with all of his critiques and visions of hope, there is also great sadness. Scholars now argue that all of this stuff in Matthew 23 about woe—and Jeremiah and Isaiah have some woes, too—isn't spoken as a threat or condemnation but as a lament. *Woe* is a funeral word. So Jesus and the prophets are not gloating over the death of Jerusalem, they're grieving. They are really sad that their beloved city has chosen the route to destruction.

XV. *But doesn't Jesus come out of the House of David, the royal line?*

In rereading the gospel stories Christians are realizing that Jesus is very uncomfortable with royal titles. He didn't like them; and in fact, he really understands himself primarily as a Torah teacher. Christians need to restore conversation with Jews so we can relearn from them what the Torah tradition is all about.

XVI. *What do you think we can learn from the Torah tradition? All that comes to mind are lists of rules and regulations.*

The Torah is the basis of the largest vision of a just human condition. The Ten Commandments are guidelines for how to maintain a human society. Now the other side of the Torah, which seems to be where your objection lies, is the discipline set out in the Torah by which the Israelites are to maintain their unique identity. Remember the great threat to Judaism was always assimilation. So the question for them was, "What daily disciplines do we need to keep from assimilating?" They settled on such things as circumcisions, Sabbath, kosher kitchens, and prayer tassels.

Those particular disciplines are not for me. But I do believe that assimilation into a consumer economy is the great threat to Christianity, so that from the Torah Christians can learn to ask, "What are the daily disciplines that will maintain our identity?" As soon as you talk about daily disciplines, you are inevitably coming very close to legalism because you're saying this is what you've got to do whether or not you understand it, like it, or feel like doing it—you've got to do it every day to remember who you are.

XVII. *Who are some modern-day prophets?*

We would probably all have something of the same list: Father Daniel Berrigan, Martin Luther King Jr., William Sloane Coffin. It is clear that a lot of prophetic figures are very local and not known among all of us. I am simply amazed at the number of people in local communities who run enormous risks regarding questions of justice and never get any publicity but get their share of abuse.

You can't really generalize, but I'd say all of those types are attentive to the concrete costs of dehumanization and are convinced that there is a larger, holy purpose to life that cannot be reduced to vested interests. These people may not articulate this idea very well, but they know enough to be able to say, "Folks, this is not right. We just can't go on this way. It's got to stop, or we're going to die."

That's what prophets do. They reimagine the human process according to the holy purposes of God, which sometimes functions as criticism and sometimes functions as enormous buoyancy in a situation of defeat and despair.

XVIII. *How can you spot a true prophet?*

The authors of Deuteronomy thought more about that problem than anybody. In Deuteronomy 18, it says the way you can tell a true prophet is
whether what the person says comes true. Well, that won't work. But in
Deuteronomy 13, it says the way you can tell true prophets is whether they
lead you into covenantal obedience; if they've led you away from the covenant, they're false. Now what I understand by covenant is the insistence
that we are woven into a common fabric—not only with God but with all
of our neighbors. And not only does that bind me to help my neighbor, it
says that I must receive my life from my neighbor.

I believe the large truth surrounding us today is that the white, male,
Western, colonial hegemony has collapsed by the mercy of God. The collapse of that hegemony means that we have a chance to reorganize and
reconfigure all social relationships. True prophets are prophets who act in
the direction of that collapse and are working at reorganizing social relationships, and false prophets are people who want to keep pretending that
they can jack up the white, male hegemony and keep it going. The pastoral
task, then, is to help people face the reality of the collapse and relinquish
those old assumptions of privilege, priority, and power.

XIX. *So when a pastor preaches that blacks and whites
should live together in harmony or men and women
should be treated equally, is he or she giving the congregation
specifics, such as hire more blacks and women?*

No, I wouldn't say so. Pastors as poets don't have the expertise to say that.
The pastor needs to say to the businessperson who is sitting there, "The
promise of the gospel is that lions and lambs shall eat together. To understand this poem you need to know that lions and lambs are metaphors.
They're not animals, they're metaphors for the big ones eating the little
ones. And the good news of the poem is that the time is over when the big
ones are going to eat the little ones."

So now it is the responsibility of the businesspeople to figure out how
that poem becomes employment policy. The preacher hasn't a clue about
that—that's the businessperson's problem—but the poem is truthful. My
inclination is to stay very close to the biblical text because businesspeople
don't need advice. What businesspeople need are some tools of metaphor

to imagine things differently. If you can imagine it differently, you can organize differently.

XX. *Isn't someone going to say to the pastor, "You have no business experience. Why should I listen to you?"*

It's an inevitable question. People want to believe that this poetry is unreality. Now the case that has to be made, which is very difficult to make, is that this poetry is not what's unreal. Why do you think the church for thousands of years has put so much effort into liturgy? What we're doing in liturgy, even if it's unintentional, is imaging the world differently. Through the liturgy we hope people will see what can come out of it to help reorganize the unreality outside the liturgy. We are really out of business as a church if we do not believe that the world enacted in the liturgy—the broken bread, the poured-out wine—is more real than the world out there. Otherwise, we're just engaging in an escapist fantasy.

I believe that what liturgy ought to do is put people in crisis and say, "This world is not like the world out there. And, my God, I have got to choose between them." But if the contrast isn't made sharp, no one is ever going to decide anything.

For a long time, establishment Christianity has thought that the claims of the gospel really fit hand-in-glove with the values of U.S. society—that this is a Christian nation. What's happening to us is that we're becoming increasingly aware that the claims of the gospel—that relationships are based on mutuality—are on a collision course with the dominant values of U.S. culture, which are premised on relationships of exploitation and based on consumerism.

XXI. *How can people adequately speak out against consumerism?*

We must hold up covenant over and against commodity. We live in a society where everything and everybody is turned into a commodity. Our neighbor becomes a commodity to be bought and sold and discarded. Now from the ground up, what biblical faith wants to argue is that you're never going to have enough commodities to be either safe or happy. You're going to have to look for your safety and your happiness somewhere else, namely in covenantal relationships.

A youth minister in a parish, for example, can raise the question, "Why do your kids go to the mall all the time? What are you looking for? Let me tell you something, what you're looking for ain't out there." It all boils down to baptism. We have been baptized, or initiated into a counterculture, a counter set of desires. What we say in baptism is that we renounce the vainglories of the world. We still may have a lust for them, but we have committed this public act of renunciation. We need to talk about what it means to have made such a renunciation. The church has available to it the freedom of imagination that is nowhere else permissible in our society. These conversations must be held because if they're not, our humanity is going to disappear.

XXII. *Can a Christian have a prophetic sense of grief and energy and hope and also have a big stake within the structure of the predominant culture?*

We are all a conundrum of compromises. I don't think there are many of us who are going to sort this out purely. It seems to me that there is great health in being able to name and acknowledge the compromises we make because only then can we change them or repent of them. And I could imagine someone, such as a politician, saying with great sensitivity, "I really can't live this way anymore. That may cause me to lose my office; but what the hell, I'm going to vote the way I understand my baptism." That's the Christian bet about liturgy and preaching—that it will insinuate itself into the imagination of laypeople and then they will make different kinds of decisions about the living of their lives.

The meeting of the Christian community is the meeting of the great compromisers. But our present practice of compromising is not the last thing in our lives. People must understand that the Christian life is a process. All of us can say to ourselves: "I've got more to do, and I've got more chances to make it different and make my compromises more life-giving. I can get a little more truth-telling in my life, a little bit at a time. And I'll see more clearly, and once in a while I'll get another cubit of courage and do something really good."

We have no right to imagine that we have committed the last adjudication because, believe me, we will be addressed again. We must be liberated from the powers of death on a daily basis. That is why I go to church and hear about Easter every week. I've got to hear it said one more time that death has been conquered and has no right to command me anymore.

Abbreviations

AB	Anchor Bible
AnBib	Analecta biblica
ANQ	*Andover Newton Quarterly*
BASOR	*Bulletin of the American Schools of Oriental Research*
BibInt	*Biblical Interpretation*
BWANT	Beiträge zur Wissenschaft vom Alten und Neuen Testament
BZAW	Beihefte zur Zeitschrift für die alttestamentliche Wissenschaft
CBQ	*Catholic Biblical Quarterly*
Dtr	Deuteronomist
EvT	*Evangelische Theologie*
FRLANT	Forschungen zur Religion und Literatur des Alten und Neuen Testaments
HSM	Harvard Semitic Monographs
ICC	International Critical Commentary
Int	*Interpretation*
JBL	*Journal of Biblical Literature*
JNSL	*Journal of Northwest Semitic Languages*
JSOT	*Journal for the Study of the Old Testament*
JSOTSup	Journal for the Study of the Old Testament Supplement Series
MT	Masoretic Text
OBT	Overtures to Biblical Theology
OTL	Old Testament Library
SBLDS	Society of Biblical Literature Dissertation Series
SBT	Studies in Biblical Theology
StABH	Studies in American Biblical Hermeneutics
ThTo	*Theology Today*

TLZ	*Theologische Literaturzeitung*
USQR	*Union Seminary Quarterly Review*
VTSup	Vetus Testamentum Supplements
WMANT	Wissenschaftliche Monographien zum Alten und Neuen Testament
ZAW	*Zeitschrift für die alttestamentliche Wissenschaft*
ZTK	*Zeitschrift für Theologie und Kirche*

Notes

Preface

1. Leo G. Perdue, *The Collapse of History: Reconstructing Old Testament Theology,* OBT (Minneapolis: Fortress Press, 1994).

2. A. R. Pete Diamond, et al., eds. *Troubling Jeremiah,* JSOTSup 260 (Sheffield: Sheffield Academic, 1999).

3. On the seductions and threats of exceptionalism, see Gary Dorrien, "Consolidating the Empire: Neoconservatism and the Politics of American Domination," *Political Theology* 6 (2005), 409–28.

1. Jeremiah: Portrait of the Prophet

1. John Skinner, *Prophecy and Religion* (Cambridge: Cambridge University Press, 1922).

2. John Bright, *Jeremiah: Introduction, Translation and Notes,* AB 21 (Garden City: Doubleday, 1956).

3. William L. Holladay, *Jeremiah: Spokesman Out of Time* (Philadelphia: United Church Press, 1974).

4. Robert R. Wilson, *Prophecy and Society in Ancient Israel* (Philadelphia: Fortress Press, 1980), 231–51.

5. Discerning studies of the person of Jeremiah, from a less critical perspective, are offered by Elie Wiesel, *Five Biblical Portraits* (Notre Dame, Ind.: University of Notre Dame Press, 1981), 97–127; and William J. Urboch, "Jeremiah: A Man for Our Seasoning," *Currents in Theology and Mission* 5:144–57 (1978).

6. Ernest W. Nicholson, *Preaching to the Exiles* (Oxford: Blackwell, 1970).

7. Robert P. Carroll, *From Chaos to Covenant: Prophecy in the Book of Jeremiah* (New York: Crossroad, 1981).

8. A. H. J. Gunneweg, "Konfession oder Interpretation im Jeremiabuch," ZTK 67 (1970): 395–416.

9. Siegfried Herrmann, "Die Bewältigung der Krise Israels," in *Beiträge zur alttestamentlichen Theologie,* ed. Herbert Donner, Robert Hanhart, and Rudolf Smend (Göttingen: Vandenhoeck and Ruprecht, 1977), 172.

10. On the "construction" of a person, see Roy Schafer, *Language and Insight* (New Haven: Yale University Press, 1978), esp. 8–18. One must make the move, of course, from Schafer's psychological interest to our concern with this historical literature. But the linkage suggests a way around the vexing and interminable critical questions on Jeremiah. Likely the portrayal of David as understood by David M. Gunn proceeds on parallel presuppositions (*The Story of King David: Genre and Interpretation*, JSOTSup 6 [Sheffield: Sheffield Academic, 1978]). We have there as well a construct of literary imagination.

11. I use the word in an active formative way, not unlike the use of *render* by Dale Patrick (*The Rendering of God in the Old Testament* [Philadelphia, Fortress Press, 1981]).

12. For one discussion of Jeremiah as a paradigm, see Sheldon H. Blank, "The Prophet as Paradigm," in *Essays in Old Testament Ethics*, ed. J. L. Crenshaw and J. T. Willis (New York: KTAV, 1974), 111–30.

13. Carroll, *From Chaos to Covenant*, chap. 2, argues this point vigorously. See his thesis statements on p. 52.

14. The poetry of 11:18-23; 12:1-6; 15:10-21; 17:12-18; 18:18-23; 20:7-13, 14-18. The most recent discussion known to me is that of Norbert Ittmann, *Die Konfession Jeremias*, WMANT 54 (Neukirchen-Vluyn: Neukirchener, 1981). See particularly the studies of Reventlow and Gerstenberger cited there. Bright has made the best case for regarding these poems as statements of personal experience ("Jeremiah's Complaints—Liturgy or Expressions of Personal Distress?" in *Proclamation and Presence*, ed. J. I. Durham and J. R. Porter [London: SCM, 1970], 189–214).

15. Abraham Heschel, *The Prophets* (New York: Harper & Row, 1962), chap. 6 and more generally chap. 12.

16. On the theme in Jeremiah, see Werner E. Lemke, "The Near and the Distant God: A Study of Jer. 23:23-24," *JBL* 100 (1981): 541–55.

17. On the formal aspects of prophets and poetry, see David Noel Freedman, "Pottery, Poetry and Prophecy: An Essay on Biblical Poetry," *JBL* 96 (1977): 5–26.

18. On the creative, original quality of poetic speech, see Carl Ratschke and Donna Gregory, "Revelation: The Poetic Imagination and the Archaeology of the Feminine," in *The Archaeology of the Imagination*, ed. C. E. Winquist, JAAR Thematic Studies 48 (Missoula: AAR, 1981), 89–104, esp. part 2.

19. On "redescribing" the world, see Paul Ricoeur, "Biblical Hermeneutics," *Semeia* 4 (1975): 31 and passim. Raschke and Gregory quote Wallace Stevens to the point: poetic metaphor "creates a new reality from which the original appears to be unreal" ("Revelation," 92).

20. On subversive imagination as a prerequisite to new social possibility, see Ricoeur, "The Language of Faith," in *The Philosophy of Paul Ricoeur*, ed. C. E. Reagan and David Steward (Boston: Beacon, 1978), 55–58.

21. On this theme, see Carroll, *From Chaos to Covenant*, 55–58.

22. Jack R. Lundbom, *Jeremiah: A Study in Ancient Hebrew Rhetoric* (Missoula: Scholars, 1975).

23. William L. Holladay, *The Architecture of Jeremiah 1–20* (Lewisburg, Penn.: Bucknell University Press, 1976).

24. James Muilenberg, "The Terminology of Adversity in Jeremiah," in *Translating and Understanding the Old Testament*, ed. H. T. Frank and W. L. Reed (New York: Abingdon, 1970), 42–63.

25. Thomas W. Overholt, *The Threat of Falsehood*, SBT 16 (London: SCM, 1970).

26. See the detailed treatment of the theme by Prescott H. Williams Jr., "Living toward the Acts of the Savior-Judge: A Study of Eschatology in the Book of Jeremiah," *Austin Seminary Bulletin* 94 (1978): 13–39.

27. Ronald Clemens has shown how this theme governs the present form of prophetic literature ("Patterns in the Prophetic Canon," in *Canon and Authority*, ed. G. W. Coats and B. O. Long [Philadelphia: Fortress Press, 1977], 42–55).

28. The standard accounts of Bright, Martin Noth, and Herrmann present the data but perhaps do not always make clear the depth of the upheaval taking place.

29. The point I am making is not the same as the older argument about "God acting in history." Rather, it is the interface of *poetic imagination* and *public events* that leads to revelatory disclosure.

30. Overholt has shown that the self-deception is not a deliberate or specific act of falsehood. Rather, it is foundational and programmatic, a good example of what Jürgen Habermas calls "systematically distorted speech" (*The Threat of Falsehood*).

31. On the function of the temple, see Samuel Terrien, *The Elusive Presence* (New York: Harper & Row, 1978), chap. 4. Terrien on the whole is positive about the temple and does not explore its temptation in any great depth. For a much more critical comment on the temple, see John L. McKenzie, "The Presence in the Temple: God as Tenant," in *God and His Temple: Reflections on Professor Samuel Terrien's* The Elusive Presence: Toward a New Biblical Theology, ed. Lawrence E. Frizzell (South Orange, N. J.: Institute of Judeao-Christian Studies, Seton Hall University, 1981), 35–38.

32. On the moral dimension of Jeremiah's words, see the rather theoretical discussion of Douglas A. Knight, "Jeremiah and the Dimensions of the Moral Life," in *The Divine Helmsman*, ed. James L. Crenshaw and Samuel Sandmel (New York: KTAV, 1980), 87–105.

33. On the vitality of the Isaiah tradition in the time of Jeremiah, see Hermann Barth, *Die Jesaja-worte in der Josiazeit* (Neukirchen-Vluyn: Neukirchener, 1977).

34. Henri Mottu, "Jeremiah vs. Hananiah: Ideology and Truth in Old Testament Prophecy," in *The Bible and Liberation: Political and Social Hermeneutics, ed. Norman K. Gottwald* (Maryknoll, N.Y.: Orbis, 1983), 58-67, has subjected this narrative to a most helpful criticism of its social intent and functions. See also Overholt, *The Threat of Falsehood*, chap. 2.

35. Norman K. Gottwald, *All the Kingdoms of the Earth* (New York: Harper & Row, 1964), 260.

36. Caution should be exercised on this point in light of the critical suggestion of Werner Lemke, "Nebuchadrezzar My Servant," *CBQ* 28 (1966): 45–50. See also

the response of Overholt, "King Nebuchadrezzar in the Jeremiah Tradition," *CBQ* 30 (1968): 39–48.

37. On the counter perception of reality, see Walter Brueggemann, "The Epistemological Crisis of Israel's Two Histories (Jer. 9:22-23)," in *Israelite Wisdom: Theological and Literary Essays in Honor of Samuel Terrein*, ed. John G. Gammie et al. (Missoula: Scholars, 1978), 85–105. The disputatious character of the prophetic word is also expressed in Isaiah 6:9-13.

38. See Wilson, *Prophecy and Society in Ancient Israel*, 233–35.

39. Finally it is the whole people who are under indictment, not simply the leaders. Thus 2:4-13 is a model of the lawsuit form. Compare Herbert Huffmon, "The Covenant Lawsuit in the Prophets," *JBL* 78 (1959): 287–88. The use of the term *rîv* (lawsuit) in Jeremiah is instructive, for the prophet seeks judgment for himself and against his people (cf. 11:20; 12:1; 18:19; 20:12). In other derivative uses the term is used for the sake of Israel against the hostile nations who warrant judgment (25:31; 50:34; 51:36).

40. On vengeance as the other side of compassion, see George Mendenhall, "The Vengeance of YHWH," in *The Tenth Generation* (Baltimore: Johns Hopkins University Press, 1973), 69–104.

41. A close parallel may be drawn to the call of Paul in the New Testament. J. Christiaan Beker has shown that Paul's call to be an apostle is completely subordinated to and derived from the mission of the gospel (*Paul the Apostle: The Triumph of God in Life and Thought* [Philadelphia: Fortress Press, 1980], esp. chap. 1). The same is clear for Jeremiah. The word rules.

42. On the paradoxical act of speaking salvation after judgment, see A. H. J. Gunneweg, "Heil im Gericht," in *Traditio-Krisis-Renovatio aus theologischer Sicht*, ed. Bernd Jospert and Rudolf Mohr (Marburg: Elwert, 1976), 1–9. See especially his last sentence indicating that to speak a word of hope when human possibility is exhausted requires belief that this is indeed the word of God.

43. This is the main point of the argument of Nicholson and Carroll. But that continuing dynamic must not be regarded as a formal literary, redactional process alone. It is at the same time a vigorous creative act of theological fidelity. Thus the portrait drawn is both imaginative and faithful.

2. The Book of Jeremiah: Meditation upon the Abyss

1. The older historical-critical scholarship is succinctly summarized by Brevard S. Childs, *Introduction to the Old Testament as Scripture* (Philadelphia: Fortress Press, 1979), 342–45.

2. Newer approaches are nicely represented in A. R. Pete Diamond, Kathleen M. O'Connor, and Louis Stulman, eds., *Troubling Jeremiah*, JSOTSup 260 (Sheffield: Sheffield Academic, 1999).

3. See chapter 1 in this volume.

4. Childs, *Introduction*, 345–54. In more recent discussions the B source has largely been merged as prose into what was the C material.

5. Ronald E. Clements, "Patterns in the Prophetic Canon," *Old Testament Prophecy: From Oracles to Canon* (Louisville: Westminster John Knox, 1996), 191–202. On Clements's approach to Jeremiah, see his *Jeremiah*, Interpretation (Atlanta: John Knox, 1988).

6. Clements, "Jeremiah 1–25 and the Deuteronomic History," in *Old Testament Prophecy*, 107–122.

7. Robert P. Carroll, *Jeremiah*, OTL (Philadelphia: Westminster, 1986); *From Chaos to Covenant: Prophecy in the Book of Jeremiah* (New York: Crossroad, 1981); and "Something Rich and Strange: Imagining a Future for Jeremiah Studies," in *Troubling Jeremiah*, ed. Diamond, O'Connor and Stulman, 423–43.

8. Louis Stulman, *Order and Chaos: Jeremiah as Symbolic Tapestry* (Sheffield: Sheffield Academic, 1998); and "The Prose as Hermeneutical Guide to Jeremiah 1–25; The Deconstruction of Judah's Symbolic World," in Diamond, O'Connor, and Stulman, eds., *Troubling Jeremiah*, 34–63.

9. Philip R. Davies (*Scribes and Schools: The Canonization of the Hebrew Scriptures* [Louisville: Westminster John Knox, 1998]) has summarized the pertinent data, albeit in an eagerly tendentious way.

10. See James Muilenburg, "Baruch the Scribe," *in Proclamation and Presence: Old Testament Essays in Honor of Gwynne Henton Davies*, ed. John I. Durham and J. R. Porter (London: SCM, 1970), 215–38.

11. See J. Andrew Dearman, "My Servants the Scribes: Composition and Context in Jeremiah 36," *JBL* 109 (1990): 403–21.

12. Moshe Weinfeld, *Deuteronomy and the Deuteronomic School* (Oxford: Clarendon, 1972).

13. It is evident that there are two persons named Shaphan in the tradition. It is of course important to recognize the difference; in the completed tradition, however, one cannot be fully sure of the distinction.

14. On the evidence for dispute in the text itself, see Christopher R. Seitz, *Theology in Conflict: Reactions to the Exile in the Book of Jeremiah*, BZAW 16 (Berlin: de Gruyter, 1989).

15. See Clements, *Old Testament Prophecy*, 123–41; and Carroll, *From Chaos to Covenant*, 198–225.

16. William McKane, *Jeremiah: 1–25*, vol. 1, ICC (Edinburgh: T. & T. Clark, 1986), 1, has famously termed the book of Jeremiah "a rolling corpus." He comments on the prose: "Since the prose of the book of Jeremiah is the product of the ongoing growth and development of a prophetic book, we should expect it to have its own character and themes" (629).

17. Since the work of Gerhard von Rad, the ceremony of Torah interpretation in Nehemiah 8 is regularly cited as an example of the kind of proclamation-interpretation reflected in the book of Deuteronomy. Thus it is plausible to link Deuteronomy and the Deuteronomic impetus in the book of Jeremiah to the movement linked to the work of Ezra.

18. On the pivotal role of chapter 25 in the book of Jeremiah, see Martin Kessler, "The Function of Chapters 25 and 50–51 in the Book of Jeremiah," 64–72; and John Hill, "The Construction of Time in Jeremiah 25 (MT)," 146–60, both in *Troubling Jeremiah*, ed. Diamond, O'Connor, and Stulman.

19. I refer deliberately to the analysis of Morton Smith, *Palestinian Parties and Politics That Shaped the Old Testament* (New York: Columbia University Press, 1971). To be sure, Smith's analysis concerned a later period in Judaism, but the lines of tension already begin to appear in this earlier context.

20. On the genre and its crucial importance for prophetic traditions, see Claus Westermann, *Basic Forms of Prophetic Speech* (Philadelphia: Westminster, 1967).

21. Basic studies of these lamentations include Kathleen M. O'Connor, *The Confessions of Jeremiah and Their Interpretation and Role in Chapters 1–25*, SBLDS 94 (Atlanta: Scholars, 1988); and A. R. Diamond, *The Confessions of Jeremiah in Context: Scenes of Prophetic Drama*, JSOTSup 45 (Sheffield: JSOT, 1987).

22. See James Muilenburg, "The Terminology of Adversity in Jeremiah," in *Translating and Understanding the Old Testament: Essays in Honor of Herbert G. May*, ed. Harry Thomas Frank and William L. Reed (Nashville: Abingdon, 1970), 42–63; and Walter Brueggemann, "The 'Uncared For' Now Cared For (Jer. 30:12-17): A Methodological Consideration," *JBL* 104 (1985): 419–28.

23. See Kathleen M. O'Connor, "The Tears of God and Divine Character in Jeremiah 2–9," 387–401; and A. R. Pete Diamond and Kathleen M. O'Connor, "Unfaithful Passions: Coding Women Coding Men in Jeremiah 2:1—4:2," 123–45, in *Troubling Jeremiah*, ed. Diamond, O'Connor, and Stulman; Angela Bauer, *Gender in the Book of Jeremiah: A Feminist-Literary Reading*, Studies in Biblical Literature 5 (New York: Peter Lang, 1999).

24. Seitz, in *Theology in Conflict*, makes the interesting suggestion that Ebedmelech (39:15-18) and Baruch (45:1-5) are specifications of the remnant that will be saved and that they function in the text as counterpoints to Joshua and Caleb as the faithful remnant in the book of Joshua.

25. Obviously the loss of that world of domination, privilege, and certitude is not a cause of rage and anxiety for everyone, for there are many who have been excluded and exploited by that power arrangement who are glad to see it go. Likely the same was the case in the ancient world of Jerusalem. The text is given us, however, by the opinionmakers who had a great stake in the ancient arrangement of power and meaning. No doubt the two cases (ancient and contemporary) are parallel in the fact that the loss is not for everyone, but the loss is deeply inscribed among the opinionmakers who tend to speak for everyone, dissent notwithstanding.

26. See Walter Brueggemann, "The Epistomological Crisis of Israel's Two Histories (Jer. 9:22-23)," in *Israelite Wisdom: Theological and Literary Essays in Honor of Samuel Terrien*, ed. John G. Gammie et al. (Missoula: Scholars, 1978), 85–105.

3. Recent Scholarship: Intense Criticism, Thin Interpretation

1. Robert P. Carroll, *Jeremiah: A Commentary*, OTL (Philadelphia: Westminster, 1986).

2. William McKane, *Jeremiah: 1–25*, vol 1, ICC (Edinburgh: T. & T. Clark, 1986).

3. William L. Holladay, *A Commentary on the Book of the Prophet Jeremiah, Chapters 1–25*, Hermeneia, (Philadelphia: Fortress Press, 1986).

4. Ronald E. Clements, *Jeremiah*, Interpretation Commentary Series (Atlanta: John Knox, 1988).

5. For a summary of the history of that critical consensus, see Brevard S. Childs, *Introduction to the Old Testament as Scripture* (Philadelphia: Fortress Press, 1979), 343–45.

6. Holladay's work has important continuity with John Bright, *Jeremiah*, AB 21 (Garden City: Doubleday, 1965), the most used English commentary of the last generation.

7. See William L. Holladay, "The Years of Jeremiah's Preaching," *Int* 37 (1983): 146–59, reprinted in *Interpreting the Prophets* (Philadelphia: Fortress Press, 1987), 130–42.

8. Carroll, *Jeremiah*, 126, 175–76, 270, 377, 487, 600.

9. Ibid., 78, 124, 128, 138, 140, 143, 177, 270, 377.

10. Ibid., 153, 158, 173, 180.

11. McKane, *Jeremiah: 1–25*, xli–xlvii.

12. Ibid., l–liii.

13. Ibid., xlix–l, stakes out his skeptical position: "My argument is that there is no comprehensive framework of literary arrangement or theological system within which the parts of 1–25 are fitted together, and that the prose does not supply such a scaffolding. There is more of accident, arbitrariness and fortuitous twists and turns than has been generally allowed for. The processes are dark and in a measure irrecoverable, and we should not readily assume them to possess such rationality that they will yield to a systematic elucidation." See also lxxxix on his skepticism concerning linkages between text and external history.

14. Ibid., xcviii–xcix.

15. Carroll, *Jeremiah*, 86.

16. Bernhard W. Anderson, "The Problem and Promise of Commentary," *Int* 36 (1982): 343–46.

17. Carroll, *Jeremiah*, 84; McKane, *Jeremiah: 1–25*, xlvii–xcix.

18. On the matter of "surplus" in the literary generation of theology, see Paul Ricoeur, *Theology of Interpretation: Discourse and the Surplus of Meaning* (Fort Worth: Texas Christian University Press, 1976).

19. Carroll, *Jeremiah*, 142.

20. Ibid., 147.

21. On the work of redescription, see Paul Ricoeur, "Biblical Hermeneutics," *Semeia* 4 (1975), 85 and passim.

22. On "YHWH alone," see Carroll, *Jeremiah*, 80. Carroll's polemical reading of that theology includes the following: "The pejorative tone of these poems indicates a highly xenophobic, narrowly defined ideological group castigating extremely imprecise practices" (139).

23. See Carroll, *Jeremiah*, 482.

24. See Carroll, *Jeremiah*, 128 on the tension between what he calls "ideology" and realpolitik.

25. On "emotive individualism" that militates against any normative communal commitments, see Alasdair MacIntyre, *After Virtue: A Study in Moral Theory* (Notre Dame, Ind.: University of Notre Dame Press, 1984).

26. On modern forms of scuttling exiles who are no longer useful, see Richard L. Rubenstein, *The Age of Triage: Fear and Hope in an Overcrowded World* (Boston: Beacon, 1984).

27. Carroll, *Jeremiah*, 84, has made a claim for such distance, and in another form McKane has as well. I understand the canonical program of Childs to be an attempt to overcome the distance that is intrinsic in a historicist approach to the texts.

4. Theology in Jeremiah: *Creatio in Extremis*

1. Gerhard von Rad, *Old Testament Theology*, vol. 2, trans. D. M. G. Stalker (London: Oliver and Boyd, 1965), 217 and passim.

2. The three-source theory that has dominated Jeremiah studies is now, of course, open to widespread question. See a summary of that scholarship in Brevard S. Childs, *Introduction to the Old Testament as Scripture* (Minneapolis: Fortress Press, 1979), 342–45.

3. Moshe Weinfeld, *Deuteronomy and the Deuteronomic School* (Oxford: Clarendon, 1972).

4. James Muilenburg, "Baruch the Scribe," in *Proclamation and the Presence: Old Testament Essays in Honour of Gwynne Henton Davies*, ed. John I. Durham and J. Roy Porter (London: SCM, 1970), 215–38. For a more rigorous historical assessment of the scribes in the world of Jeremiah, see J. Andrew Dearman, "My Servants the Scribes: Composition and Context in Jeremiah 36," *JBL* 109 (1990): 403–21.

5. For the locus of Hosea (and derivatively Jeremiah) in the circles of levitical priests derived from Mosaic traditions and voiced in the Deuteronomists, see Hans Walter Wolff, "Hoseas geistige Heimat," *TLZ* 81 (1956): 83–94. It is surely more compelling to conclude that Jeremiah was nourished and evoked in these circles than to imagine that the Deuteronomic focus was artificially imposed on the tradition of Jeremiah.

6. See William P. Brown and S. Dean McBride Jr., eds., *God Who Creates: Essays in Honor of W. Sibley Towner* (Grand Rapids, Mich.: Eerdmans, 2000). The essays in this volume are reflective of a radically shifted paradigm in Old Testament interpre-

tation. See Walter Brueggemann, "The Loss and Recovery of Creation in Old Testament Theology," *ThTo* 53 (1996): 177–90, and "A Shifting Paradigm: From 'Mighty Deeds' to 'Horizon,'" in *The Papers of the Henry Luce III Fellows in Theology*, ed. Gary H. Gilbert (Atlanta: Scholars, 1996), 7–47.

7. Leo G. Perdue, *The Collapse of History: Reconstructing Old Testament Theology*, OBT (Minneapolis: Fortress Press, 1994), 141–50.

8. More generally on the so-called Scythian Songs, see Brevard S. Childs, "The Enemy from the North and the Chaos Tradition," *JBL* 78 (1959): 187–98; on the Oracles against the Nations, see Childs, *Introduction*, 352–53.

9. Frank Moore Cross, "The Divine Warrior," in *Canaanite Myth and Hebrew Epic: Essays in the History of the Religion of Israel* (Cambridge: Harvard University Press, 1973), 91–112; Patrick D. Miller Jr., *The Divine Warrior in Early Israel*, HSM 5 (Cambridge: Harvard University Press, 1973); Paul D. Hanson, *The Dawn of Apocalyptic* (Philadelphia: Fortress Press, 1975), 123–26, 182–85 and passim; von Rad, *Old Testament Theology*, vol. 2, 199.

10. See Walter Brueggemann, "Israel's Sense of Place in Jeremiah," in *Rhetorical Criticism: Essays in Honor of James Muilenburg*, ed. Jared J. Jackson and Martin Kessler (Pittsburgh: Pickwick, 1974), 149–65; Peter Diepold, *Israel's Land*, BWANT 15 (Berlin: Kohlhammer, 1972).

11. The terms *limit expression* and *limit experience* that are crucial to my argument are drawn from Paul Ricoeur, "Biblical Hermeneutics," *Semeia* 4 (1975): 107–45.

12. On this larger unit of poetry, see Childs, *Introduction*, 352–53.

13. See Childs, *Introduction*, 345–54, and more specifically, Ronald E. Clements, "Patterns in the Prophetic Canon," in *Canon and Authority: Essays in Old Testament Religion and Theology*, ed. George W. Coats and Burke O. Long (Philadelphia: Fortress Press, 1977), 42–55.

14. William L. Holladay, in *Jeremiah* (vol. 1, Hermeneia [Philadelphia, Fortress Press, 1986–89], 163), speaks of "the stark sublimity" of the poem. The use of the term "sublime" recalls the sense of Immanuel Kant and Rudolph Otto that "the Sublime" is not only awesome in beauty but also profound in its threat. Thus *sublime* is exactly the correct term here.

15. Childs ("The Enemy from the North and the Chaos Tradition") has paid careful attention to the term *r'š* that occurs in this text and links it to the ancient tradition of chaos.

16. Perdue, *The Collapse of History*, 143.

17. On that contemporary judgment, see the commentaries of Robert P. Carroll, William L. Holladay, and William McKane. In older scholarship, Paul Volz and Wilhelm Rudolph held to the early authenticity of the oracles.

18. Herbert B. Huffmon, "The Impossible Word of Assurance: Jer. 31:34-35 (35-37)," paper delivered at the Society of Biblical Literature meeting in New Orleans, 1996.

19. It is perhaps not unimportant that the double use of *pnh* (face) has a counterpart in 4:26 wherein the destruction of creation is "from before YHWH." That

both the destruction and the assurance are "before YHWH" points to the Yahwistic, theonomous focus of both realities.

20. On such a "two-stage" presentation of Judah's theological reality in the tradition of Isaiah (with special reference to Isa. 8:23b), see Hugh G. M. Williamson, "First and Last in Isaiah," in *Of Prophets' Visions and the Wisdom of Sages: Essays in Honour of R. Norman Whybray on His Seventieth Birthday*, ed. Heather A. McKay and David J. A. Clines, JSOTSup 162 (Sheffield: Sheffield Academic, 1993), 95–108. It is likely that such a two-stage presentation became dominant and canonical for the prophetic perspective in general.

21. Robert P. Carroll, *Jeremiah: A Commentary*, OTL (Philadelphia: Westminster, 1986), 616.

22. I use the term *subsequent* because it is not possible in the tradition of Jeremiah to deny that there was a rejection in the events of 587; see Walter Brueggemann, "A Shattered Transcendence? Exile and Restoration," in *Biblical Theology: Problems and Perspectives*, ed. Steven J. Kraftchick et al. (Nashville: Abingdon, 1995), 169–82. The subsequent character of the assurance is more explicit in Isa. 54:9 with its "never again" (*'ôd*), see also Gen. 9:11.

23. The intimate connection between creation and wisdom reflection is now commonplace, as in Perdue's discussion (*The Collapse of History*). Reference may also be made to the works of von Rad and Walther Zimmerli.

24. R. Norman Whybray, *Wisdom in Proverbs*, SBT 45 (Naperville, Ill.: Allenson, 1976), 75.

25. William McKane, *Proverbs*, OTL (Philadelphia: Westminster, 1970), 296–97; Whybray, *Wisdom in Proverbs*, 75, 95–104.

26. It is clear that this articulation has close linkages to materials in Second Isaiah. It is not possible, however, to demonstrate the direction of influence.

27. One of the primary grounds for taking 10:1-6 as later is the theme of the treatment of idols. Such a literary judgment based so tightly upon a view of the history of Israelite religion, however, is not necessary. Current interpretation is not inclined to hold literary judgments so closely to historical judgments, if indeed it matters much anyway about what is early and what is late.

28. See James L. Crenshaw, *Hymnic Affirmation of Divine Justice*, SBLDS 24 (Missoula: Scholars, 1975).

29. See Alice Ogden Bellis, *The Structure and Composition of Jeremiah 50:2—51:58* (Lewiston, N.Y.: Mellen, 1995), 136–39.

30. Bellis regards these verses as a belated intrusion in the text.

31. William McKane, *Jeremiah: 26–52*, vol. 2, ICC (Edinburgh: T. & T. Clark, 1996), 1309.

32. See Walter Brueggemann, "A 'Characteristic' Reflection of What Comes Next (Jer. 32:16-44)," in *Prophets and Paradigms: Essays in Honor of Gene M. Tucker*, ed. Stephen Breck Reid, JSOTSup 229 (Sheffield: Sheffield Academic, 1996), 16–32.

33. On the category of impossibility, see Walter Brueggemann, "'Impossibility' and Epistemology in the Faith Tradition of Abraham and Sarah (Gen. 18:1-15),"

in *The Psalms and the Life of Faith*, ed. Patrick D. Miller Jr. (Minneapolis: Fortress Press, 1995), 167–68.

34. On motivation, see Patrick D. Miller, *They Cried to the Lord: The Form and Theology of Biblical Prayer* (Minneapolis: Fortress Press, 1994), 114–26.

35. The lead verb in the other two uses of 10:12 and 51:15 is a participle.

36. It is worth observing that the phrase "outstretched arm" has been characteristically taken as exodus terminology. This is yet another case where the historical paradigm has dictated the term of interpretation when, under another paradigm, the phrasing may relate to creation. Terence Fretheim ("The Plagues as Ecological Signs in Historical Disaster," *JBL* 110 [1991]: 385–96) has proposed a rereading of the exodus narrative in the categories of creation. Such a rereading would, in a small detail, reassign this phrasing to creation theology.

37. Gerhard von Rad, "The Theological Problem of the Old Testament Doctrine of Creation," in *The Problem of the Hexateuch and Other Essays* (New York: McGraw-Hill, 1966), 142.

38. It is clear that von Rad took his cue from the categories of Karl Barth. For a polemical review of Barth's categories, see James Barr, *Biblical Faith and Natural Theology: The Gifford Lectures for 1991* (Oxford: Clarendon, 1993). Of particular interest is Barr's assertion, "Thus the understanding of pro-Nazi theology as basically a kind of natural theology was probably a vast misdiagnosis" (112–13).

39. G. Ernest Wright, *The Old Testament against Its Environment*, SBT 2 (London: SCM, 1950); and *God Who Acts: Biblical Theology as Recital*, SBT 8 (London: SCM, 1952).

40. It may be possible to suggest an analogue between the losses of sixth-century Judah and contemporary losses in the immense suffering in Auschwitz, Hiroshima, and Vietnam, to name only the most prominent examples. Robert Jay Lifton has identified "psychic numbing," that is, to cease to notice or care, as a strategic response to evil that threatens to overwhelm. He suggests that psychic numbing produces a "symbol gap," wherein there are no adequate symbols to mediate the experience. Such a situation of deficiency of speech and expression requires fresh utterances to break the numbing. *Mutatis mutandis*, I suggest that the limit expressions of the Jeremiah tradition are addressed to the limit experiences of Judah that perhaps produced such numbing.

41. Quoted in David E. Purpel, *The Moral and Spiritual Crisis in Education: A Curriculum for Justice and Compassion in Education*, Critical Studies in Education Series (New York: Bergin and Garvey, 1989), xiii.

42. Martin Buber, *I and Thou* (New York: Scribner, 1937); Emmanuel Levinas, *Totality and Infinity: An Essay on Exteriority* (Pittsburgh: Duquesne University Press, 1969).

43. I am glad to join in a salute to Sib Towner, longtime friend and colleague. Sib's way in our common scholarship is deeply marked by gentleness, caring, and humaneness, a model for us in an enterprise permeated with tension and dispute.

5. Next Steps in Jeremiah Studies

1. A. R. Pete Diamond, Kathleen M. O'Connor, and Louis Stulman, eds., *Troubling Jeremiah*, JSOTSup 260 (Sheffield: Sheffield Academic, 1999).

2. William L. Holladay, *Jeremiah 1: A Commentary on the Book of the Prophet Jeremiah, Chapters 1–25*, Hermeneia (Philadelphia: Fortress Press, 1986); and *Jeremiah 2: A Commentary on the Book of the Prophet Jeremiah, Chapters 26–52*, Hermeneia (Minneapolis: Fortress Press, 1989).

3. Robert P. Carroll, *Jeremiah: A Commentary*, OTL (Philadelphia: Westminster, 1986).

4. William McKane, *Jeremiah: 1–25*, vol. 1, ICC (Edinburgh: T. & T. Clark, 1986); and *Jeremiah: 26–52*, vol. 2, ICC (Edinburgh: T. & T. Clark, 1996).

5. Leo G. Perdue, *The Collapse of History: Reconstructing Old Testament Theology*, OBT (Minneapolis: Fortress Press, 1994). In *Troubling Jeremiah*, see Perdue's essay and Thomas Overholt's response to it.

6. See the document of Rolf Rendtorff, "The Book of Isaiah: A Complex Unity: Synchronic and Diachronic Reading," in *New Visions of Isaiah*, ed. Roy F. Melugin and Marvin A. Sweeney, JSOTSup 214 (Sheffield: Sheffield Academic, 1996), 40, who speaks of "a reversal of scholarly priorities: The latter reading, which I am sympathetic with, does not imply a denial of diachronic questions but a change—and perhaps a reversal—of scholarly priorities."

7. A. R. Pete Diamond, *The Confessions of Jeremiah in Context: Scenes of Prophetic Drama*, JSOTSup 45 (Sheffield: JSOT, 1987); Kathleen M. O'Connor, *The Confessions of Jeremiah: Their Interpretation and Role in Chapters 1–25*, SBLDS 94 (Atlanta; Scholars, 1988); and Mark S. Smith, *The Laments of Jeremiah and Their Contexts: A Literary and Redactional Study of Jeremiah 11–20* (Atlanta: Scholars, 1990).

8. Ronald E. Clements, "Jeremiah 1–25 and the Deuteronomistic History," in *Old Testament Prophecy: From Oracles to Canon* (Louisville: Westminster John Knox, 1996), 107–22.

9. Diamond, "Introduction," in *Confessions*, 16, 32.

10. See Louis Stulman, "The Prose Sermons as Hermeneutical Guide to Jeremiah 1–25: The Deconstruction of Judah's Symbolic World," 34–63; Else K. Holt, "The Potent Word of God: Remarks on the Composition of Jeremiah 37–44," 161–70; Roy D. Wells Jr., "The Amplification of the Expectations of the Exiles in the MT Revisions of Jeremiah," 272–92, in *Troubling Jeremiah*.

11. See A. R. Pete Diamond and Kathleen M. O'Connor, "Unfaithful Passions: Coding Women Coding Men in Jeremiah 2:1—4:2," 123–45; Kathleen M. O'Connor, "The Tears of God and Divine Character in Jeremiah 2–9," 387–403.

12. Brevard S. Childs, *Introduction to the Old Testament as Scripture* (Philadelphia: Fortress Press, 1979), 351.

13. Ronald E. Clements, "Patterns in the Prophetic Canon," in *Canon and Authority: Essays in Old Testament Religion and Theology*, ed. George W. Coats and Burke O. Long (Philadelphia: Fortress Press, 1977), 42–55 (48).

14. See n. 7.

15. See Mark Coleridge, "Life in the Crypt, or, Why Bother with Biblical Studies?" *BibInt* 2 (1994): 139–51.

16. Philip Fisher, "American Literary and Cultural Studies since the Civil War," in *Redrawing the Boundaries: The Transformation of English and American Literary Studies*, ed. Stephen Greenblatt and Giles Gunn (New York: Modern Language Association of America, 1992), 232–33.

17. Ibid., 233.

18. Christopher R. Seitz, *Theology in Conflict: Reactions to the Exile in the Book of Jeremiah*, BZAW (Berlin: de Gruyter, 1989).

19. On the notion of "bids," see Rowan Williams, "The Literal Sense of Scripture," *Modern Theology* 7 (1991): 121–34.

20. See the other essays in A. R. Pete Diamond, Kathleen M. O'Connor, and Louis Stulman, eds., *Troubling Jeremiah*, JSOTSup 260 (Sheffield: Sheffield Academic, 1999). In particular, the essay of Raymond F. Person Jr. suggests a different kind of sensitivity to oral rhetoric to which attention must be paid.

21. Clifford Geertz, "Ideology as a Cultural System," in *The Interpretation of Cultures: Selected Essays* (New York: Basic, 1973), 193–233. For a helpful review of the topic, see Paul Ricoeur, *Lectures on Ideology and Utopia* (New York: Columbia University Press, 1986). Norman K. Gottwald, "Ideology and Ideologies in Israelite Prophecy," in *Prophets and Paradigms: Essays in Honor of Gene M. Tucker*, ed. Stephen Breck Reid, JSOTSup 229 (Sheffield: Sheffield Academic, 1996), 136–49, has helpfully reconsidered the theme with reference to the prophets.

22. See Peter L. Berger and Thomas Luckmann, *The Social Construction of Reality: A Treatise in the Sociology of Knowledge* (Garden City, N.Y.: Doubleday, 1967).

23. Robert P. Carroll, "Jeremiah, Intertextuality, and *Ideologiekritik*," *JNSL* 22 (1996): 26, 27.

24. Phyllis Trible, "The Gift of a Poem: A Rhetorical Study of Jeremiah 31:15-22," *ANQ* 17 (1976): 271–80; and *God and the Rhetoric of Sexuality*, OBT (Philadelphia: Fortress Press, 1978), 41–50; Kathleen O'Connor, "Jeremiah," in *The Women's Bible Commentary*, ed. Carol A. Newsom and Sharon H. Ringe (Louisville: Westminster John Knox, 1992), 169–77; and "'Speak Tenderly to Jerusalem': Second Isaiah's Reception and Use of Daughter Zion," *Princeton Seminary Bulletin* (1999): 281–94.

25. Gale A. Yee, *Poor Banished Children of Eve: Woman as Evil in the Hebrew Bible* (Minneapolis: Fortress Press, 2003).

26. Renita J. Weems, *Battered Love: Love, Marriage, Sex, and Violence in the Hebrew Prophets*, OBT (Minneapolis: Fortress Press, 1995).

27. See John Hill, "The Construction of Time in Jeremiah 25 (MT)," 146–60, and Martin Kessler, "The Function of Chapters 25 and 50–51 in the Book of Jeremiah," 64–72, in *Troubling Jeremiah*.

28. See Susan A. Handelman, *The Slayers of Moses: The Emergence of Rabbinic Interpretation in Modern Literary Theory* (Albany: SUNY Press, 1982).

29. As much as anyone, Elie Wiesel has shown the possibility of testimony as a legitimate alternative mode of knowledge. Wiesel is of course concerned with the evidence of the Nazi death camps that depends, finally, upon the witnesses. More generally on testimony as a reliable mode of knowledge, see C. A. J. Coady, *Testimony: A Philosophical Study* (Oxford: Clarendon, 1992).

30. I refer deliberately to Arthur Allen Cohen, *The Tremendum: A Theological Interpretation of the Holocaust* (New York: Crossroad, 1981).

31. I fully share the judgment that the narrative of chapter 36 is a fictive construct designed to authorize the book and the voice of the prophet who speaks there. Of course the fictive character of the narrative does not diminish its importance for the processes and claims of authority for the literature.

32. This quality of "knowledge" of YHWH has been well probed by Samuel Terrien, *The Elusive Presence: Toward a New Biblical Theology* (San Francisco: Harper & Row, 1978).

33. Abraham Heschel, *The Prophets* (New York: Harper & Row, 1962). See also Kazo Kitamori, *Theology of the Pain of God* (Richmond: John Knox, 1965).

34. Robert P. Carroll, *From Chaos to Covenant: Prophecy in the Book of Jeremiah* (New York: Crossroad, 1981), 279.

35. Walter Brueggemann, "Jeremiah: Intense Criticism/Thin Interpretation," *Int* 42 (1988): 268–80. See also chapter 3 of this volume.

36. George Steiner, "Critic/Reader," *New Literary History* (1979): 423–52 (442).

37. Ibid., 445.

38. Ibid., 447.

6. The Prophetic Word of God and History

1. On the problem in relation to the assumptions of modernity, see Owen C. Thomas *God's Activity in the World: The Contemporary Problem* (Chico, Calif.: Scholars, 1983); and Werner E. Lemke, "Revelation through History in Recent Biblical Theology," *Int* 36 (1982): 34–46.

2. In this sentence, I have moved from God's "action" to God's "speech." The two matters, act and word, are intimately linked with each other. James Barr, in particular, has taught us to pay attention to God's speech rather than God's actions.

3. The most helpful general discussion of modernity known to me is Stephen Toulmin, *Cosmopolis: The Hidden Agenda of Modernity* (New York: Free Press, 1990).

4. I am glad to acknowledge the impact upon my thinking of George A. Lindbeck, *The Nature of Doctrine: Religion and Theology in a Postliberal Age* (Philadelphia: Westminster, 1984). I have carried my own thinking in directions Lindbeck would not pursue, but his work has been enormously suggestive to me.

5. On this text and the theological trajectory that derives from it, see Walter Brueggemann, "'Impossibility' and Epistemology in the Faith Traditions of Abraham and Sarah (Genesis 18:1-15)," in *The Psalms and the Life of Faith*, ed. Patrick D.

Miller Jr. (Minneapolis: Fortress Press, 1995), 167–68; and Claus Westermann, *The Promises to the Fathers: Studies on the Patriarchal Narratives* (Philadelphia: Fortress Press, 1980), 11–12, 60–61.

6. There are, to be sure, many scholarly suggestions about sociohistorical antecedents to the existence of Israel. Without denying the importance or validity of those antecedents, it is unmistakable (a) that Israel is a genuine *novum*, no matter what historical-critical judgments might be made, and (b) that Israel understands itself as a *novum* in world history. On the continuities with Canaanite antecedents, see the several essays in *Ancient Israelite Religion: Essays in Honor of Frank Moore Cross,* ed. Patrick D. Miller et al. (Philadelphia: Fortress Press, 1987). On the theological, methodological issues of Israel as a theological *novum,* see M. Douglas Meeks, *Origins of the Theology of Hope* (Philadelphia: Fortress Press, 1974), 67–69 and passim.

7. Martin Buber, *Moses* (Atlantic Highlands, N.J.: Humanities, 1988), 75–76. See the derivative discussions of Buber's theme by Emil Fackenheim, *God's Presence in History* (New York: Harper & Row, 1972); and Walter Brueggemann, *Abiding Astonishment: Psalms, Modernity, and the Making of History* (Louisville: Westminster John Knox, 1991).

8. Michael Walzer, *Exodus and Revolution* (New York: Basic, 1985).

9. On the human leadership of Moses, see Aaron Wildavsky, *The Nursing Father: Moses as a Political Leader* (Birmingham, Ala.: University of Alabama Press, 1984).

10. On nontheological factors in understanding the prophets as regards psychology, sociology, and anthropology respectively, see Johannes Lindblom, *Prophecy in Ancient Israel* (Philadelphia: Muhlenberg, 1962); Robert R. Wilson, *Prophecy and Society in Ancient Israel* (Philadelphia: Fortress Press, 1980); and Thomas W. Overholt, *Channels of Prophecy: The Social Dynamics of Prophetic Activity* (Minneapolis: Fortress Press, 1989).

11. On YHWH versus the idols, see Pablo Richard et al., *The Idols of Death and the God of Life: A Theology* (Maryknoll, N.Y.: Orbis, 1983). More generally on the interface of idolatry and ideology, see Walter Brueggemann, *Israel's Praise: Doxology against Idolatry and Ideology* (Philadelphia: Fortress Press, 1988).

12. On the dialectic of hurt and hope in the character and will of God, see Walter Brueggemann, "The Rhetoric of Hurt and Hope: Ethics Odd and Crucial," *The Annual, Society of Christian Ethics,* ed. D. M. Yeager (Knoxville: Society of Christian Ethics, 1989), 73–92.

13. For summary statements on the cruciality of hope for ancient Israel, see Walter Zimmerli, *Man and His Hope in the Old Testament,* SBT 2nd Ser. 20 (Naperville, Ill.: Allenson, n.d.); and Hans Walter Wolff, *Anthropology of the Old Testament* (Philadelphia: Fortress Press, 1974), 149–55. More generally, see Donald E. Gowan, *Eschatology in the Old Testament* (Philadelphia: Fortress Press, 1986); and Walter Brueggemann, *Hopeful Imagination: Prophetic Voices in Exile* (Philadelphia: Fortress Press, 1986). It has been Jürgen Moltmann (*Theology of Hope: On the Ground and the Implications of a Christian Eschatology* [New York: Harper & Row, 1967]) who has

most fully considered the larger theological dimensions of the hope of ancient Israel, on which see also Meeks, *Origins.*

14. In *Abiding Astonishment,* I have argued that the impact of modernity upon the speech (and faith) of the church is not an irreversible cultural development but the exercise of an option. This means that a recovery of such speech (and faith) that moves against modernity is also a choosable option. Indeed, I have suggested that the prerational historical recital of ancient Israel may not be an early speech mode that was superseded by more rational thought but rather a subversive response to that more rational thought that was a mode of political interpretation exercising an option in its mode of speech.

15. On the phrase, see Brueggemann, *Abiding Astonishment,* and the references to Buber and Fackenheim.

16. One dramatic example of the way in which technique can overcome speech is a recent incident in Germany. Protesting youths have systematically taken to writing graffiti as a social counterstatement. To combat this, the government has developed and utilized a new chemical mix that has the capacity to erase the graffiti without damaging the surfaces on which they are written.

17. On the history-making word, see Walter Brueggemann, *Hope within History* (Atlanta: John Knox, 1987), 49–71.

18. On this view of technology, see Jacques Ellul, *The Humiliation of the Word* (Grand Rapids: Eerdmans, 1985), and his more programmatic statement, *The Technological Society* (New York: Knopf, 1965).

19. Alasdair MacIntyre, *Whose Justice? Which Rationality?* (Notre Dame, Ind.: University of Notre Dame Press, 1988), has provided a compelling analysis of the way in which every ethical "given" is in fact embedded in a narrative history that relativizes its claim and makes it available for criticism. Although MacIntyre does not explicitly dwell on the claims of a technological ideology, the categories of his argument are pertinent for such a critique.

20. See Brueggemann, "Living toward a Vision: Grief in the Midst of Technique," in *Hope within History,* 72–91.

21. In "Vine and Fig Tree: A Case Study in Imagination and Criticism," *CBQ* 43 (1981), 188–204, I have reflected specifically on the way in which Israel's prophets engaged in the twin tasks of criticism and the imagination of an alternative.

22. Francis Fukuyama, "The End of History?" *The National Interest* (Summer 1989): 3–18. What Fukuyama prefers to judge "the end of history" is given a much more discerning, ambiguous assessment by Theodore H. von Laue, *The World Revolution of Westernization: The Twentieth Century in Global Perspective* (New York: Oxford University Press, 1987).

23. In addition to my paper cited in n. 12, see my paper, "Bodied Faith and the Body Politic," in *Old Testament Theology: Essays on Structure, Theme, and Text* (Minneapolis: Fortress Press, 1992), 67–94.

24. On this text, see Gerhard von Rad, *Wisdom in Israel* (Nashville: Abingdon, 1972). Von Rad writes: "Its aim is, rather, to put a stop to the erroneous concept that

a guarantee of success was to be found simply in practicing human wisdom and in making preparations. Man must always keep himself open to the activity of God, an activity which completely escapes all calculation, for between the putting into practice of the most reliable wisdom and that which then actually takes place, there always lies a great unknown" (101). "They also knew that the world is encompassed within the incalculable mystery of God" (234). "For this reason, all objects of human knowledge were on the one hand knowable and, on the other, subject to a divine mystery to which God could at any time recall them, thus concealing them from man" (310).

7. An Ending That Does Not End

1. See Louis Stulman, *Order amid Chaos as Symbolic Tapestry*, Biblical Seminar 57 (Sheffield: Sheffield Academic, 1998), 26–27 and passim.

2. A case is readily made that in their canonical form the prophetic books have been ordered according to the themes of judgment and hope; see Brevard S. Childs, "Jeremiah," in *Introduction to the Old Testament as Scripture* (Philadelphia: Fortress Press, 1979), 345–54; and Ronald E. Clements, "Patterns in the Prophetic Literature," in *Canon and Authority*, ed. George W. Coats and Burke O. Long (Philadelphia: Fortress Press, 1977), 42–55. While helpful, such an approach of necessity must ignore many of the nuances that here concern us.

3. In addition to Stulman, *Order amid Chaos*, see especially Christopher R. Seitz, *Theology in Conflict: Reactions to the Exile in the Book of Jeremiah*, BZAW 176 (Berlin: de Gruyter, 1989).

4. Critical judgment on the nature of the crisis of 587 covers a broad range and spectrum, from the maximal view of D. L. Smith-Christopher, "Reassessing the Historical and Sociological Impact of the Babylonian Exile (597/587–539 B.C.E)," in *Exile: Old Testament, Jewish and Christian Conceptions*, ed. James M. Scott (Leiden: Brill, 1997), 7–36, to the skepticism of H. M Barstad, *The Myth of the Empty Land: A Study in the History and Archaeology of Judah during the 'Exilic' Period* (Oslo: Scandinavian University Press, 1996). For a review of the problem from a skeptical perspective, see Lester L. Grabbe, ed., *Leading Captivity Captive: "The Exile" as History and Ideology*, JSOTSup 278 (Sheffield: Sheffield Academic, 1998).

5. On the question of blame, see Stulman, *Order amid Chaos*, 120–36. Stulman shows how the object of blame varies from text to text.

6. The case of Hananiah in chapter 28 indicates that some did not go deeply at all into the crisis. Hananiah, moreover, is to be understood not simply as "false" but as a practitioner of Zionist ideology that assumed Jerusalem's long-term guarantee against disaster.

7. It is, of course, an anachronism to use the term *modern* in this way. The notion of a "Solomonic Enlightenment," moreover, has been largely dismissed by current scholars. Given both of these realities, it is nonetheless clear that the Solomonic enterprise did indeed shift the basic assumptions of society; the embrace of those new assumptions symbolized by Solomon's temple is exactly what is placed in jeopardy by the events around 587.

8. I intend to beg all questions of historicity concerning the person of the prophet and what he may have uttered. See chapter 1 in this volume.

9. James Muilenburg ("The Terminology of Adversity in Jeremiah," in *Translating and Understanding the Old Testament: Essays in Honor of Herbert Gordon May*, ed. Harry Thomas Frank and William L. Reed [Nashville: Abingdon, 1970], 42–63) has explored the use of images and metaphors in the judgment motif in Jeremiah. More recently my colleague Kathleen O'Connor has gone more poignantly into some of these metaphors: see "The Broken Family Mended: Jeremiah 31:1-36" (Society of Biblical Literature Annual Meeting, 1996); and "Unfaithful Passions: Coding Women Coding Men in Jer. 2:1—4:2," *Biblical Interpretation* 4 (1996), 288–310 (with Pete Diamond).

10. Abraham Heschel, *The Prophets* (New York: Harper & Row, 1962), chs. 16–17 and passim.

11. All scripture quotations in this chapter are from the NRSV unless otherwise noted.

12. There is likely a play on the two terms *devour* (*'kl*) and *consume* (*klh*).

13. William L. Holladay, *Jeremiah 1: A Commentary on the Book of the Prophet Jeremiah Chapters 1–25*, Hermeneia (Philadelphia: Fortress Press, 1986), 166–67.

14. Holladay, *Jeremiah 1*, 183, following Wilhelm Rudolph, *Jeremia*, 3rd ed., Handbuch zum Alten Testament 1/12 (Tübingen: Mohr [Siebeck], 1968). Holladay notes that because of "inconcinnity," LXX adopts a different maneuver for the text.

15. Patrick D. Miller (*Sin and Judgment in the Prophet: A Stylistic and Theological Analysis* [Chico, Calif.: Scholars, 1982], 67) lists this text among those in prophetic utterances in which the anticipated judgment matches in detail the affront.

16. Again notice the play on *klh* and *'kl*, the latter occurring four times in the preceding verse.

17. The facts did not speak for themselves but awaited construal. The problematic character of the "facts" is evident in the work I have cited in n. 4. Indeed, the much talk there of "ideology" is an argument that the "facts" have been wrongly construed, thus insisting upon yet a different construal that is taken to be as more congruent with "what happened." Indeed, Robert P. Carroll, "Exile! What Exile? Deportation and the Discourses of Diaspora," in *Leading Captivity Captive: "The Exile" as History and Ideology*, ed. Lester L. Grabbe, JSOTSup 278 (Sheffield: Sheffield Academic, 1998), 64 n. 8, comments on "this obsession" with "the Bible as history." The appeal to "facts" against theological interpretation, of course, is itself also an ideological enterprise, only slightly different in texture.

18. See Walter Brueggemann, "Shattered Transcendence? Exile and Restoration," in *Biblical Theology: Problems and Perspectives, in Honor of J. Christiaan Beker*, ed. Steven J. Kraftchick et al. (Nashville: Abingdon, 1995), 169–82.

19 A postmodern approach is not greatly interested in authorial intent but is more likely to proceed from "the final form of the text."

20. As a case in point, see the comments of Timothy Beal, "The System and the Speaking Subject in the Hebrew Bible: Reading for Divine Abjection," *BibInt* 2 (1994): 171–89, concerning the way in which Julia Kristeva has given a single reading in order to read against that single reading. Beal shows that the initial judgment of a single reading in the Micah text is itself a distortion of the text.

21. That is, according to my judgment, the problem is not simply a problem with a text that is not single, but with the God witnessed to in the text as unresolved, that is, not single in intent.

22. On "second naiveté," see Mark I. Wallace, *The Second Naiveté: Barth, Ricoeur, and the New Yale Theology*, StABH 6 (Macon: Mercer University Press, 1990). For an example of such a reading, see Walter Brueggemann, "The 'Uncared For' Now Cared For (Jeremiah 30:12-17): A Methodological Consideration," in *Old Testament Theology: Essays on Structure, Theme, and Text* (Minneapolis: Fortress Press, 1992), 296–306.

23. William McKane, *Jeremiah: 1–25*, vol 1., ICC (Edinburgh: T. & T. Clark, 1986), 1–lxxxiii.

24. The phrase, of course, is from Frank Kermode, *The Sense of an Ending: Studies in the Theory of Fiction* (Oxford: Oxford University Press, 1968).

25. On alternative endings, see the nice phrase concerning chapters 45 and 52 by Stulman, *Order amid Chaos*, 69–71: "endings with embryonic beginnings."

26. See Gerhard von Rad, *Old Testament Theology*, vol. 1 (San Francisco: Harper & Row, 1962), 84, 343; Martin Noth, *The Deuteronomic History*, JSOTSup 15 (Sheffield: JSOT, 1981), 12, 72, 98; and Hans Walter Wolff, "The Kerygma of the Deuteronomic Historical Work," in *The Vitality of Old Testament Traditions*, ed. Walter Brueggemann and Hans Walter Wolff, 2nd ed. (Atlanta: John Knox, 1982), 86, 100. See also more recently the intertextual approach of Jan Jaynes Granowski, "Jehoiachin at the King's Table: A Reading of the Ending of the Second Book of Kings," in *Reading between Texts: Intertextuality and the Hebrew Bible*, ed. Danna Nolan Fewell, Literary Currents in Biblical Interpretation (Louisville: Westminster John Knox Press, 1992), 173–88.

27. On the shape of the Greek text of Jeremiah, see J. Gerald Janzen, *Studies in the Text of Jeremiah*, HSM 6 (Cambridge: Harvard University Press, 1973).

28. See James Muilenburg, "Baruch the Scribe," in *Proclamation and Presence: Old Testament Essays in Honour of Gwynne Henton Davies*, ed. John I. Durham and J. R. Porter (London: SCM, 1970), 215–38; J. Andrew Dearman, "My Servants the Scribes: Composition and Context in Jeremiah 36," *JBL* 109 (1990): 403–21; and more broadly, Philip R. Davies, *Scribes and Schools: The Canonization of the Hebrew Scriptures* (Louisville: Westminster John Knox, 1998).

29. Seitz (*Theology in Conflict*, 280 and passim) suggests that Baruch, along with Ebed-Melek, is "singled out as exceptions to the respective judgments." That is, they are exempted from the general condemnation and as such open a way to the future because not all are to be destroyed.

8. A Second Reading of Jeremiah after the Dismantling

1. See the various positions taken by John Bright, *Jeremiah*, AB 21 (Garden City, N.Y.: Doubleday, 1965); William L. Holladay, *Jeremiah: Spokesman Out of Time* (Philadelphia: United Church Press), 1974; E. W. Nicholson, *Preaching to the Exiles* (Oxford: Blackwell, 1970); and Robert P. Carroll, *From Chaos to Covenant* (New York: Crossroad, 1981). The more radical view taken by Nicholson and Carroll seems at present to have considerable momentum among scholars.

2. Much of the material in Jeremiah appears to be set in the interim period after Zedekiah between 598 and 587. The point is not important for us because either dating of deportation can function paradigmatically as the moment of dismantling.

3. See especially chapter 4 in *Preaching to Exiles*.

4. Brevard S. Childs, *Introduction to the Old Testament as Scripture* (Philadelphia: Fortress Press, 1979), 339–54. See also Ronald E. Clements, "Patterns in the Prophetic Canon," in *Canon and Authority*, ed. George W. Coats and Burke O. Long (Philadelphia: Fortress Press, 1977), 42–55.

5. Holladay and Bright represent a more conservative posture of this matter contrasted especially with that of Carroll. See now especially Peter R. Ackroyd ("The Book of Jeremiah—Some Recent Studies," *JSOT* 28 [1984]: 47–59), who adds his important support to the radical view of Carroll.

6. On one important theological aspect of the various developments of these traditions, see Peter Diepold, *Israel's Land*, BWANT 15 (Berlin: Kohlhammer, 1972).

7. Childs (*Introduction*, 311–38) tends to make the same kind of argument about the book of Isaiah. See the discussion in Walter Brueggemann, "Unity and Dynamic in the Isaiah Tradition," *JSOT* 29 (1984): 89–107. The radical concern to determine which words are not from the prophet and to assign as much as possible to other voices seems to me to be simply a negative form of the old quest for the "actual words" of the prophets, only now the stress and valuing is negative rather than positive. Carroll seems to have zeal to deny such words to the prophet. I am not convinced that putting the question in such a way is very helpful.

8. See Karl-Friedrich Pohlmann, *Studien zum Jeremiabuch*, FRLANT 118 (Göttingen: Vandenhoeck and Ruprecht, 1978), 31.

9. Henning Graf Reventlow, *Liturgie und prophetisches Ich bei Jeremia* (Gutersloh: Mohn, 1963), 88.

10. On "redescription," see Paul Ricoeur, "Biblical Hermeneutics," *Semeia* 4 (1975): 31, 127 and passim. Sallie McFague (*Metaphorical Theology* [Philadelphia: Fortress Press, 1982]) has shown in a most compelling way how language functions theologically to do the work of redescribing.

11. On the doing of evil and receiving commensurate evil, see Patrick D. Miller, *Sin and Judgment in the Prophets* (Chico, Calif: Scholars, 1982).

12. See Diepold, *Israel's Land*, and Walter Brueggemann, "Israel's Sense of Place in Jeremiah," in *Rhetorical Criticism*, ed. by Jared J. Jackson and Martin Kessler (Pittsburgh: Pickwick, 1974), 149–65.

13. Reventlow, *Liturgie und prophetische Ich bei Jeremia*, 89–92.

14. On the weight of this usage, see Gerhard von Rad, "Faith Reckoned as Righteousness," in *The Problem of the Hexateuch and Other Essays* (New York: McGraw-Hill, 1966), 125–30.

15. This use of the term *'akir* is particularly important. It suggests a decree that goes against the facts and against normal expectation. The term is used negatively to warn against partiality in judgment (Deut. 1:17, 16:19; Prov. 24:23). In our passage, the term suggests an intentional act of partiality by YHWH. That is, this judge handles justice in a new way by issuing this verdict.

16. On the "new thing" in this literature, see Gerhard von Rad, *Old Testament Theology*, vol. 2 (New York: Harper & Row, 1965), 263–77. Now see the striking suggestion of Childs (*Introduction*, 328–30) who sees the new thing as consolation after judgment. This meaning would be supported by this text.

17. In "Unity and Dynamic in the Isaiah Tradition," I have suggested some aspects of the dynamic of the community that permits hope to follow judgment. Surely more must be said than a simple literary juxtaposition. I suggest that my argument there bears upon the movement in Jeremiah as well.

18. Without reason being given, the verdict reverses the statement of 21:10, 44:27.

19. See Prescott Williams, "Living toward the Acts of the Savior-Judge: A Study of Eschatology in the Book of Jeremiah," *Austin Seminary Bulletin* 94 (1978): 13–39.

20. On "knowing" as acknowledgement, see Herbert Huffmon, "The Treaty Background of Hebrew *yada*," *BASOR* 181 (1966): 31–37. See the radical exposition of the term by Jose Miranda, *Marx and the Bible* (Maryknoll, N.Y.: Orbis, 1974), 44–53.

21. For a most incisive treatment of the language of knowing YHWH, see Walter Zimmerli, *I Am Yahweh* (Atlanta: John Knox, 1982). On the juxtaposition of knowing and the covenant formula, see Rudolf Smend, *Die Bundesformel*, Thelogische Studien 68 (Zürich: EVZ, 1963).

22. The verb is *nathan*, which is not a weak verb. But one has the impression that the verb is not so peculiarly used as in the earlier *'akîr*.

23. The usage is of interest because it indicates how the same rhetorical arrangements can be mobilized in different directions, here with reference to a foreign nation.

24. On the literary history of this chapter, see Joseph G. Ploger, *Literarkritische, formgeshichtliche und stilkritische Untersuchungen zum Deuteronomium*, Bonner Biblische Beiträge 26 (Bonn: Peter Hanstein, 1966), 130–217. See also John V. M. Sturdy, "The Authorship of the 'Prose Sermons' of Jeremiah," in *Prophecy: Essays Presented to Georg Fohrer*, ed. by J. A. Emerton, BZAW 150 (New York; de Gruyter, 1980), 143–50.

25. On the curse formulae more generally, see Delbert Hillers, *Treaty-Curses and the Old Testament Prophets*, Biblica et Orientalia 16 (Rome: Pontifical Biblical Institute, 1964).

26. This is an interesting methodological point. Historical critical methods tend only to go so far as an analysis of the formulae. But just where that method ends, we arrive at the critical point, namely, the peculiar use made of the formulae. Currently we in the scholarly guild are seeking to find a method to discipline this move toward the theological claim of the text.

27. For a very helpful analysis of the historical factors, see Sara Japhet, "People and Land in the Restoration Period," in *Das Land Israel in biblischer Zeit*, ed. Georg Strecker (Göttingen: Vandenhoeck & Ruprecht, 1983), 103–25.

28. On cunning, see the use made of Hegel's phrase by Richard L. Rubenstein (*The Cunning of History: Mass Death and the American Future* [New York: Harper & Row, 1975]), who has shown how the waywardness of history is used and channeled by inhumane technical and political processes.

29. This conventional judgment is supported by the reports of 2 Kings 24:14-16 and Jeremiah 52:24-25. It is attested in 2 Kings 24:12, Jeremiah 52:16 that some of the poorest were left in the land. But we should at least notice the fact that Jeremiah 52:15 reports that some of the poorest were deported. That verse at least gives us pause with our usual judgment. The text is not secure, and in any case our argument does not depend on the claim that some exiles were poor. It is a cultural reality that anyone deported to a new context begins in a state of disadvantage that is not unlike poverty.

30. See the comment of Carroll, *From Chaos to Covenant*, 202.

31. The notice cited in 52:15 makes it impossible to read the distinction in terms of economic or cultural advantage because there may have been "poor" in both groups. But the disadvantage of the exiles is overriding both experientially in being displaced and deported and symbolically since exile has been regarded as punishment for a very long time.

32. See Nehemiah 1:4, surely linked to the Psalm. While Psalm 137 suggests despair, that status of Nehemiah suggests otherwise. But theologically and liturgically, this community regards itself as the "displaced poor" who must grieve. Only such a self-understanding provided impetus for the Reconstruction to come.

33. For a most important New Testament extrapolation from this same theological trajectory, see John H. Elliott, *A Home for the Homeless: A Sociological Exegesis of 1 Peter, Its Situation and Strategy* (Philadelphia: Fortress Press, 1981).

34. I am not closely equating the Deuteronomic move with canon-building, but it is likely that they are not unrelated to each other. In fact the powerful force of the Deuteronomist seems to have been crucial for the emergence of canon. This may be especially important in seeing how the political judgments in the tradition of Jeremiah come to be taken as abiding theological judgments.

35. Gene M. Tucker ("Prophetic Superscriptions and the Growth of a Canon," in *Canon and Authority*, 56-70) has traced in a formal way the process of making literature canonical. What Tucker describes as a formal process is here embodied substantively. We can observe how a specific historical judgment becomes an amazing theological affirmation with an enduring claim for the future.

36. About its cruciality, see Walter Brueggemann, *The Land: Place as Gift, Promise, and Challenge in Biblical Faith*, 2nd ed., OBT (Minneapolis: Fortress Press, 2002). The matter has been given a somewhat different nuance by W. D. Davies, *The Territorial Dimension of Judaism* (Berkeley: University of California Press, 1982).

37. On exilic notions of land redistribution, see Ezekiel 47:13—48:29, and the commentary by Ralph W. Klein, *Israel in Exile* (Philadelphia, Fortress Press, 1979), 90–92.

38. On the text from the Medellín Conference set in historical and cultural context, see Gustavo Gutiérrez, *The Power of the Poor in History* (Maryknoll, N.Y.: Orbis, 1983).

9. A Shattered Transcendence: Exile and Restoration

1. J. Maxwell Miller and John H. Hayes (*A History of Ancient Israel and Judah* [Philadelphia: Westminster, 1986]) write: "The fall of the city and the exile of its citizens marked a watershed in Judean history and have left fissure marks radiating throughout the Hebrew Scriptures. The 'day of judgment' heralded in prophetic announcements had not just dawned, it had burst on Judah with immense ferocity" (416).

2. See the data summarized by Miller and Hayes, *A History of Ancient Israel and Judah*, 416–36; and John Bright, *A History of Israel* (Philadelphia: Westminster, 1981), 343–72.

3. Daniel L. Smith, *The Religion of the Landless: The Social Context of the Babylonian Exile* (Bloomington, Ind.: Meyer Stone, 1989).

4. See Jacob Neusner, *Understanding Seeking Faith: Essays on the Case of Judaism* (Atlanta: Scholars, 1986), 137–41 and passim; and Paul Joyce, *Divine Initiative and Human Response in Ezekiel*, JSOTSup 51 (Sheffield: JSOT, 1989): 12–17.

5. See the analysis of Richard Elliott Friedman (*The Exile and Biblical Narrative* [Chico, Calif.: Scholars, 1981]) on the two great narrative responses to the crisis of exile.

6. See Peter R. Ackroyd, *Exile and Restoration*, OTL (Philadelphia: Westminster, 1968); Ralph W. Klein, *Israel in Exile*, OBT (Philadelphia: Fortress, 1979); Enno Janssen, *Juda in der Exilszeit* (Göttingen: Vandenhoeck & Ruprecht, 1956); and Joyce, *Divine Initiative*.

7. The reality of exile may have led some to despair but not in the community that generated the text. Elaine Scarry (*The Body in Pain: The Making and Unmaking of the World* [New York: Oxford University Press, 1985]) has shown how speech counters the dismantling of personhood. In parallel fashion I submit that text counters despair, both as text-making and text-reading. The exilic community was intensely engaged in text-making and text-reading as a counter to despair.

8. I take this to be a widely accepted judgment. James Sanders (*Torah and Canon* [Philadelphia: Fortress Press, 1972]) has argued this case effectively. Canon criticism, he writes,

> begins with questions concerning the function of those ancient traditions
> which were viable in the crucifixion-resurrection experience of the sixth
> and fifth centuries B.C. and which provided the vehicle for Judaism's birth
> out of the ashes of what had been. . . . But if one's interest is rather in the
> actual history of how the Bible came to be, what events gave rise to the
> collecting of the materials actually inherited, and why these traditions
> were chosen and not others, then two main historical watersheds impose
> themselves. The Bible comes to us out of the ashes of two Temples, the
> First or Solomonic Temple, destroyed in 586 B.C., and the Second or
> Herodian Temple, destroyed in A.D. 70. (xix, 6)

See the discerning statement by Donn F. Morgan (*Between Text and Community: The "Writings" in Canonical Perspective* [Minneapolis: Fortress Press, 1990]) on the canonical power of the exilic experience.

9. This is the essential dynamic of Gerhard von Rad's two-volume *Old Testament Theology*; see esp. vol. 2 (New York: Harper & Row, 1965), 263–77 and passim. See also Paul D. Hanson, "Israelite Religion in the Early Postexilic Period," in *Ancient Israelite Religion*, ed. Patrick D. Miller et al. (Philadelphia: Fortress Press, 1987), 485–508.

10. For a careful review and assessment of the contribution of Wellhausen and his dominant paradigm, see the essays in Douglas A. Knight, ed., *Julius Wellhausen and His Prolegomena to the History of Israel, Semeia* 25 (1983).

11. It should be possible to acknowledge some crucial discontinuity between ancient Israel and emergent Judaism without a judgment of inferiority. But to assert discontinuity without "bootlegging" inferiority requires an important break with the assumptions of the Wellhausen paradigm. Hanson ("Israelite Religion") has enunciated the discontinuity without suggesting inferiority.

12. Peter R. Ackroyd, *Continuity: A Contribution to the Study of the Old Testament Religious Tradition* (Oxford: Blackwell, 1962), reprinted in *Studies in the Religious Tradition of the Old Testament* (London: SCM, 1987), 3–16; "Continuity and Discontinuity: Rehabilitation and Authentication," in *Tradition and Theology in the Old Testament*, ed. Douglas A. Knight (Philadelphia: Fortress Press, 1977), 215–34, reprinted in *Studies in the Religious Traditions*, 31–45; "The Temple Vessels: A Continuity Theme," VTSup 23 (1972): 166–81, reprinted in *Studies in the Religious Tradition*, 46–60; and "The Theology of Tradition: An Approach to Old Testament Theological Problems," *Bangalore Theological Forum* 3 (1971): 49–64, reprinted in *Studies in the Religious Traditions*, 17–30.

13 Intertextuality, as reflected in the work of Michael Fishbane, provides a powerful way to maintain a flexible continuity in contexts of discontinuity.

14. Ackroyd, "Continuity," *Studies in the Religious Tradition*, 15.

15. Such a statement makes no assumptions about inspiration, revelation, or authority. I refer to such "theological realism" in terms of the claims made by the text itself. The ground for such a claim is of course theological, but in the first instance, it can be heeded on the grounds of the text as a "classic" that requires our attendance.

16. On such an understanding of the text, see Dale Patrick, *The Rendering of God in the Old Testament*, OBT (Philadelphia: Fortress Press, 1981). This approach understands theology as dramatic rendering and proceeds by bracketing out metaphysical questions.

17. On the notion of "covenantal discourse," see Harold Fisch, *Poetry with a Purpose: Biblical Poetics and Interpretation* (Bloomington, Ind.: Indiana University Press, 1988), 118–31. The gain of Fisch's assertion is that it takes seriously the claim of the text itself without excessive historical-critical reservation. See Fisch's "theological realism" concerning the Psalms (108–14).

18. On the question of continuity and discontinuity, see Ernst Käsemann, "Blind Alleys in the 'Jesus of History' Controversy," in *New Testament Questions Today* (London: SCM, 1969), 23–65; Ernst Fuchs, *Studies of the Historical Jesus*, SBT (Napierville, Ill.: Allenson, 1964), 11–31; and James D. G. Dunn, *Unity and Diversity in the New Testament: An Inquiry into the Character of Earliest Christianity* (Philadelphia: Westminster, 1977). See J. Chriastiaan Beker's theological discussion of the question, *Paul the Apostle: The Triumph of God in Life and Thought* (Philadelphia: Fortress Press, 1980), 192–208.

19. J. Christiaan Beker, *Suffering and Hope: The Biblical Vision and the Human Predicament* (Philadelphia: Fortress Press, 1987).

20. For the purposes of my argument, it cannot be insisted upon too strongly that the mode of God's self-presentation is dramatic, and that we are witnessing the character of God through a drama. The warrant for such a mode of discourse is that the text itself proceeds in this way.

21. On the several theological resources from the Exile that give different voice to God, see the works of Ackroyd and Klein cited in n. 6 and Friedman in n. 5.

22. A. D. H. Mayes, "Deuteronomy 4 and the Literary Criticism of Deuteronomy," *JBL* 100 (1981): 23–51, supported by the argument of G. Braulik, has made a strong case for the literary unity and coherence of the passage. See Norbert Lohfink, *Höre Israel! Auslegung von Texten aus dem Buch Deuteronomium* (Dusseldorf: Patmos, 1965), 87–120; and G. Braulik, *Die Mittel deuteronomischer Rhetorik*, AnBib 68 (Rome: Biblical Institute, 1978).

23. See Frank M. Cross, *Canaanite Myth and Hebrew Epic* (Cambridge, Mass: Harvard University Press, 1973), 274–89; and Richard D. Nelson, *The Double Redaction of the Deuteronomistic History*, JSOTSup 18 (Sheffield: JSOT, 1981).

24. See Hans Walter Wolff, "The Kerygma of the Deuteronomic Historical Work," in *The Vitality of Old Testament Traditions*, Walter Brueggemann and Hans Walter Wolff (Atlanta: John Knox, 1975), 96–97.

25. Phyllis Trible, *God and the Rhetoric of Sexuality*, OBT (Philadelphia: Fortress Press, 1978), 31–59.

26. On the double movement, see Zechariah 1:15-17 and Isaiah 60:10-14. The former text has important parallels to our text. On the "hidden face" of God, see Samuel E. Balentine, *The Hidden God: The Hiding of the Face of God in the Old Testament* (New York: Oxford University Press, 1983), esp. 148; and Lothar Perlitt,

"Die Verborgenheit Gottes," *Probleme biblischer Theologie*, ed. Hans Walter Wolff (München: Christian Kaiser, 1971), 367–82.

27. On the double theme in Jeremiah, see J. Lust, "'Gathering and Return' in Jeremiah and Ezekiel," in *Le Livre de Jeremie*, ed. M. Bogaert (Leuven: Leuven University Press, 1981), 119–42; and Thomas M. Raitt, *A Theology of Exile: Judgment and Deliverance in Jeremiah and Ezekiel* (Philadelphia: Fortress Press, 1977).

28. Hans W. Frei (*The Identity of Jesus Christ: The Hermeneutical Bases of Dogmatic Theology* [Philadelphia: Fortress Press, 1975]) holds a magisterial view of the single story of God focused on Jesus Christ. That single and magisterial story necessarily asserts the profound and universal continuity. Against such a claim of any "great story," see the protest of Jean-François Lyotard, *The Postmodern Condition: A Report on Knowledge*, Theory and History of Literature 10 (Minneapolis: University of Minnesota Press, 1984). See the judicious comments of William C. Platcher (*Unapologetic Theology: A Christian Voice in a Pluralistic Conversation* [Louisville: Westminster John Knox, 1989], 156 and passim) concerning a "universal" story and the Christian narrative.

29. John Calvin, *Commentary on the Book of the Prophet Isaiah* (Grand Rapids, Mich.: Baker, 1979), 140.

30. Kornelis H. Miskotte, *When the Gods Are Silent* (New York: Harper & Row, 1967), 405. See also Karl Barth, *Church Dogmatics* 2/1, no. 30 (Edinburgh: T. & T. Clark, 1957), 372–73.

31. Compare, for example, Exodus 33:5; Isaiah 26:20, 47:9; Psalm 30:6; and Lamentations 4:6.

32. Compare 1 Corinthians 15:52.

33. Miskotte, *When the Gods Are Silent*, 405. Miskotte understands that the move from abandonment to compassion happens only through God's deep pathos, that is, through the "breaking of his own heart." Claus Westermann (*Isaiah 40–66: A Commentary*, OTL [Philadelphia: Westminster, 1969]) is not as explicit but alludes to the same reality: "A change has come over God. He ceases from wrath, and again shows Israel mercy" (274). In his comment, however, Westermann speaks of the way Israel's "heart throbbed," but does not draw God's heart into the trouble in the same way.

34. Much of the Noah Flood story is from P, and therefore from the Exile. Thus, it is not unexpected that that flood narrative should be on the horizon of this exilic poet.

35. For example, the "again" (*'od*) of Isaiah 54:9 is clearly reminiscent of the same word in Genesis 9:11, with the same intention.

36. Bernhard W. Anderson ("From Analysis to Synthesis: The Interpretation of Genesis 1–11," *JBL* 97 [1978]: 23–29) has shown that Genesis 8:1 is the pivot of the Flood narrative, for instance, when God remembers Noah. In the structure of the narrative, that decisive *remembering* is preceded by God's *forgetting* of Noah. In the same way, in Isaiah 54, God's act of compassion is preceded by a real act of

abandonment. Thus the analogy of our text to that of the Flood narrative applies to the entire dramatic structure of the narrative.

37. On the "covenant of peace," see Bernard F. Batto, "The Covenant of Peace: A Neglected Ancient Near Eastern Motif," *CBQ* 49 (1987): 187–211.

38. For that reason, this text does not need an *'od* of reassurance. That is, this text entertains no discontinuity and therefore there is no need for reassertion and new promise.

39. In Isaiah 54:9-10, the claim for the future is based on *'od*.

40. On the late dating of vv. 35-37, see Robert P. Carroll, *Jeremiah: A Commentary*, OTL (Philadelphia: Westminster, 1986), 115–16; and William L. Holladay *Jeremiah 2: A Commentary on the Book of the Prophet Jeremiah, Chapters 26–52*, Hermeneia (Minneapolis: Fortress Press, 1989), 199. Holladay dates the text to the time of Nehemiah. My argument, however, is that in doing theology, one must move beyond such critical judgment to take the realistic assertion of the text. Such a posture, I suppose, is one of "second naiveté."

41. Such "common theology" necessarily interprets exile simply as punishment in a sharper system of retribution. On "common theology," see Norman K. Gottwald, *The Tribes of Yahweh* (Maryknoll, N.Y.: Orbis, 1979), 667–91; and Walter Brueggemann, "A Shape for Old Testament Theology, I: Structure Legitimation," *CBQ* 47 (1985): 156–68.

42. The new resolve of God in our texts is not unlike the new resolve of God in the Flood narrative (Gen. 8:20-22; 9:8-17). In the Flood narrative, no reason is given for that new resolve, as none is given here.

43. Critically the changes can be explained by the identification of distinct literary sources. Such distinctions, however, often violate the intention of the final form of the text, which is the proper material for doing biblical theology.

44. Jürgen Moltmann (*The Crucified God* [New York: Harper & Row, 1974]) has most powerfully insisted upon this dialectic of crucifixion and resurrection, refusing to let the resurrection overcome or nullify the centrality of the Crucifixion in the story of God's life.

45. On getting from Friday to Sunday, George Steiner (*Real Presences: Is There Anything in What We Say?* [London: Faber & Faber, 1989]) concludes with a pathos-filled statement:

> There is one particular day in Western history about which neither historical record nor myth nor Scripture make report. It is a Saturday. And it has become the longest of days. We know of that Good Friday which Christianity holds to have been that of the Cross. But the non-Christian, the atheist knows of it as well. That is to say that he knows of the injustice, of the interminable suffering, of the waste, of the brute enigma of ending. . . . We know also about Sunday. To the Christian, that day signifies an intimation, both assured and precarious, both evident and beyond

comprehension, of resurrection, of a justice and a love that have conquered death. If we are non-Christian or non-believers, we know of that
Sunday in precisely analogous terms.... The lineaments of that Sunday
carry the name of hope (there is no word less deconstructible).

But ours is the long day's journey of the Saturday. Between suffering,
aloneness, unutterable waste on the one hand and the dream of liberation
on the other. In the face of the torture of a child, of the death of love which
is Friday, even the greatest art and poetry are almost helpless. In the Utopia of the Sunday, the aesthetic will, presumably, no longer have logic or
necessity. The apprehensions and figurations ... which tell of pain and of
hope, of the flesh which is said to taste of ash and of the spirit which is said
to have the savor of fire, are always Sabbatarian. They have risen out of an
immensity of waiting which is that of man. Without them, how could we
be patient? (231–32)

Steiner's poignant statement from outside the Christian faith (as a Jew) is paral-
leled from inside the Christian community by Nicholas Lash (*Easter in Ordinary:
Reflections on Human Experience and the Knowledge of God* [Charlottesville: University Press of Virginia, 1988]), who writes: "In a fascinating section of *What Is Man?*
Buber distinguishes between 'epochs of habitation and epochs of homelessness.'
Whether we like it or not, ours is an epoch of homelessness.... But homelessness
is the truth of our condition, and the 'gifts of the spirit,' gifts of community and
relationships, forgiveness and life-giving, are at least as much a matter of promise,
of prospect, and of the task that is laid upon us, as they are a matter of past achievement or present reality" (216, 268).

Both Steiner and Lash voice the discontinuity and affirm that our current habitation is in the homelessness between. The Old Testament moment of exile is indeed
one long Saturday, which afterward may seem to have been "a moment."

46. Moltmann underscores the abandonment that overrides every claim of transcendence. Thus, "The Fatherlessness of the Son is matched by the Sonlessness of
the Father" (*The Crucified God*, 243).

47. Lyotard, in *The Postmodern Condition*, insists that there are only concrete nar-
ratives and claims in communities of testimony. The reality of Israel's struggle with
God requires the giving up of every universal. See his appeal on p. 40 to a figure from
Ludwig Wittgenstein that a town consists of many little houses, squares, and streets.
See the remarkable argument by Stephen Toulmin, *Cosmopolis: The Hidden Agenda
of Modernity* (New York: Free Press, 1990), 31–32 and passim.

48. See Richard L. Rubenstein, "Job and Auschwitz," *USQR* 25 (1970): 421–37.

49. Emil Fackenheim (*To Mend the World: Foundations of Future Jewish Thought*
[New York: Schocken, 1982]), has most eloquently characterized our new, post-
Holocaust theological situation, which requires theology to lower its voice back to

more concrete claims that are brought to speech only in communities of hurt and risk.

50. Beker (*Suffering and Hope*, 91) concludes: "Finally, a biblical theology of hope allows us to be realistic and honest about the poisonous reality of death and dying in our world. . . . And so the biblical vision still offers a promissory word in the face of suffering due to the power of death." Beker's final affirmation is rooted exactly in the testimony of exiles who discern God making promises to exiles, in exile, beyond exile.

It was a delight originally to join in congratulations to Chris Beker and in expressing gratitude for his work through this essay. His own study, marked by pain, candor, and hope, was a model for doing exilic theology that mediates new possibility. Our common work in Old Testament, New Testament, and systematic theology now is gathered around new questions, new modes of discourse, and new public possibilities. If we are able to get beyond ourselves, we may discern clues in our own "break point," that God's old transcendence is at risk, and that God may make new compassion-shaped resolves. Both God's risk and God's new compassion-shaped resolve refuse and resist domestication, either through our certitude or through our despair.

11. Prophetic Ministry: A Sustainable Alternative Community

1. For recent bibliography on the book of Jeremiah, see Leo G. Perdue and Brian W. Kovacs, eds., *A Prophet to the Nations: Essays in Jeremiah Studies* (Winona Lake, Ind.: Eisenbrauns, 1983); and James L. Crenshaw, "A Living Tradition: The Book of Jeremiah in Current Research," in *Interpreting the Prophets*, ed. James Luther Mays and Paul J. Achtemeier (Philadelphia: Fortress Press, 1987), 100–112. In the latter volume, see also the essays by Walter Brueggemann, William L. Holladay, and Thomas M. Raitt.

2. Barbara W. Tuchman (*The March of Folly* [New York: Ballantine, 1984]) has characterized such a relentless way to death as a "march of folly." While she does not take up the case of ancient Israel in any detail, she does allude to the case of King Rehoboam as an example of her thesis (8–11). One of Tuchman's criteria for "folly" is that there must be clearly voiced warnings to the leadership. Judah's move toward self-destructiveness meets that criterion. Israel and Judah pursued their self-destructive policies in the face of clear warnings and opposition from the prophets, and of them, most poignantly from Jeremiah.

3. In speaking of the "person of Jeremiah," I shall refer to the "portrait" or "persona" of the prophet as it is given to us in the book of Jeremiah. I have no doubt that the "person" of Jeremiah presented to us in the book is a constructed, crafted portrait, created for tendentious theological reasons, albeit rooted in a historical character. See chapter 1 in this volume; and Timothy Polk, *The Prophetic Persona: Jeremiah and the Language of the Self*, JSOTSup 32 (Sheffield: JSOT, 1984).

While I am not dismissive of historical rootage as is Robert P. Carroll (*Jeremiah*, OTL [Philadelphia: Westminster, 1986]), I intend here to beg "historical questions" about Jeremiah and deal with the person of Jeremiah as offered to us in the book of Jeremiah.

4. Jeremiah's situation was one in which the "known world" of the Jerusalem establishment was disintegrating. *Mutatis mutandis*, I suggest that our situation is one in which the domination of Western Christendom is collapsing, with enormous epistemological as well as economic implications.

5. On the general relation of prophets to the older tradition of covenant, see Gerhard von Rad, *Old Testament Theology*, vol. 2 (San Francisco: Harper & Row, 1965); and Ronald E. Clements, *Prophecy and Covenant*, SBT 43 (Naperville: Allenson, 1965). More precisely on Jeremiah, see William L. Holladay, "The Background of Jeremiah's Self-Understanding: Moses, Samuel, and Psalm 22," *JBL* 83 (1964): 153–64. The larger connection between the tradition of Moses and the book of Jeremiah is mediated through the Deuteronomic theological traditions, on which see Carroll, *Jeremiah.*

6. See Robert R. Wilson, *Prophecy and Society in Ancient Israel* (Philadelphia: Fortress Press, 1980), 157–252. The apparent and specific connection between Moses and Jeremiah is the work of the Deuteronomist, who also connected King Josiah to Moses.

7. On the cruciality of recital, see Gerhard von Rad, *Old Testament Theology*, vol. 1 (San Francisco: Harper & Row, 1962); and Amos N. Wilder, "Story and Story-World," *Int* 37 (1983): 353–64.

8. On the loss of the story, see Hans W. Frei, *The Eclipse of Biblical Narrative* (New Haven: Yale University Press, 1974). Frei deals with a modern problem, but the same problem is evident even in ancient Israel. Jeremiah's contemporaries had also lost confidence in their normative narrative.

9. See Walter Brueggemann, "Israel's Sense of Place in Jeremiah," in *Rhetorical Criticism*, ed. J. J. Jackson and Martin Kessler (Pittsburgh: Pickwick, 1974), 149–65; and Peter Diepold, *Israel's Land*, BWANT 15 (Berlin: Kohlhammer, 1972).

10. The phrase "know me" has been taken by scholars to have two distinct meanings. On the one hand, Herbert B. Huffmon ("The Treaty Background of Hebrew *Yada'*," *BASOR* 181 [1966]: 31–37) has shown that it may mean to acknowledge as covenant lord, that is, to acknowledge that one is in a relationship requiring obedience. On the other hand, Hans Walter Wolff ("'Wissen um Gott' bei Hosea als Urform von Theologie," *EvT* 12 [1952/53]: 533–54) has shown that at least in Hosea the phrase means to know the actual recital of saving deeds. Either or both of these meanings may be operative in the use of the formula in Jeremiah. Judah does not acknowledge YHWH's sovereignty, and Judah does not know or take seriously the old recital that gives identity. Compare Jeremiah 9:3 (MT 9:2), 22:16, 31:34.

11. On Moses' practice of intercession, see Exodus 32:11-13, 31-32; Numbers 11:11-15; 14:13-19.

12. Christopher R. Seitz ("The Prophet Moses and the Canonical Shape of Jeremiah," *ZAW* 101 [1989]: 3–27) has a most suggestive hypothesis concerning Jeremiah's intercession and the prohibition against intercession. However, see Samuel E. Ballentine ("The Prophet as Intercessor: A Reassessment," *JBL* 103 [1984]: 161–73) for an argument that the prophets were not intercessors.

13. On the "divine council" see Patrick D. Miller, *Genesis 1–11: Studies in Structure and Theme*, JSOTSup 8 (Sheffield: JSOT, 1978), 9–16; and E. Theodore Mullin Jr., *The Divine Council in Canaanite and Early Hebrew Literature* (Chico, Calif.: Scholars, 1980).

14. On the formal analysis of the "messenger formula," see Eugene W. March, "Prophecy," in *Old Testament Form Criticism*, ed. John H. Hayes (San Antonio: Trinity University Press, 1974), 156–57.

15. The "call narrative" is heavily stylized. See also Norman Habel, "The Form and Significance of the Call Narratives," *ZAW* 77 (1965): 297–323; and the derivative comments by Robert P. Carroll, *From Chaos to Covenant: Prophecy in the Book of Jeremiah* (New York: Crossroad, 1981), 31–51. It may be, given a different perspective, that this "call narrative" does not concern the "experience" of the prophet as it purports, but rather is a literary device that serves for the theological authorization of the *book*.

16. See Henri Mottu, "Jeremiah vs. Hananiah: Ideology and Truth in Old Testament Prophecy," in *The Bible and Liberation*, ed. Norman K. Gottwald (Maryknoll, N.Y.: Orbis, 1983), 235–51; and more generally, James A. Sanders, *From Sacred Story to Sacred Text* (Philadelphia: Fortress Press, 1987), 87–105.

17. See Kazo Kitamori, *Theology of the Pain of God* (Richmond: John Knox, 1965); and more generally Abraham Heschel, *The Prophets* (New York: Harper & Row, 1962).

18. See the poignant discussion of this text by Emil Fackenheim, "New Hearts and Old Covenant," in *The Divine Helmsman*, ed. James L. Crenshaw and Samuel Sandmel (New York: KTAV, 1980), 191–205.

19. Dorothee Soelle, *The Strength of the Weak* (Philadelphia: Westminster, 1984), 90–91. On the cruciality of pain for critical theology, see the programmatic essay of Rebecca S. Chopp, "Theological Persuasion: Rhetoric, Warrants and Suffering," in *Worldviews and Warrants: Plurality and Authority in Theology*, ed. William Schweiker and Per M. Anderson (Lanham, Md.: University Press of America, 1987), 17–31.

20. This language is one aspect of the "limit expression" that goes with "limit experience," according to the categories of Paul Ricoeur, "Biblical Hermeneutics," *Semeia* 4 (1975): 108–45.

21. On the several dimensions of hope in exile, see Ralph W. Klein, *Israel in Exile* (Philadelphia: Fortress Press, 1979).

22. On the Christian appropriation of this promise, see Hans Walter Wolff, *Confrontations with Prophets* (Philadelphia: Fortress Press 1983), 49–62.

23. See Walter Brueggemann, "The 'Uncared For' Now Cared For (Jer. 30:12-17): A Methodological Consideration," *JBL* 104 (1985): 419–28.

24. See Peter L. Berger and Thomas Luckmann, *The Social Construction of Reality* (Garden City, N.Y.: Doubleday, 1966); and Walter Brueggemann, *Israel's Praise: Doxology against Idolatry and Ideology* (Philadelphia: Fortress Press, 1988), chap. 1.

25. On the organizational aspects of the Mosaic revolution, see Norman K. Gottwald, *The Tribes of Yahweh*, (Maryknoll, N.Y.: Orbis, 1979).

26. See Josef Scharbert, "Jahwe in frühisraelitischen Recht," in *Gott, der Einzige: Zur Entstehung des Monotheismus in Israel*, ed. E. Haag (Freiburg: Herder, 1985), 160–83; and Paul D. Hanson, "The Theological Significance of Contradiction within the Book of the Covenant," in *Canon and Authority*, ed. George W. Coats and Burke O. Long (Philadelphia: Fortress Press, 1977), 110–31.

27. See H. G. M. Williamson, *Ezra and Nehemiah*, Old Testament Guides (Sheffield: Sheffield Academic, 1987).

28. Jochen Vollmer (*Geschichtliche Rückblicke und Motive in der Prophetie des Amos, Hosea, and Jesaja*, BZAW 119 [Berlin: de Gruyter, 1971]) has argued this understanding of the prophets.

29. Martin Buber, *The Prophetic Faith* (New York: Harper, 1949).

30. On the Deuteronomic reshaping of the tradition of Jeremiah, see Brevard S. Childs, *Introduction to the Old Testament as Scripture* (Philadelphia: Fortress Press, 1979), 345–48. Older, important discussions of the problem include those of John Bright, "The Date of the Prose Sermons in Jeremiah," *JBL* 70 (1951): 15–35; and H. H. Rowley, "The Prophet Jeremiah and the Book of Deuteronomy," *Studies in Old Testament Prophecy*, ed. H. H. Rowley (New York: Scribners, 1950), 157–74.

31. On the recasting, see chapter 1 in this volume; and more programatically, Carroll, *Jeremiah*.

32. On the form, see Claus Westermann, *Basic Forms of Prophetic Speech* (Philadelphia: Westminster, 1967).

33. On such studied correspondence between sin and punishment, see Patrick D. Miller, *Sin and Judgment in the Prophets* (Chico, Calif.: Scholars, 1982).

34. The prohibition against intercession prayer thus nullifies the Mosaic function of mediation. See the reference to Seitz in n. 12. Indeed the prohibition brings to dramatic end the whole speaking-answering structure of covenant. See Isaiah 65:24 for its subsequent resumption.

35. This passage has important connections to the later text of Nehemiah 5. On the more general issue of the social process of generating poverty, see D. N. Premnath, "Latifundialization and Isaiah 5:8-10," *JSOT* 40 (1988): 49–60.

36. A. Vanlier Hunter (*Seek the Lord! A Study of the Meaning and Function of the Exhortations in Amos, Hosea, Isaiah, Micah, and Zephaniah* [Baltimore: St. Mary's Seminary and University, 1982]) has shown how the appeal for reform in Jeremiah is each time aborted. Every apparent invitation to reform offered by the prophets is in fact a previous offer of reform that has been rejected by the people. In each case what was an offer of reform has now become a judgment in light of *failed reform*.

37. Jeremiah's controversy with established leadership seems to include every office of leadership (cf. 2:8). For more narrative specificity, see his conflict with the king (36), with a royal prophet (27–28), and with a priest (21:1-6).

38. On the crucial use of metaphor for adequate theological conversation, see the exquisite lecture by Robert J. O'Connell, *Imagination and Metaphysics in St. Augustine* (Milwaukee: Marquette University Press, 1986). On the crucial use of imagination for the practice of faith, see the splendid discussion of Garrett Green, *Imaging God: Theology and the Religious Imagination* (San Francisco: Harper & Row, 1989).

39. See James Muilenburg, "The Terminology of Adversity in Jeremiah," in *Translating and Understanding the Old Testament*, ed. H. T. Frank and W. L. Reed (Nashville: Abingdon, 1970), 42–63.

40. Heschel (*The Prophets*, 107–15) has seen this most clearly and expressed it most poignantly.

41. See Thomas W. Overholt, *The Threat of Falsehood*, SBT 162 (London: SCM, 1970).

42. Gerhard von Rad (*Old Testament Theology*, vol. 1 [San Francisco: Harper & Row, 1962], 69–85) had seen that the Deuteronomistic and Priestly traditions were in fact statements of old, normative memories in the time of the exilic upheaval. My argument seeks to build upon von Rad at two points. First, I do not think that von Rad fully stated how polemical and disputatious was the restatement of the old tradition. The restatement is not simply a different reading, but it is a reading of present reality that intends to dispute the common, popular reading of the present. Second, the tradition of Jeremiah is a crucial vehicle through which this polemical rereading is presented. This means that the book of Jeremiah in its canonical form is an urgent polemical statement. While there is a clear overlay of Deuteronomic polemic, this general intent may not be far removed from the work of the prophet Jeremiah, though the prophet obviously proceeded in an idiom very different from that of the Deuteronomists.

43. See Walter Brueggemann, "The Epistemological Crisis of Israel's Two Histories (Jer. 9:22-23)," in *Israelite Wisdom*, ed. John G. Gammie et al. (Missoula: Scholars, 1978), 85–105.

44. See the judicious statement of John Bright ("Jeremiah's Complaints—Liturgy or Expressions of Personal Distress?" in *Proclamation and Presence*, ed. John I. Durham and J. R. Porter [London: SCM, 1970], 189–214), which likely represents something of a consensus opinion. We are fortunate now to have in translation for the first time the classic statement of Walter Baumgartner, *Jeremiah's Poems of Lament* (Decatur, Ga.: Almond, 1987). Seitz ("The Prophet Moses," 7–12) shrewdly suggests that it is the prohibition against intercession that evokes the lamentations. Thus, if not in one form, then in another the prophet will be a voice of prayer.

45. The study of Kitamori cited in n. 17 is focused primarily on this verse.

46. See Walter Brueggemann, *Hopeful Imagination: Prophetic Voices in Exile* (Philadelphia: Fortress Press, 1986), 9–47.

47. See Prescott Williams Jr., "Living toward the Acts of the Saviour-Judge," *Austin Seminary Bulletin* 94 (1978): 13–39.

48. On the phrase, see John M. Bracke, "The Coherence and Theology of Jeremiah 30–31," (Ph.D. Diss., Union Theological Seminary, Richmond, 1983), 148–55.

14. Prophets and Historymakers

1. John Hall Elliott, *A Home for the Homeless: A Sociological Exegesis of 1 Peter, Its Situation and Strategy* (Philadelphia: Fortress Press, 1981).

Index of Names

Index of Biblical References

Index of Biblical References